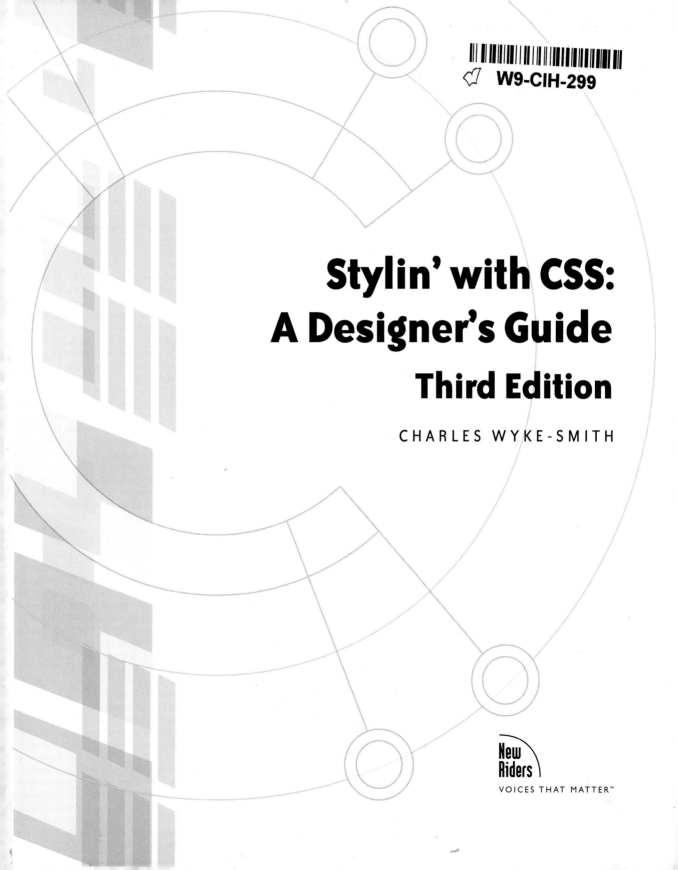

Stylin' with CSS:
A Designer's Guide
Third Edition

CHARLES WYKE-SMITH

New
Riders

VOICES THAT MATTER™

Stylin' with CSS: A Designer's Guide, Third Edition
Charles Wyke-Smith

New Riders
Find us on the Web at: www.newriders.com
To report errors, please send a note to errata@peachpit.com

New Riders is an imprint of Peachpit, a division of Pearson Education

Project Editor: Nancy Peterson
Development Editor: Beth Bast
Technical Editor: Curtis Blanton
Production Editor: Katerina Malone
Proofreader: Darren Meiss
Indexer: Karin Arrigoni
Compositor: Beth Bast
Cover design: Aren Straiger
Interior design: Mimi Heft

ISBN 13: 978-0-321-85847-4
ISBN 10:   0-321-85847-6

9 8 7 6 5 4 3 2 1

Printed and bound in the United States of America

Acknowledgements

My thanks and appreciation to the Peachpit team: Michael Nolan for encouraging me to write the third edition and getting it green-lighted, to my project editor Nancy Peterson for her guidance, insight, and patience, and to publisher Nancy Ruenzel for seven years of publishing my books.

On the development team, my thanks go to proofer Darren Meiss for his meticulous grammar, production editor Katerina Malone for her management skills, and Karin Arrigoni for the detailed work on the index.

A big thank you goes to my good friend and technical editor of this book, Curtis Blanton, for his detailed feedback and suggestions on the code and the explanations—a really great job, Curtis! Thanks also to programmers, Jeffrey Johnson and Isaac Shapira, for their advice and support.

Finally, a very special thanks goes to my wife Beth Bast who, as both development editor and compositor, has endlessly read and edited my drafts, created the book's graphics, and laid out the entire book in InDesign. It has been an intense five months of work and her efforts and attention to detail are in every page of this book. Thanks, my love, I couldn't have done it without you.

A big hug for my daughters, Jemma and Lucy, who have been very patient while their parents have focused on writing this book. We love you both.

—Charles Wyke-Smith
Charleston, South Carolina, September 24, 2012

About the Author

Photo–Kelly Roper
Photography, Charleston, SC

Charles Wyke-Smith has been involved in media production for his entire career. In the mid-80s, he co-founded PRINTZ Electronic Design, an early, all-computerized design studio in San Francisco. He has worked in management and consulting roles at Wells Fargo, ESPN Videogames, and Benefitfocus, where he was Director of User Experience. In 2009, he co-founded PeopleMatter, an HR platform for the services industries. He is currently CEO of a new startup, Bublish, a book discovery platform.

Charles is a performing musician and author of several Web development books, including *Stylin' with CSS, Codin' for the Web, Scriptin' with AJAX,* and *Visual Stylin' with CSS3*. He lives in Charleston, South Carolina with his wife and two daughters.

Contents

Introduction

This is an exciting time to be a Web designer. The Web is now the way we consume almost all media, as cable TV, CDs, and DVDs are replaced by on-demand Web-delivered services like Hulu, Netflix, Pandora, and Spotify.

We also have a variety of devices on which to consume this media—desktop computers, laptops, tablets, smartphones, and massive 60-inch flat screen displays.

Supporting the delivery of content across all these different devices and media is an emerging technology standard—centered around browsers that use HTML5, CSS3, and JavaScript.

When I wrote the second edition of *Stylin' with CSS* almost five years ago, a rigid and complex XML-based version of HTML, called XHTML, had become the standard. Because XHTML was unsuited to the free-wheeling and fast-moving world of Web development, Apple, Mozilla, and Opera formed the Web Hypertext Application Technology Working Group. The purpose of this organization was to revive the development of HTML that the World Wide Web Consortium had abandoned after HTML4 in favor of XHTML. The phoenix that arose from the ashes became known as HTML5, and in the last three years, the move from XHTML to HTML5 has occurred swiftly and with good reason.

HTML5 is designed for today's multimedia Web, with a rich set of APIs (Application Programming Interfaces) that provide built-in support for video, audio, graphics, geo-location, data storage, and much more. HTML5 also offers many new elements for better of structuring documents (`section`, `article`, `nav`, and so on). Previously, semantically meaningless divs with identifying classes and IDs had been used for this purpose, which limited the portability and meaning of the markup.

During HTML's transition from HTML4 to XHTML and then to HTML5, CSS3 has been steadily implemented by every browser. The visual-rendering toolbox that is CSS3 is a massive set of recommendations, so large that it has been divided into numerous modules so that different teams can plan how each module will work.

Finally, you can utilize long-awaited CSS3 features, such as gradients, transitions, transformations, shadows, and radiused corners, and be confident that the vast majority of users will see these features correctly rendered. For older browsers, where CSS3 is not fully supported, Modernizr, a JavaScript file that you link to your pages, enables you to detect support for specific CSS3 features. You can then provide fallbacks (alternative code) or polyfills (JavaScript code that simulates build-in CSS3 functionality) for those features. You can learn more about these fallbacks and polyfills in the Appendix section of this book.

Today, the Web is a much more user-friendly, and developer-friendly, place than it has ever been. Writing this latest version of *Stylin' with CSS* has, as always, been a labor of hundreds of hours of coding and writing, countless late nights and endless cups of tea, but it has also felt like a kind of celebration. That's because, behind the examples and exercises, this book describes a new state of the Web—the realization of a vision that has long been imagined. Thanks to the work and advocacy of Jeffrey Zeldman, Ian Hicks, and countless others, the long quest for Web standards appears to have been realized. It's like inching your way up the side of a mountain and suddenly realizing you're at the top. The fact that I no longer have to write (and waste pages of this book teaching you to write) hacks for older browsers for even the most simple layouts; that I can create shadows or radiused corners with a single line of CSS instead of using complex graphics and layers of divs; that every current browser displays my pages in a complete and consistent way—is a massive breakthrough.

So, in this book, I am looking forward to the future. Rather than spend pages showing you how to work around old browser incompatibilities as I did in previous editions, I am focusing on the vast scope of what is possible now and in the future with HTML5, CSS3, and modern browsers. Internet Explorer 9 and up, and Firefox, Chrome, Safari, and Opera (which automatically update users to the latest versions) all behave in remarkably consistent ways. The number of users on older browsers (specifically IE8 and below) decreases every day. I provide information in the Technical Notes in the Appendix about how to work with older browsers, but the main narative of this book is to show you how CSS works today and in the future.

A Focus on Essential Techniques

You don't need to be a brilliant artist or a computer programmer to be successful with CSS, although both those abilites can be put to good use. What you do need to do is have a solid grounding in the workings of HTML and CSS, and understand some key techniques and best practices. This book is designed to provide you with this understanding and provide a strong foundation for building your skills. CSS3 is so extensive that there are many features of it I didn't even mention in this book. No matter, I believe that once you have read and worked thought the examples in this book, you will be able to rapidly extend your knowledge and skills—that at least is the sincere objective in what I have written here.

Download My Code, Don't Rewrite It

All the code shown in this book is available for download at the book's Web site, www.stylinwithcss.com. I recommend you use the download code rather than copying the code from the book; not only is it much quicker and easier to do that, but I will also update the download code to correct any errors that are found. I will also run an errata section on the site and post any reported inaccuracies in the book. The site will have a new blog that I am starting, so please come by for information and maybe inspiration, and post comments and make suggestions for articles you would like to see.

Thanks for buying this book. I hope it's a big help to you, and good luck with your Web endeavors.

CHAPTER 1

HTML Markup and Document Structure

THIS BOOK IS ABOUT CSS, which is why the first chapter is about HTML, the Hypertext Markup Language!

The reason I start with HTML is that the purpose of CSS is to style HTML markup, so you first need to know how to write and structure your HTML markup so that it can be readily styled with CSS. Every Web page begins life as HTML because the first task in building a Web page is to mark up the content. Content is all the stuff you want to deliver to your audience, such as text, images, audio, and video.

The purpose of HTML markup is semantic; that is, it gives your content meaning to the user agents, such as browsers, screen readers, and Web crawlers, that display, speak, or analyze it. HTML provides a mechanism of tags to mark up your content and each tag defines the content within it. The most commonly used tags define headings, paragraphs, links, and images. There are currently 114 HTML tags in total, but the 80/20 rule applies here: you use the same small set of about 25 tags for 80% of your markup needs. You can find a complete list of HTML tags at www.stylinwithcss.com.

Once you have marked up your content, CSS can then be used to style the tags based on tag names, tag attributes such as IDs and classes, and each tag's relationship to other tags in the markup. HTML tags also create a document hierarchy, which allows you to use CSS to lay out the page, and to style each element in any way you wish.

HTML5, the latest version of HTML, brings a new set of structural tags for grouping related sets of content tags to better define the overall structure of your Web pages. The names of these tags include header, nav (navigation), article, section, aside, and footer. For example, you would use the nav tag to group a list of links that enable navigation to different pages of your site. Within an `article` tag, you might organize a group of headings and paragraphs that make up a blog entry.

Before HTML5, creating page structure required the use of semantically meaningless tags, such as `div` and `span`, but now there are tags specifically for this purpose.

To illustrate all of these ideas, I'll show how content is marked up, and show how your HTML creates a hierarchy of tags on which CSS and JavaScript can operate.

The Basics of Markup

Each content element—a heading, a paragraph, or an image, for example—is marked up in one of two ways, with an enclosing tag or a non-enclosing tag, dependant upon whether or not the tag's content is text.

Enclosing Tags for Text

The basic format of an enclosing tag is

```
<tagName>Some text content</tagName>
```

Attributes can be added to the tag

```
<tagName attribute_1="value" attribute_2="value">Some text content</tagName>
```

Text elements, such as headings and paragraphs, have enclosing tags, that is: one opening tag and one closing tag, like this:

```
<h1>Words by Dogsworth</h1>
```

```
<p>I wandered lonely as a dog.</p>
```

You can see that a tag is comprised of angle brackets that contain the name of the tag. The tag name is typically a single letter or an abbreviation that represents the type of content. The closing tag contains a slash before the tag name to differentiate it from the opening tag.

In between the opening and closing tag is the content that is displayed in the browser; the tags themselves do not display.

The opening and closing tags make it clear where the heading and paragraph text starts and ends. Note that the heading has a 1 in its tag, as there are six levels of headings in HTML, with h1 being the top-level heading.

Non-Enclosing Tags for Referenced Content

```
<tagName attribute_1="value" attribute_n="value" />
```

Non-text content is displayed using non-enclosing tags. The difference between enclosing and non-enclosing tags is that an enclosing element encloses the actual content that will be displayed, whereas a non-enclosing element simply provides the browser with a *reference* to the content that will be displayed. The browser makes additional requests to the server as the HTML page loads to get the content referenced in non-enclosing tags.

Here, an image is marked up with a non-enclosing tag.

```
<img src="cisco.jpg" alt="My dog Cisco">
```

Closing Tags

XHTML was strict about all tags being closed, but HTML5 is more lax, and allows you to omit certain closing tags. You can read the syntax overview at http://dev.w3.org/html5/html-author/#syntactic-overview.

For example, your code will still validate as HTML5 and display correctly onscreen if you just open a new paragraph tag without closing the previous one. However, I always close every tag, as this helps me better see the organization of my markup, and ensures I never fail to close the tags that should always be closed. I recommend that you do the same for all elements, as I show in this book.

With non-enclosing tags, XHTML required you to write

```
<img src="images/cisco.jpg" alt="My dog Cisco" />
```

With HTML5, you don't need the closing slash and can write

```
<img src="images/cisco.jpg" alt="My dog Cisco">
```

However, I still write a non-enclosing tag with the closing space-slash; HTML5 simply ignores it, and as I scan my code for structure, I get instant visual confirmation that the tag is closed and does not enclose the next tag.

Attributes

alt tags are read aloud for visually impaired users who are using a screen reader, so it is essential that you always add meaningful alt attribute text to images.

Attributes provide the browser with additional information about a tag. For example, the `img` tag in the preceding example has two attributes. The first, `src`, has an attribute name of `src` (source) and an attribute value of `cisco.jpg`. This attribute defines that the source of the image is a file with the name `cisco.jpg`. The second attribute, `alt`, defines the alternative text that will display onscreen if the image fails to load for some reason.

Attributes can be added to every HTML tag. As you will see when we start marking up the examples later, some attributes, such as class and ID, can be added to almost any tag, while others, for example `src`, can only be added to a tag such as `img` that references the source file.

You can find a complete reference of HTML tags and attributes at the HTML Dog site http://htmldog.com/ reference/htmltags.

HTML Elements Used in This Chapter

Here are the block and inline HTML tags I use in this chapter. I'll explain the difference between block and inline elements a little later in the chapter.

BLOCK-LEVEL TEXT ELEMENTS

`h1`, `h2`, `h3`, `h4`, `h5`, `h6` (Six heading levels—h1 is the most important)

`p`	paragraph
`ol`	ordered list
`li`	list item
`blockquote`	stand-alone quotation

INLINE TEXT ELEMENTS

`a`	link (anchor)
`img`	image
`em`	italic
`strong`	importance
`abbr`	abbreviation
`cite`	citation
`q`	quotation within text

Headings and Paragraphs

By far the most common text tags you will use are headings and paragraphs. Typically, you start your page with an h1 heading and add text within it that tells the reader what the page is about. Then you use an h2 heading for the next level of content, and if there are subheadings within the h2 content, then use h3 and so on.

Not only will h1 be the largest and most prominent heading (unless you change its appearance with CSS), but search engines seem to look for h1 as a source of additional keywords after the title tag.

Paragraphs are used for body text and are the general workhorse tag for any text elements. In short, if you have text that doesn't belong in one of the other text tags, put it in a paragraph.

Let's now move on to document flow and inline and block-level elements, and discover how each element creates a box on the page. These aspects of HTML are the foundation for quickly and efficiently styling the document to your desired layout and visual appearance with CSS.

Compound Elements

Not only does HTML enable markup of basic content like headings, images, and paragraphs, but also enables the creation of more complex user interface components such as lists, tables, and forms, by using compound elements—sets of tags that are designed to work together.

For example, the li list item is only valid within two of the three list type tags, ol (ordered list), ul (unordered list), but not dl (definition list). Here's a simple ordered list <ol> that contains three list items <li>.

```
<ol>
    <li>Save HTML file</li>
    <li>Move file to Web server via FTP</li>
    <li>Preview in browser</li>
</ol>
```

Figure 1.1 shows how this looks in the browser.

FIGURE 1.1 A simple ordered list. The browser numbers the items of an ordered list automatically.

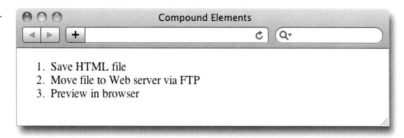

There are two things to observe here. First, certain tags, like ol, require other tags to be used in concert with them—in this case li tags. Second, the li list items are said to be "nested" inside the ol ordered list element, because the ordered list tag opens before the list items, and closes after them. Nesting of tags is a crucial concept to understand.

About Nested Tags

In the example above, the li tags are said to be children of the ol tag because they are nested inside it, and the ol tag is said to be the parent tag of the li tags, because it contains those tags.

Here's a simple example that uses the em (emphasis) tag to emphasize a word in a paragraph. Unfortunately, the em child tag is incorrectly nested inside the parent p tag.

```
<p>That car is <em>fast</p>.</em>
```

Here is how it should be written.

```
<p>That car is <em>fast</em>.</p>
```

If you nest a tag, that is, open a new tag before the preceding one is closed, you must close that second tag before closing the first. This is incorrectly done in the first example above, but is correctly done in the second example.

The overall structure of a document is created by the way tags are nested inside one another, and "parent-child" relationships between the tags are thereby created. Let's see all this in action as I show you how an HTML document is structured.

Anatomy of an HTML Document

The overall structure of an HTML document has been greatly simplified with HTML5. Those of you with even a few years of Web development experience will remember the complex options for doctypes for HTML and XHTML, for transitional and strict options, and for meta-content data. These have been replaced with simpler syntax that you can start using today and that will be backward compatible with earlier versions of HTML.

There are some HTML elements that must be present on every HTML document, aka Web page. These elements provide the framework in which your content can be successfully displayed. You can think of these required elements as a template with which you start every page that you build. Many Web coding applications, such as Adobe Dreamweaver, can automatically generate this template every time you create a new HTML page.

An HTML Template

Today, a bare-bones template of an HTML page using HTML5 syntax looks like this:

```
<!DOCTYPE html>
<html>

    <head>

    <meta charset="utf-8" />

    <title>An HTML Template</title>

    </head>

    <body>

        <!-- your Web page content here -->

    </body>
</html>
```

The HTML comments tag lets you add notes for yourself and others who might work on this page in the future. HTML comments begin with `<!--` and end with `-->`. You add your comment text in between. Comments are ignored when the page loads and do not display in the browser.

The first line is the new, simplified DOCTYPE that simply states this is an HTML document. Note that this tag does not need to be closed.

Next comes the html tag. It is known as the root level tag because all other tags on the page are nested inside it; it doesn't close until the end of the page. It has only two immediate child tags: head and body.

The Title Tag

Search engines weigh the title tag heavily, that is, importance is placed on the words within it. It also appears as the heading of the search results. Don't waste your title tag with something like *Welcome to my Web Page!* Ensure it contains the short description and keywords that your audience will use when searching for the topics or services offered by your site.

The head tag contains tags that help the browser understand how to display the page. In this bare-bones example, there are just two tags in the head: the meta tag with a charset attribute that tells the browser to use UTF-8 character encoding, and the title tag, whose text will appear along the top of the browser window when the page is displayed. I have added the text "An HTML Template" into the title tag.

The body tag contains all the HTML elements that make up your content. Let's start by replacing the comment with a couple of content tags and then take a look at the page displayed in a browser.

Inside the body tag of the template above, I add:

```
<body>

    <h1>Stylin' with CSS</h1>

    <p>Great Web pages start with great HTML markup!</p>

</body>
```

Figure 1.2 shows how the page displays in the browser.

FIGURE 1.2 A simple Web page with a headline and a paragraph displayed in the browser.

The browser lays out the elements one after another down the page starting from the top left corner. Observe that the headline and the paragraph each display in different sizes of the font Times Roman, with spacing between them—some kind of basic styling is clearly being applied to them. This initial (default) styling comes from a

CSS style sheet that is built into the browser and visually renders each HTML element in an appropriate if rather dull way.

Let's now add two more common HTML elements—a link and an image.

```
<body>

    <h1>Stylin' with CSS</h1>

    <p>Great Web pages start with great HTML markup!</p>

    <a href="http://www.stylinwithcss.com">My Books</a>

    <img src="images/cisco.jpg" alt="My dog Cisco" />

</body>
```

Figure 1.3 shows how the page looks now.

FIGURE 1.3 The page now contains four elements: a headline, a paragraph, a link, and an image.

A link is created with the a (anchor) tag, which has one required attribute, the href (hyperlink reference) containing the URL of the page to which the link points.

I introduced the image tag earlier and here you see it in action. It uses the src (source) attribute instead of an href, but its value is also a URL that locates the image.

Notice that while the headline and paragraph stack under each other, the link and the image sit side by side. The reason for this is that the headline and the paragraph are block-level elements, but the link and image are inline elements.

Block and Inline Elements

The preceding figure illustrates the effect of what is known as the document flow, which defines the way that HTML elements sequentially "flow" down the page in the order they appear in the markup. The purpose of the document flow, provided by the browser's style sheet, is to ensure that the document will display in a plain but usable way if simply marked up correctly with HTML. The art of CSS is to transform this utilitarian default display of HTML markup into an inviting and intuitive page design.

Almost all HTML elements have a `display` property of either `block` or `inline`. The most notable exceptions are table elements, which have their own special `display` properties.

Block elements, such as headings and paragraphs, stack underneath each other down the page, each visually forming a new line. Inline elements, such as links and images, sit next to each, and only move down on to a new line if they do not have room to do so.

As you learn about each HTML element, your first question should always be: Is this a block or an inline element? Knowing this allows you, as you write the markup, both to predict how an element will position itself initially, and to plan how you will reposition it later with CSS.

BUILDING A PAGE WITH BLOCK AND INLINE ELEMENTS

Here is a page made up entirely of headings and paragraphs. I am keeping the paragraphs very short here for clarity in the screenshots and code.

Here is the markup.

```
<!DOCTYPE html>
<html>

<head>
   <meta charset="utf-8" />
   <title>Block and Inline Elements</title>
</head>

<body>
   <h1>Types of Guitars</h1>
   <p>Guitars come in two main types: electric and
   acoustic.</p>
   <h2>Acoustic Guitars</h2>
   <p>Acoustic guitars have a large hollow body that
   projects the sound of the strings.</p>
   <h3>Nylon String Acoustic Guitars</h3>
   <p>Descendants of the gut-strung instruments of yore,
   nylon string guitars have a mellow tone.</p>
   <h3>Steel String Acoustic Guitars</h3>
   <p>Steel string guitars first appeared in country music
   and today most acoustic guitars have steel strings.</p>
   <h2>Electric Guitars</h2>
   <p>Electric guitars have a solid or hollow body with
   pickups that capture the string vibration so it can be
   amplified.</p>
   <h3>Solid Body Electric Guitars</h3>
   <p>Solid body electric guitars are commonly used in rock
   and country music.</p>
   <h3>Hollow Body Electric Guitars</h3>
   <p>Hollow body acoustic guitars are commonly used in
   blues and jazz.</p>
</body>

</html>
```

The content of this page is marked up as headings and paragraphs.
Normally-present structural tags such as article have been omitted for clarity.

Figure 1.4 shows this code displayed in the browser.

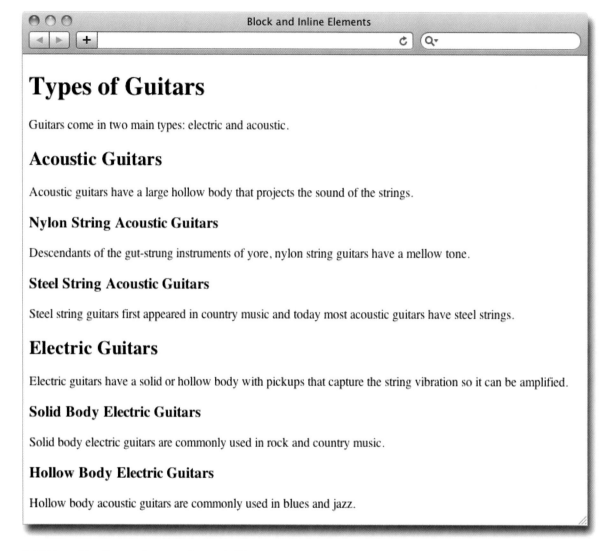

FIGURE 1.4 Headings and paragraphs create this page.

In the code and the screenshot, you can see that there are three levels of headings. The browser styles each of these at different sizes so that the hierarchy of the page's content is apparent. Each element starts a new line because headings and paragraphs are block-level elements.

Note also that a margin of space is added around the edge of the page so that the text does not touch the edge of the browser window. Also, space is added between the lines of text. Before looking at this spacing in more detail, let's add some images to this page as shown in **Figure 1.5**. Images, as you now know, are inline elements.

FIGURE 1.5 Two inline elements are added to the page.

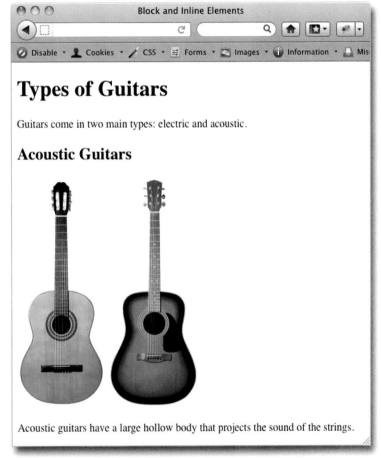

The fact that the img tags are on separate lines in the markup has no effect on the display of the images. They are inline elements, so they will sit next to each other. White space (such as tabs, returns, and spaces) between tags is ignored, so you can freely add line breaks and spaces to lay out your code for easy reading. As good practice, child tags are indented from their parent tag.

Here is the code for the illustrated part of the page showing that two images were added into the markup. The images are inline elements so they sit next to each other.

```
<body>

    <h1>Types of Guitars</h1>

    <p>Guitars come in two main types: electric and
    acoustic</p>
```

```
<h2>Acoustic Guitars</h2>

<img src="images/acoustic_nylon.jpg" alt="nylon string
acoustic guitar" />

<img src="images/acoustic_steel.jpg" alt="steel string
acoustic guitar" />

<p>Acoustic guitars have a large hollow body that
projects the sound of the strings.</p>

</body>
```

At this point, let's deepen our understanding of block and inline elements by doing a little investigation of this page using one of my favorite development tools, the Web Developer extension. This is an add-on for Firefox, and it adds a menu of useful tools to examine HTML, CSS, and JavaScript.

FIGURE 1.6 Here I select from the Web Developer toolbar *Outline* menu.

You can download and install *Web Developer* by selecting Add Ons *from the* Firefox *Tools menu, searching on the* Add Ons *site for Web Developer, and then selecting* "Add" *on the Web Developer page.*

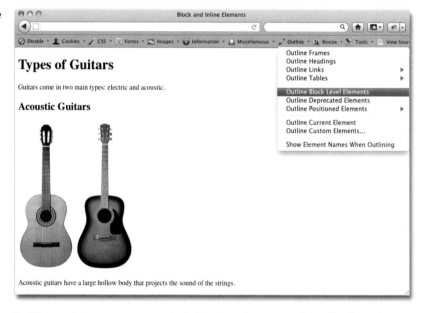

In **Figure 1.6**, you can see the Web Developer toolbar displayed along the lower edge of the window chrome. One of the many things that it can do is help you more clearly see the placement of the elements and their relationships to one another. In the screenshot, I am selecting *Outline Block Level Elements* from the *Outline* menu, which displays the outline of the block-level elements' boxes.

FIGURE 1.7 Selecting *Outline Block Level Elements* shows the actual size of the elements' boxes and the space between them. The inline images are not outlined.

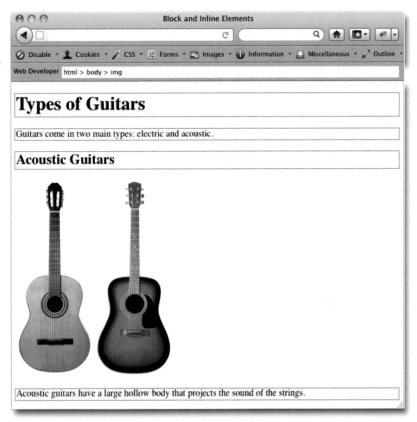

With the outlines of the block-level elements displayed, you can see in **Figure 1.7** that the element boxes are much bigger than the text they contain. While each element's height is just slightly greater than the height of its content; its width is the width of the browser window!

A block-level element box expands to the width of its parent element.

In this case, the parent of all these elements is body, which, by default, is the width of the browser window (less a small default margin). So all these elements are the width of the browser window also. Now you can understand why block-level elements always create a new line; they are full width, so there is no room for another element to sit next to them.

Web Developer doesn't allow me to select all of the page's inline elements in the same way as I can select block-level elements, but

I can select *Outline Custom Elements* from the *Outline* menu to see their element boxes. Inline element boxes behave in the opposite manner to block elements.

An inline element box "shrink-wraps" its content, and fits around it as tightly as possible.

Now you can understand why inline elements will sit next to each other, but block elements always start a new line.

Nested Elements

Let's now see the onscreen effect of nesting HTML elements in the markup. All the elements in the preceding example share the same parent—body. The required body element is always present, so Web Developer doesn't normally show it, but you can display the body element by selecting *Outline Custom Elements* from the *Outline* menu as shown in **Figure 1.8**.

FIGURE 1.8 Select *Outline Custom Elements* and then, in the next window, specify which element to display and which color to display it in.

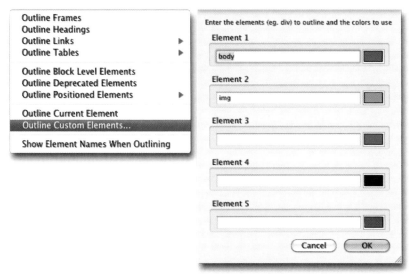

Figure 1.9 shows you that the box of the parent element body (blue) literally nests, that is encloses, all the child element boxes (red). These block-level child elements expand to fit the body element, which by default is the width of the browser window (less a tiny margin).

When you nest HTML tags in your markup, you are nesting boxes inside of one another onscreen.

FIGURE 1.9 The parent body element surrounds its child elements.

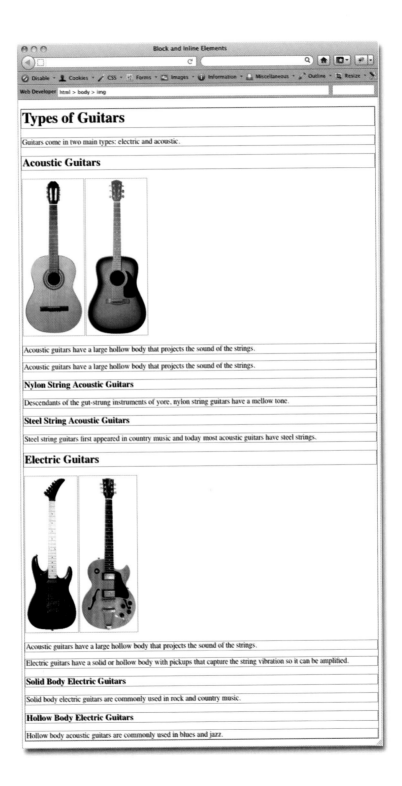

In a page with many elements, this nesting of boxes can go many layers deep, so organizing your HTML to indicate page structure in the markup of the code helps you ensure that tags are correctly nested. Indicate nesting with indenting. It's good practice to use four spaces to indent each level, represented here with dots.

```
<nav id="toc">

....<ol>

........<li><a href="#">Introduction</a></li>

........<li><a href="#">Chapter 1</a></li>

........<li><a href="#">Chapter 2</a></li>

........<li><a href="#">Chapter 3</a></li>

....</ol>

</nav>  <!-- end table of contents -->
```

Some HTML editors, such as Dreamweaver, will add four spaces when you press Tab, saving you keystrokes and aiding consistency.

TWO EXAMPLES OF NESTING IN MARKUP

Let's look at another nesting example, this time using a blockquote. A blockquote element is used for a quotation that is a separate visual element on the page. Note the use of HTML entities to create the curly quote marks.

```
<blockquote>&ldquo;Sometimes you want to give up the guitar,
you'll hate the guitar. But if you stick with it, you're
gonna be rewarded.&rdquo;
    <cite>Jimi Hendrix</cite>
</blockquote>
```

a citation is used for the author's name

Figure 1.10 shows how this looks onscreen, with both elements outlined.

FIGURE 1.10 A blockquote is indented by default.

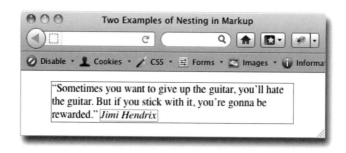

HTML Entities

HTML entities are typically used to generate the typographical characters that are not printed on the keys of your keyboard, such as ™, †, ©, and so on. HTML entities start with an ampersand and end with a semicolon, and contain a string of characters that represent the entity. In the preceding example, the entity names are abbreviations of left-double-quote and right-double-quote.

Fellow Peachpit author, Elizabeth Castro, whose books I highly recommend, lists the commonly used HTML entities at http://www.elizabethcastro.com/html/extras/entities.html.

Note that because entities start with an ampersand, the ampersand's usage is restricted to that purpose. Because of this, you must use the `&amp;` entity for every occurrence of & in the text enclosed within your HTML tags; for example, `Johnson &amp; Johnson`. This displays as Johnson & Johnson.

The `blockquote` tag is, as its name suggests, a block-level element: its purpose is to be a stand-alone element on the page, so this makes perfect sense.

Nested inside the blockquote (outlined in red), after the quoted text, is the citation (outlined in green), marked up with the inline tag `cite`. It has room to sit inline after the paragraph text. You can see that the `cite` tag is by default styled with italics.

Also in this example, you will see two HTML entities: `&ldquo;` and `&rdquo;` which create typographically correct left-double-quote and right-double-quote quotation marks. Using these quote entities, instead of the straight-up-and-down basic quotation marks created by pressing Shift-' (Shift-quote) on the keyboard, gives a professional touch to your page.

As a second example, let's take a look at this little bit of markup that uses three inline elements within a block-level element.

```
<p>It is <strong>absolutely critical</strong> that
<em>everyone</em> does this <abbr title="as soon as
possible">ASAP</abbr>!</p>
```

Figure 1.11 shows how this displays in Firefox.

FIGURE 1.11 A paragraph marked up with tags to indicate importance, emphasis, and an abbreviation.

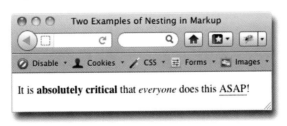

Figure 1.12 shows the same text with the element boxes displayed.

FIGURE 1.12 Three inline elements are enclosed in a block-level element.

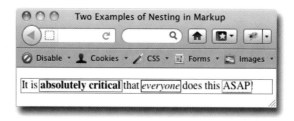

Besides the obvious sense of urgency, there's a lot you can take away from this short example.

•   The text is marked up as a paragraph and encloses three inline tags.

•   The strong tag indicates importance, and is styled by default as bold text.

•   The em tag indicates emphasis and is styled by default as italic text.

•   The abbr tag indicates an abbreviation and, in Firefox, is by default underlined with dots.

You have seen how HTML markup creates boxes on the page, and that nesting the markup nests the onscreen boxes, now let's move on to the HTML overview—the Document Object Model.

The Document Object Model

The last piece of HTML knowledge you need before we start looking at CSS is that the structure of your HTML creates the Document Object Model, hereafter referred to as the DOM. This is the browser's view of the elements on the page, and state of every element's properties, from which it can determine the family-tree relationships between the elements. By referencing a specific location in the DOM model with CSS, you can select an HTML element and then modify its style properties.

Let's start learning about the DOM with this example.

```
<body>

  <section>

    <h1>The Document Object Model</h1>

    <p>The page's HTML markup structure defines the DOM.</p>

  </section>


</body>
```

HTML code, correctly indented to indicate the hierarchy of the tags

FIGURE 1.13 A simple DOM hierarchy representation of the markup..

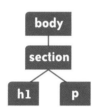

The code example above and **Figure 1.13** depict a typical page structure, where a structural tag (in this case, section) contains a number of child content tags (here h1 and p). The indenting of the code indicates the family hierarchy. This hierarchy can also be represented in a vertical orientation, just like any good family tree.

Figure 1.14 shows the HTML code with the elements outlined

FIGURE 1.14 This figure shows that body (outlined in red encloses the green section, which in turn encloses two child elements, heading and paragraph, both outlined in blue.

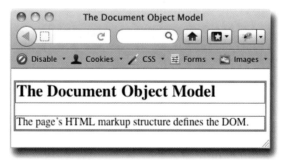

Here's what we can say about this DOM hierarchy:

• section is the **parent** of h1 and p—the immediate ancestor above them

• h1 and p are the **children** of section—the immediate descendants below it

- h1 and p are **siblings**—they share a parent, section
- section, h1, and p are **descendants** of body—elements below (nested somewhere within it)
- section and body are **ancestors** of h1 and p—elements above them (nesting them at some level)

I will use the terms child, parent, sibling, ancestor, and descendant frequently in the coming chapters, so it's worth being sure you know what they mean, and fully understanding how the nesting of your HTML creates the hierarchy of the DOM.

CSS manipulates the DOM by first selecting an element or set of elements and then changing those elements' properties. If you use CSS to modify an element's property, such as its width, or insert a pseudo-element into the markup, those changes are made to the DOM, which then updates the page.

In short, you construct the DOM with HTML markup, and then can modify the DOM using CSS as the page first loads and as the user interacts with the page.

Summary

In this chapter, you learned how HTML tags provide structure to content, and that each element creates an onscreen box. You learned the difference between block and inline HTML elements. You also learned that when elements are nested inside one another, a hierarchical relationship is created between them. You learned that the nesting of HTML elements in the markup creates nested boxes onscreen. Finally, you learned that the DOM is the browser's view of the document, and that CSS can change the style properties of elements in the DOM and thereby change the layout and appearance of the page itself. This knowledge is the foundation for successfully styling HTML with CSS. In Chapter 2, I'll cover the rules and mechanics of CSS and how they operate on HTML markup.

How CSS Works

YOU SAW IN CHAPTER 1 how the structure of a document is created with HTML. In this chapter, I will show you how CSS rules are used to style HTML, and explain the workings of the Cascade, which is how CSS resolves which style is applied when more than one style affects an element property.

Each HTML element has style properties that can be set with CSS. These properties relate to the different visual aspects of the element, such as its position onscreen, the width of its border, the size, color, and fonts of its text, and so on. CSS is a mechanism for selecting HTML elements and then setting the selected elements' CSS properties. Each CSS selection and the associated styles that are applied is called a CSS rule.

So let's look at CSS rules and how to apply them to HTML elements. Follow along at home by adding the examples I will show you into this simple HTML5 template, or just open the examples in the code download, which you can find at http://www.stylinwithcss.com.

```
<!DOCTYPE html>
<html>

<head>

<meta http-equiv="Content-Type" content="text/html;
charset=UTF-8" />

<title>HTML5 Template</title>

<style>

  /* CSS rules go inside the style tags */

</style>

</head>

<body>
```

This code example illustrates the difference in the formatting of comments in CSS and HTML

```
<!-- HTML elements go between the body tags -->
</body>
</html>
```

Here you see the use of the HTML `style` tag. This tag allows you to add (or to use the technical term, embed) CSS styles directly into the document. The browser will apply the CSS styles within the `style` tag to the HTML elements within the `body` tag.

The Anatomy of a CSS Rule

A rule is the term for a complete CSS instruction; a rule states the element to be modified and the styles that will be applied to it.

Here's an example of a CSS rule that will set the color of a paragraph to red.

```
p {color:red;}
```

Applied to this HTML markup

```
<p>This text is very important!</p>
```

the element's text will display red as shown in **Figure 2.1**.

FIGURE 2.1 A simple CSS tag selector styles an HTML element.

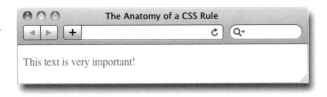

Find this HTML template and all the code examples in this book at http://www.stylinwithcss.com.

Here's how this code fits into in an HTML5 page template.

```
<!DOCTYPE html>
<html>

<head>

<meta charset="utf-8" />

<title>HTML5 Template</title>

<style>

continues
```

Three Ways to Add Styles to Your Document

There are three ways to add CSS to your Web pages: inline, embedded, and linked from a CSS style sheet.

INLINE STYLES

Inline style declarations are added to a tag using the HTML `style` attribute, like this

```
<p>This paragraph simply takes on the browser's default paragraph style.</p>
```

```
<p style="font-size: 12px; font-weight:bold; font-style:italic; color:red;">By adding inline CSS styling to this paragraph, you override the default styles.</p>
```

The scope of inline styles is very restricted. An inline style affects only the tag to which it is attached, and will always override the embedded styles and styles in a linked style sheet.

EMBEDDED STYLES

Embedded CSS styles are placed in the head of your HTML document, like this

```
<head>
<!-- other head elements (e.g., meta tags, title) go here -->
<style type="text/css">
  h1 {font-size:16px;}
  p {color:blue;}
</style>
</head>
```

The scope of embedded styles is limited to the page. Page styles override style sheet styles, but lose out to inline styles. It can be convenient to develop styles for a component, such as a menu, using embedded styles, as I do in the early demos in this book, so that you have both the HTML and the CSS in one page, but once the CSS is functional, you will want to move those styles into a style sheet so they can be shared by other pages.

LINKED STYLES

When creating a site of more than one page, you will want to place your styles in a separate document known as a style sheet. A style sheet is simply a text file with the .css extension. You can link your style sheet to as many HTML pages as you want with a single line of code in the head tag of each page:

```
<link href="styles.css" rel="stylesheet" type="text/css" />
```

The scope of linked styles is site-wide. Simply use the HTML link tag to link the style sheet to each page that will use the styles. When you change a style in a style sheet, it can affect a selected element wherever it appears in the site which makes for consistent page-to-page stylings and easy site-wide updates.

Style sheets can also be linked to other style sheets using the `@import` at-rule, like this

```
@import url(css/styles2.css)
```

Note that `@import` at-rules must appear before any other CSS rules in the style sheet, or the `@import`-referenced style sheets won't load.

continued

CSS is nested inside the style ⎯⎤
tags in the page head

```
        p {color:red;}

</style>

</head>

<body>
```

HTML goes between the ⎯⎯⎯⎯⎤
body tags

```
        <p>This text is very important!</p>

</body>
</html>
```

> *Style tags are not needed in style sheets. Style sheet styles will not load if you do this.*

It's important to note that CSS styles are embedded in the page using the style tag. When the browser encounters an opening style tag, it switches from interpreting the code as HTML and starts interpreting the code as CSS. When it encounters the closing style tag, it switches back to HTML.

Use this template to try the examples that follow in this chapter. Add the template above into a text file and save it with a .html file extension, then paste each example's CSS and HTML into the templates as illustrated above. Save, and then open the text file in a Web browser to view the result.

CSS Rule Naming Conventions

FIGURE 2.2 There are two main elements of a CSS rule—a selector and a declaration. The declaration is made up of two sub-elements—a property and a value. Curly brackets open and close the declarations.

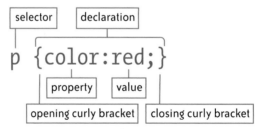

A CSS rule is made up of two parts: the selector, which states the element the rule selects—in this case, a paragraph—and the declaration. The declaration is made up of two parts: a property, which states what aspect of the element is to be affected—here, the color of the text—and a value, which defines the property's new state—here, red.

Observe that the selector is followed by an opening curly bracket. The property and its value are separated by a colon and the declaration ends with a semicolon. The rule ends with the closing curly bracket.

It's worth taking a good look at **Figure 2.2** so that you are absolutely clear on these terms; you'll be seeing them a lot more as we move forward.

This basic rule structure can be extended in three ways:

1. Multiple declarations can be contained within a rule.

```
p {color:red; font-size:12px; font-weight:bold;}
```

Now the paragraph text is red, 12 pixels high, and bold.

Note that each declaration ends with a semicolon to separate it from the next. The last semicolon before the closing curly bracket is optional, but I always add it so that I can tack on more declarations later without having to remember it.

You may be wondering what other values properties, such as font-size and color, may have. For example, you might want to know if you can specify a color using RGB (red, green, blue) instead of a color name. (The answer is yes, you can.) First, I will show you how selectors work. Then, later in this chapter, I'll discuss the declaration part of the rules.

2. Multiple selectors can be grouped. If, say, you want text for h1, h2, and h3 tags to be blue and bold, you could type all this

```
h1 {color:blue; font-weight:bold;}
```

```
h2 {color:blue; font-weight:bold;}
```

```
h3 {color:blue; font-weight:bold;}
```

However, you can avoid this kind of repetition by grouping selectors into a single rule like this

```
h1, h2, h3 {color:blue; font-weight:bold;}
```

Be sure to put a comma after each selector except the last. The spaces between the selectors are optional, but they make the code easier to read.

3. Multiple rules can be applied to the same selector. If, having written the previous rule, you decide that you also want just the h3 tag to be italicized, you can write a second rule for h3, like this

> In this book, multiple CSS declarations are placed on a single line to save space. You may want to break each declaration onto its own line for clarity in your CSS. Note that CSS ignores white space between declarations so you can add line breaks, spaces, and tabs to format your CSS to your liking.

```
h1, h2, h3 {color:blue; font-weight:bold;}

h3 {font-style:italic;}
```

These three types of rule structures form the basis of the more complex selections you will want to make. For example, when coding your CSS, you will likely want a specific element such as a paragraph to display differently in a sidebar than in an article, and the rules we have seen so far affect all the tags of the kind stated throughout the document. So now let's learn how to write rules that can target specific areas of your markup.

These more specific selectors fall into three main groups.

- **Contextual selectors**—select an element based on an ancestor or sibling element

- **ID and class selectors**—select an element based on ID and class attributes that you add to it

- **Attribute selectors**—select an element based on information in its attributes

Contextual Selectors

Let's imagine you may want paragraph text to display at one size in an article in the main content area of your page, and to display at a different size when used in a sidebar. This "location-based" variation of styles for a specific tag is achieved with contextual selectors, which you will learn about next.

```
tag1 tag2 {declarations}
```

tag2 is only selected if it has a *tag1* ancestor.

Contextual selectors, technically known as *descendant combinator selectors*, state a sequence of space-separated tag names. Their purpose is to let you select tags that are descendants of specified ancestors.

```
article p {font-weight:bold;}
```

In this example of a contextual selector, only p tags that are descendants of article tags will be affected by this rule. Put another way, the targeted tag in the above rule is a p tag that is in the context of (i.e. a descendant of) an article tag.

 Let's look at this concept in more detail using this piece of markup

```
<body>

  <article>

    <h1>Contextual selectors are <em>very</em> selective</h1>

    <p>This example shows how to target a <em>specific</em>
    tag.</p>

  </article>

  <aside>

    <p>Contextual selectors are <em>very</em> useful!</p>

  </aside>

</body>
```

This markup, without any CSS styling, displays like **Figure 2.3** in the browser.

FIGURE 2.3 Markup styled with the defult browser styles.

The markup creates the DOM (Document Object Model) represented in this hierarchy diagram (**Figure 2.4**).

FIGURE 2.4 A DOM hierarchy diagram of the markup.

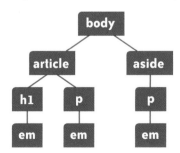

Figure 2.5 shows the corresponding box structure that this DOM hierarchy creates on the page.

FIGURE 2.5 Each level of the hierarchy creates a box around its child elements.

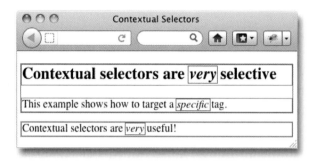

You will find it helpful to refer to the preceding hierarchy diagram as I show you CSS rules that target specific elements within this example's markup.

I displayed the box outlines by selecting Outline Block Level Elements *and* Outline Custom Elements *(where I entered the names of the inline elements) in the Developer Toolbar for Firefox.*

I'll start with a simple one-tag selector.

```
em {color:green;}
```

This rule selects all em tags on the page, so the text of all three em tags is green (**Figure 2.6**).

FIGURE 2.6 A simple one-tag rule colors all the em elements' text green.

Let's modify this contextual selector to be a little more specific about the tags we are selecting.

```
p em {color:green;}
```

Remember that, unlike the group selectors you saw earlier, contextual selectors have spaces, not commas, between the selectors.

Now the p is the context, and the em, because it's stated last, is the tag to be selected. What this rule means is "select any em tag with a p tag ancestor." Take a look at the hierarchy diagram—which tags will be selected by this rule?

The answer is that this rule selects the em tags inside the two paragraphs, but the em within the heading is unaffected; that tag does not have a paragraph as an ancestor and therefore the rule does not apply (**Figure 2.7**).

FIGURE 2.7 With a paragraph as context, the rule does not affect the em tag in the heading.

Figure 2.8 illustrates a variation on this single-context selector idea. Let's change the CSS rule to read

```
article em {color:green;}
```

which displays

FIGURE 2.8 When the context is the article tag, the em tag in the aside is unaffected.

Now I am using the article tag as the context, so the em text in article's h1 heading and in its paragraph is green. The em text in the aside tag is unaffected, because the em in aside does not have an article ancestor. Note that it doesn't matter that there is a p tag in-between the article and the em—the em simply has to have an article ancestor somewhere higher in the hierarchy for the selector to work.

If I want to target only the em tag within the heading, I need to be more specific with the context.

```
article h1 em {color:green;}
```

Now I am stating that only an `em` tag that is descended from an `h1` tag that is descended from an `article` tag will be selected.

FIGURE 2.9 Using two contextual selectors enables more specific selection of a tag.

As **Figure 2.9** shows, sometimes you have to string contextual selectors together to specify a particular tag you want to target.

Specialized Contextual Selectors

So far, you have seen tags with contextual selectors that use ancestor tags for context. As long as that tag has the context somewhere "upstream" in its hierarchy, that element is selected. It doesn't matter how many other tags appear in the hierarchy between the stated selectors. Sometimes, though, you want to be more specific than just "some ancestor"; what if you want to select an element based on the tag name of its immediate parent or its preceding sibling?

Let's use a new piece of markup to demonstrate some specialized contextual selectors.

```
<section>
  <h2>An H2 Heading</h2>
  <p>This is paragraph 1</p>
  <p>Paragraph 2 has <a href="#">a link</a> in it.</p>
  <a href="#">Link</a>
</section>
```

Child Selector >

tag1 > tag2

tag2 must be the child of *tag1*, or to put another way, *tag1* must be the parent of *tag2*. Unlike a regular contextual selector, this rule does not apply if a *tag1* ancestor is further up the hierarchy.

```
section > h2 {font-style:italic;}
```

Figure 2.10 shows how this looks in the browser.

FIGURE 2.10 h2 is selected because it is a child of section.

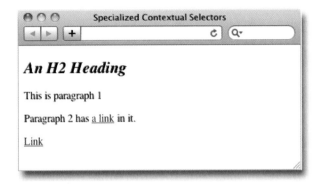

Adjacent Sibling Selector +

tag1 + tag2

tag2 must immediately follow its sibling *tag1*.

```
h2 + p {font-variant:small-caps;}
```

Figure 2.11 shows how this looks in the browser.

FIGURE 2.11 First p is selected because it is the first sibling of h2.

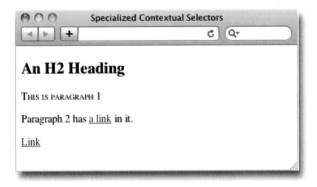

General Sibling Selector ~

Type the ~ (tildé) character using Shift and the key located to the left of the 1 key.

tag1 ~ tag2

tag2 must follow (not necessarily immediately) its sibling *tag1*.

```
h2 ~ a {color:red;}
```

Figure 2.12 shows how this looks in the browser.

FIGURE 2.12 Only the sibling link tag is selected.

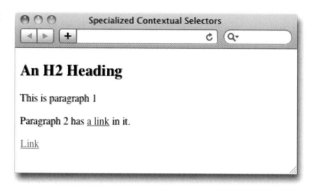

The Universal Selector *

* (Press Shift-8)

The * universal selector (commonly known as the star selector) is a wildcard; it matches any element, so if you use

```
* {color:green;}
```

the text of all elements (text and borders) will be green. Generally, you use the * selector with another selector

```
p * {color:red;}
```

This makes the text of all elements within a p tag red.

An interesting use for this selector is as the inverse of the child selector—a not-a-child selector, if you will.

```
section * a {font-size:1.3em;}
```

The color *property sets the foreground color which affects both text and border color, but is typically used to color only text.*

FIGURE 2.13 The link that is the grandchild is selected, but the link that is the child is not.

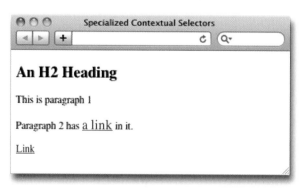

As **Figure 2.13** shows, any a tag that is at least a grandchild of the section tag, but not a child, is selected; it doesn't matter what the a's parent tag is.

In summary, a CSS rule with a single selector tag selects every instance of that tag on the page, and you can use contextual selectors to specify a tag's required ancestors or siblings.

IDs and Classes

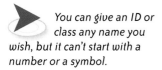

You can give an ID or class any name you wish, but it can't start with a number or a symbol.

IDs and classes give you a second approach to styling your document—one that can operate without regard for the document hierarchy. You can use classes and IDs to target specific areas of your document directly by first adding IDs and class attributes to the tags in your HTML markup and then referencing those IDs and classes in your CSS selectors.

The Class Attribute

A class attribute can be added to any HTML element within the body tag. Here's a piece of markup that illustrates the use of an HTML class attribute.

```
<h1 class="specialtext">This is a heading with the
<span>same class</span> as the second paragraph.</h1>
<p>This tag has no class.</p>
<p class="specialtext"> When a tag has a class attribute,
you can target it <span>regardless</span> of its position in
the hierarchy.</p>
```

Figure 2.14 shows how this displays.

FIGURE 2.14 The default styling of the markup.

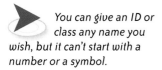

This is a heading with the same class as the second paragraph.

This tag has no class.

When a tag has a class attribute, you can target it regardless of its position in the hierarchy.

Note that when you write a class selector, you precede the name of the class with a . (period). Do not put a space between the period and the class name.

Note that I've added the class attribute `specialtext` to two of these tags.

THE CLASS SELECTOR

`.classname`

An HTML class name is referenced in CSS by directly preceding it with a . (period).

Let's apply these two CSS styles.

```
p {font-family:helvetica, sans-serif; font-size:1.2em;}
```

```
.specialtext {font-style:italic;}
```

Figure 2.15 shows how this affects the markup.

FIGURE 2.15 The text of the paragraphs is now in Helvetica and larger. The heading and second paragraph both have the specialtext class, so now both are italicized.

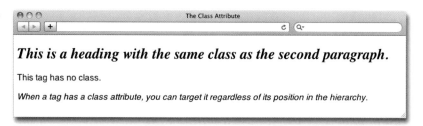

These rules result in both paragraphs displaying in the Helvetica font (or the browser's generic sans-serif font if Helvetica is not available), and the paragraph with the `specialtext` class also displaying italicized. The text in the `h1` tag remains in the browser's default font (usually Times) because the Helvetica style is only applied to paragraphs, but it is now italicized because it has the `specialtext` class. Note that the `span`, a tag that has no default styles, simply inherits its parent's styling, because I didn't explicitly style it.

TAG-WITH-CLASS SELECTOR

If you only want to target the paragraph with the class, you create a selector that combines the tag name and the class, like this

```
p {font-family:helvetica, sans-serif; font-size:1.2em;}
```

```
.specialtext {font-style:italic;}
```

```
p.specialtext {color:red;}
```

FIGURE 2.16 By combining a tag name and class name, you make the selector more specific.

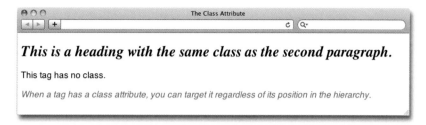

As shown in **Figure 2.16**, the highlighted CSS selects a p tag with the class of specialtext. Combining a tag and class name like this lets you be even more specific about which tag you want to select.

Let's add another rule to take this idea one step further.

```
p {font-family:helvetica, sans-serif; font-size:1.2em;}

.specialtext {font-style:italic;}

p.specialtext {color:red;}

p.specialtext span {font-weight:bold;}
```

As you can see in **Figure 2.17**, the word "regardless" is italicized and bold because it is in a span tag that is in a paragraph with the specialtext class, as the rule specifies. All four rules contribute to the styling of this span tag, because the span inherits the styles in the first three rules from its paragraph parent—I'll explain inheritance in detail later in this chapter.

FIGURE 2.17 By adding a second selector, you can be very specific about which tag is styled.

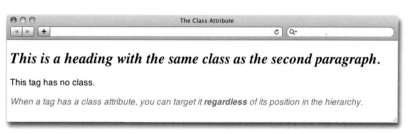

MULTIPLE CLASSES SELECTOR

You can add multiple classes to an element, like this

```
<p class="specialtext featured">Here the span tag <span>may
or may not</span> be styled.</p>
```

You can see that the specialtext and the featured class names are placed in the same set of quotes with a space between them. Put more technically, the HTML class attribute can have multiple values, separated with spaces. To select an element where both class names must be present, you would write

```
.specialtext.featured {font-size:120%;}
```

Observe that there is no space between the two classes in the CSS because I am stating that only an element with *both* classes is selected. A space in-between would state the ancestor/descendant relationship of a contextual selector.

It is a common mistake to add a separate HTML `class` attribute for each class, instead of using a single class attribute with multiple values, as shown in the markup above. You will see practical uses for multiple class names in later chapters.

The ID Attribute

IDs are written in a similar way to classes, and you use a # (hash symbol) to indicate an ID in the same way as you use a . (period) to indicate a class.

IDs for In-Page Navigation

IDs are also used for in-page navigation links. Here's the HTML for a link that targets a location within the same page.

```
<a href="#bio">Biography</a>
```

Note that the # (hash) sign before the `href`'s value indicates that this link's target is a location within the page; it will not trigger the browser to load a page of this name, as it would if the # sign were not present.

Using the same `#IDname` syntax used in CSS selectors, the `href` points to a target ID on the same page. Further down the page is the target.

```
<h3 id="bio">Biography</h3>

<p>I was born when I was very young…</p>
```

Note there is no hash tag on the target ID value. It's just a regular ID.

When this link is clicked, the page will instantly scroll to bring the `h3` element with the ID `bio` to the top of the page. A link with only # as an `href` value will scroll the page back to the top.

```
<a href="#">Back to Top</a>
```

To do this, you don't even need a target element with an ID of #—it just works.

Note that a link doesn't act like a link if the `href` value is left blank, so it's accepted practice to use the # symbol as a placeholder value in an `href` if you don't yet know what URL will go there. Often, a programmer on the team will later add a middleware, e.g., PHP, variable in its place to accept a URL from a database.

If a paragraph is marked up with an ID, like this

```
<p id="specialtext">This is the special text.</p>
```

then the corresponding selector looks like this

```
#specialtext {some CSS rules here}
```

or

```
p#specialtext {some CSS rules here}
```

Other than this, IDs work in the same way as classes, and (almost) everything in our previous discussion of classes applies equally to IDs. So what's the difference?

When to Use an ID and When to Use a Class

At first glance, classes and IDs might appear to be interchangeable—they are both HTML attributes used to identify specific tags within the markup—but they serve very different purposes.

WHEN TO USE AN ID

> You can also use an ID to associate JavaScript with a tag (for example, to run a script that activates an animation when the user mouses over a link). It's especially important that you ensure JavaScript-related IDs have unique names within a page, or the JavaScript may behave unpredictably.

The purpose of an ID is to uniquely identify an element within the page. Because of this, every ID attribute you use in a page must have a unique value (name). Or, put another way, each ID name can only be used once in a page.

```
<nav id="mainmenu">
```

In this case, there cannot be another element on the page with the ID name of mainmenu. To identify a part of your page's markup, such as the main navigation menu, you might use an ID on a nav (navigation element) that encloses the menu's elements.

```
<nav id="mainmenu">
  <ul>
    <li><a href="#">Yin</a></li>
    <li><a href="#">Yang</a></li>
  </ul>
</nav>
```

This ID uniquely identifies this menu on the page to allow you to target each of the different types of tags within it with a simple contextual selector. For example, you could color the menu's a links orange, without affecting other links on the page, using

```
#mainmenu a {color:orange;}
```

With its unique ID, you can easily target just this element and its children with your CSS. Going forward, you will see that I usually add an ID on the top-level element of each section of the page, to give me an unambiguous context, so that I can write CSS rules that only select tags within that part of the HTML.

So now that you understand that an ID indicates a unique HTML element within the page, let's look at when to use classes.

WHEN TO USE A CLASS

The purpose of a class is to identify a number of elements that will share a set of characteristics, as you saw with the specialtext example earlier in the chapter.

In this list of baby names, I want to make the boy's names blue and the girl's names pink. First, I use classes to identify the gender of the names in the markup.

```
<nav>

  <ul>
    <li class="boy"><a href="#">Alan</a></li>

    <li class="boy"><a href="#">Andrew</a></li>

    <li class="girl"><a href="#">Angela</a></li>

    <li class="boy"><a href="#">Angus</a></li>

    <li class="girl"><a href="#">Anne</a></li>

    <li class="girl"><a href="#">Annette</a></li>

  </ul>

</nav>
```

Then I color the links with CSS

```
blue ─────────────────┤ .boy a {color:#6CF;}

pink ─────────────────┤ .girl a {color:#F9C;}
```

The first rule selects any a element that has an ancestor with the class boy, and the second rule selects any a element that has an ancestor with the class `girl`. In both cases, that ancestor is the link's parent `li` element.

Don't Go Crazy with Classes

Avoid what Web maven, Jeffrey Zeldman, describes as "classitis—the measles of markup," where you add a unique class to just about every tag in your markup and then write a rule for each one. If you are already in the habit of slapping classes on every tag, as most of us do when we enthusiastically jump into CSS without the knowledge of how inheritance and contextual selectors operate, then you are probably repeating many of the same styles for each tag (such as stating the same font for every tag on that page). Inheritance and contextual selectors allow you to share styles between tags and thereby minimize the CSS that you have to write and maintain.

IDs and Classes Summary

The purpose of an ID is to uniquely identify a specific element in the page's markup. This provides the required context to let you write CSS rules that filter out the rest of the markup and select only the tags within that context.

In contrast, a class is a common identifier that can be applied to any number of HTML elements and across multiple pages, so they can be assigned the same set of CSS rules. A class also allows you to apply the same style rules to elements that have different tag names.

Attribute Selectors

So far I've shown how contextual selectors, and IDs and classes, are used to make HTML selections with CSS. A third method of making selections is with attribute selectors. Attribute selectors select elements based on the attributes of the HTML tags. Here are the two useful examples.

The Attribute Name Selector

tagName[attributeName]

Selects any tag of type *tagName* that has the attribute name *attributeName*.

This CSS

```
img[title] {border:2px solid blue;}
```

causes any HTML img tag with a title attribute, like this

```
<img src="images/yellow_flower.jpg" title="yellow flower"
alt="yellow flower" />
```

to display a blue, two-pixel border around it; it doesn't matter what the value of the title attribute is, just that there is one. You might use such a style to indicate to the user that if he points at this image, a tooltip (pop-up text generated by the title attribute) displays. It's common practice to use the same text value for the alt and title attributes. The alt tag text displays if the image does not load, or can be read by a screen reader, while the title displays a tooltip that displays if the user points at the image.

The Attribute Value Selector

With HTML5, quotes are optional on attribute values. I add them for clarity.

```
tagName[attributeName="attributeValue"]
```

Selects any tag with an attribute *attributeName* that has the value *attributeValue*.

This selector lets you be specific about what the attribute's value should be. For example, the rule

```
img[title="red flower"] {border:4px solid green;}
```

puts the border around the image if the image's title attribute is red flower; in other words, if it has this title attribute

```
<img src="images/red_flower.jpg" title="red flower" alt="red
flower" />
```

You can find the complete list of attribute selectors at www.stylin-withcss.com.

Summary of Attribute Selectors

Selecting by attribute name and other aspects of an element's attributes gives you a means to differentiate between tags of the same type. By planning ahead, you can create markup that can be readily selected using attribute selectors.

One common aspect of the selectors you have seen so far is that they all are targeting something in the markup—a tag name, a class, an ID, an attribute, or an attribute value. But you can also use CSS to change the styling of an element when certain events occur, such as the user pointing at (hovering over) a link. This is achieved with pseudo-classes.

Pseudo-Classes

Named for the fact that they work like class selectors, even though those classes aren't actually attached to tags in the markup, pseudo-classes fall into two groups.

- **UI (User Interface) pseudo-classes** cause rules to be applied to the markup when an HTML element is in a certain state, such as the cursor being over a link.

- **Structural pseudo-classes** cause rules to be applied to the markup when certain structural relationships exist in the markup, such as an element being first or last in a related group of elements.

UI Pseudo-Classes

UI pseudo-classes are applied based on the state of a particular HTML element. They are most commonly used with hyperlinks (a tags), enabling style changes such as a change in a link's color or removing its underline when rolled over, but can also be used to provide a variety of responses, such as displaying an informational panel when the user rolls over an element, as you will see in the chapter on interface components.

LINK PSEUDO CLASSES

There are four UI pseudo-classes for anchor links, as links are always in one of these four states:

- **Link.** The link is just sitting there and waiting for someone to click on it.

- **Visited.** The user has previously clicked on the link.

- **Hover.** The link is currently being pointed at (rolled over).

Because these four pseudo-classes all have the same specificity (to be discussed later in this chapter), browsers may not display the desired result if the four selectors are not listed in the order shown here. The mnemonic "LoVe? HA!" is an easy, if cynical, way to remember the order in which to write these pseudo-classes for each set of links.

The single colon (:) is used to designate pseudo-classes, but a double colon (::) is required for new pseudo-elements introduced in CSS3. Although browsers currently support the use of the single colon for CSS1 and CSS2 pseudo-elements, you should get into the habit of using the double colon as the single colon for these pseudo-elements may eventually be phased out. You can read more at http://www.w3.org/ TR/2005/WD-css3-selectors-20051215/#pseudo-elements.

- **Active.** The link is currently being clicked (the mouse is pressed down on the element but has not been released).

Here are the corresponding pseudo-class selectors for these states (using the a selector with some sample declarations):

```
a:link {color:black;}

a:visited {color:gray;}

a:hover {text-decoration:none;}

a:active {color:red;}
```

The distinctive : (colon) in the selector screams (at least, indicates) "I am a pseudo-class!"

According to the declarations above, links are initially black (and underlined by default). When the mouse rolls over them (the hover state), the underlining is removed, and they stay black, because no color is defined here for the hover state. When the user holds the mouse down on the link (the active state), it turns red. Once the links has been clicked, meaning the mouse was pressed down and released over the same element, triggering its URL, then forever after (or more accurately, until the browser's history of the visit to the link's URL expires or is deleted by the user), the link displays in gray.

You don't have to define all four of these states. If you just want to define a link and a hover state, that's fine, and often all that makes sense. If, for example, you have a long, table-of-contents set of links, it's very helpful to show, perhaps with a lighter color, which ones have already been visited (clicked). However, changing the color of clicked links doesn't make sense for a navigation bar.

Typically, I just define an a state and a :hover state; the latter, to let the user know that the element is clickable when it's rolled over.

Having the ability to style link states in this way is all very nice, but the real power comes when you start using these link pseudo-classes as elements of contextual selectors. Then you can create different looks and behaviors for various groups of links in your design—for example, it's easy to make links look and behave differently within nav, footer, sidebar, and article elements, as you will see later.

Note you can use any element with these pseudo-classes, not just a, to create all kinds of rollover effects. In this example, the paragraph's background turns gray when the mouse rolls over it.

```
p:hover {background-color:gray;}
```

THE :FOCUS PSEUDO-CLASS

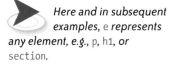 *Here and in subsequent examples, e represents any element, e.g.,* p, h1, *or* section.

e:focus

An element such as a text field of a form has focus when the user clicks it; that's where the characters appear when the user types. For instance, the code

```
input:focus {border:1px solid blue;}
```

puts a blue border around such a field when the cursor is in the field. This can help the user understand where characters will appear when she types.

THE :TARGET PSEUDO-CLASS

e:target

If the user clicks a link that points to an element elsewhere on the page, that element is the target and it can be selected using the :target pseudo class.

In the case of this link

```
<a href="#more_info">More Information</a>
```

an element somewhere on the page that has the ID more_info is the target. That element might look like this

```
<h2 id="more_info">This is the information you are looking for.</h2>
```

This CSS rule

```
#more_info:target {background:#eee;}
```

adds a gray background to an element with the ID more_info when the user clicks the link to navigate to it.

Wikipedia uses :target extensively for its citations. Wikipedia citation links are unobtrusive numbers styled as links within the text. The citations themselves are in a long list at the bottom of the page.

Without the highlight that `:target` provides, you wouldn't know which of the many citations listed relates to the link you clicked.

You can find additional UI pseudo-classes at www.stylinwithcss.com.

Structural Pseudo-Classes

Structural pseudo-classes enable styles to be applied based on the structure of the markup, such as the element's immediate parent or its preceding sibling.

:FIRST-CHILD AND :LAST-CHILD

e:first-child

e:last-child

A `:first-child` is the first-listed element of a set of sibling elements, and a `:last-child` is the last. For example, if this rule

```
ol.results li:first-child {color:blue;}
```

was applied to this markup

```
<ol class="results">
  <li>My Fast Pony</li>
  <li>Steady Trotter</li>
  <li>Slow Ol' Nag</li>
</ol>
```

then the text "My Fast Pony" would be blue. If the selector read

```
ol.results li:last-child {color:red;}
```

then the text "Slow Ol' Nag" would be red.

:NTH-CHILD

e represents an element name and *n* represents a number (the keywords odd and even can also be used)

e:nth-child(*n*)

For example,

```
li:nth-child(3)
```

would select every third item of a set of list items.

A very common use of `nth-child` is to improve the readability of tables by striping their rows with alternate background colors, as you will see in Chapter 6.

There are several other structural pseudo-classes, and you can find a complete listing of them at www.stylinwithcss.com.

Pseudo-Elements

Pseudo-elements, as the name suggests, provide the effect of extra elements magically appearing in your document's markup. Here are examples of the two most useful ones, and you can find a complete list of pseudo-elements at www.stylinwithcss.com.

In order to create this first-letter effect without the pseudo-element, you would have to wrap a span *element around the letter and then style the span. Instead, the pseudo-element effectively adds this invisible markup.*

THE ::FIRST-LETTER PSEUDO-ELEMENT

e::first-letter

This CSS, for example:

p::first-letter {font-size:300%;}

enables you to create a large letter at the start of a paragraph as shown in **Figure 2.18**.

FIGURE 2.18 The ::first-letter pseudo-element allows you to create large letters.

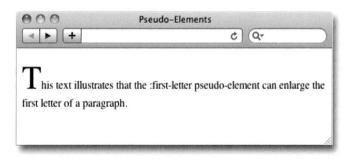

THE ::FIRST-LINE PSEUDO-ELEMENT

e::first-line

enables you to style the first line of (usually) a paragraph of text. For example,

p::first-line {font-variant:small-caps;}

results in the first line displaying in small capital letters (**Figure 2.19**).

FIGURE 2.19 The ::first-line pseudo-element styles the first line as uppercase letters. Note that the ::first-line pseudo-element selection changes as the browser window is resized and the line length changes.

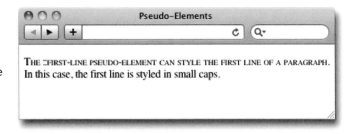

THE ::BEFORE AND ::AFTER PSEUDO-ELEMENTS

These two pseudo-elements

`e::before` and `e::after`

cause specified content to be added before and after an element. This markup

`<p class="age">25</p>`

and these styles

`p.age::before {content:"Age: ";}`

`p.age::after {content:" years.";}`

result in text that reads:

Age: 25 years.

Note that a space is added into each of the content values to produce the desired word spacing in the output.

This technique is most useful when the tag's content is being generated as a result of a database query; if all the result contains is the number, then these selectors allow you to provide that data point with descriptors when you display it for the user.

Search engines can't pick up pseudo-element content (because it doesn't appear in the markup), so don't use these elements to add important content that you want search engines to index.

This example provides a basic, although useful, application of the `::before` and `::after` pseudo-elements. However, later I will demonstrate the power of these two pseudo-elements in creating new elements "on-the-fly" that hang off the element to which they are applied, to provide some interesting styling possibilities.

This completes an overview of the various types of CSS selectors. Now it's time to take a deeper dive into how CSS works.

In a large style sheet, any number of rules might select and attempt to set the same property of the same element. For example, a paragraph with a class attribute might have a font assigned to it by a rule that uses its tag name, while another rule uses the element's class name to assign a different font. Of course, this font property can only have one value at any given time, so CSS has three related mechanisms for resolving such conflicts and determining which of the rules will "win" and actually set that property. These mechanisms are inheritance, the Cascade, and specificity. Let's now look at each of these in turn.

Inheritance

Just like the money you hope you'll get from rich Uncle Dick some day, inheritance in CSS involves passing something down from ancestors to descendants: the values of CSS properties. You will remember from my discussion on the document hierarchy in Chapter 1 that the body tag is the great-ancestor of them all—all the tags in your markup descend from it. So, thanks to the power of CSS inheritance, if you style the body tag like this

```
body {font-family:helvetica, arial, sans-serif;}
```

then every text element in your document inherits these styles and it displays in Helvetica (or in one of the other choices if Helvetica is not available) no matter how far down the hierarchy it is. The efficiency that inheritance offers is obvious; rather than specify the same font-family for every single tag in your markup, you set the font at the top of the hierarchy as the primary font for the entire site. Then you only need additional font-family properties for elements that need to be in a different font.

Many CSS properties are inherited in this way, most notably those that relate to text, such as color, font, and size. However, many other CSS properties are not inherited because inheritance doesn't make sense for them. These non-inherited properties primarily relate to the positioning and display of box elements, such as borders, margins, and padding, which you will learn about in the next chapter.

For example, imagine that you want to create a sidebar box with lists of links in it. You might do this by writing a nav with a list of child links, and styling the nav with a font size and a border, say a two-pixel red line. While it is very convenient that every link's font size will be inherited from the div, it makes no sense for every one of those list items to inherit the div's red border too. And they won't—border properties are not inherited.

Because font and text styling are inherited, you must be careful when working with relative font sizes such as percentages and ems. If you style a tag's font size to be 80 percent and it's descended from a tag whose text is also sized at 80 percent, its text size will be 64 percent (80 percent of 80 percent), which may not be the effect you want. In Chapter 4, I'll cover the pros and cons of absolute and relative text sizing.

I'll continue to demonstrate the effect of inheritance in later examples and show you how to leverage inherited styles so that you write the minimum amount of CSS necessary to achieve your desired result.

The Cascade

OK, now you have enough information to have a meaningful discussion about the Cascade. As its name suggests, the Cascade in Cascading Style Sheets involves styles falling down from one level of the hierarchy of your document to the next, and its function is to let the browser decide which of the many possible sources of a particular property value for a tag is the one to use.

The Cascade is a powerful mechanism. Understanding it helps you write CSS in the most economical and easily editable way and enables you to create documents that are viewed as you want them to be seen, while leaving appropriate control of aspects of the document's display, such as overall font sizes, with users who have special needs.

Sources of Styles

Styles can come from many places. First, it's not hard to accept that there must be a browser style sheet (the default style sheet) hidden away inside the browser, because every tag manifests styles without you writing any. For example, h1 tags create large bold type, em tags create italicized type, and lists are indented and have bullets or numbers for each item.

Then there is the user style sheet. The user can create a style sheet, too, although very few do. This capability is handy, for example, for the visually impaired, as they can increase the overall size of displayed text of all sites that load in their browser, or force text to be in colors that they can better differentiate. A visually impaired user might add a style like

```
body {font-size:200%;}
```

that doubles the size of all text—inheritance at work again.

See the sidebar, Three Ways to Add Styles to Your Document, *earlier in this chapter.*

Then there are author style sheets, which are written by you, the author of the page. I have already discussed the sources of author styles: linked style sheets, embedded styles within a page, and inline styles that are attached to tags.

Here's the order in which the browser looks at, or cascades through, the various locations:

- Default browser style sheet
- User style sheet
- Author style sheets (in the order that they are linked to the page)
- Author embedded styles
- Author inline styles

The browser updates its settings for each tag's property values (if defined) as it encounters them while looking sequentially through the rules in each location. Whatever each element's properties are set to at the end of this process determines how the element is displayed onscreen.

If, for example, the author style sheet style defines the p tag's font-family to be Helvetica but an embedded (page) style uses the same selector to define it as Verdana, the paragraph will be displayed in Verdana—the embedded styles are read after the author style sheet. However, if there is no font style for paragraphs defined in either the user or the author style sheet, then paragraphs will display in Times, because that's the style defined in all default browser style sheets.

All this will make more sense as you learn the Cascade rules that determine which styles are applied to the page's elements.

Get more info on the Cascade at the W3C site (www.w3.org/TR/CSS2/cascade. html).

The Cascade Rules

Here are the rules that define how the Cascade works.

Cascade Rule 1: Find all declarations that apply to each element and property. As it loads each page, the browser looks at every CSS rule and identifies which HTML elements are affected.

Cascade Rule 2: Sort by order and weight. The browser sequentially checks each of the five sources, setting any matched properties as it goes. If a matched property is defined again further down the sequence, the browser updates the value and does this repeatedly, if necessary, until all five possible locations of properties for each tag in that page have been checked. Whatever a particular property is set to at the end of this process, is how it's displayed.

There is also the weight of the declaration. You can add to the weight (power) of a rule if you define it as important, like this

```
p {color:green !important; font-size:12pt;}
```

The word `!important` follows a space after the style you want to make important but before the ; (semicolon) separator.

This style defines the text's green color as important, and therefore, it will always display green, even if it is declared as a different color further down the Cascade. Essentially, you are saying: This style gets applied, no matter what. Think carefully before you force a particular style on the user with an `!important` rule definition, because you may be messing up someone's personal style sheet, which may be set that way for a very good reason. If you think you need to use it, take a long look at your CSS first and you will usually find a better alternative. To give this some perspective, I rarely, if ever, use the `!important` declaration.

Cascade Rule 3: Sort by specificity. Besides being very hard to pronounce, specificity determines just how specific a rule is. Without specificity, you would be constantly changing the order of the styles in your style sheet to ensure the right style wins.

As you saw, if a style sheet contains both this rule

```
p {font-size:12px;}
```

and this rule

```
p.largetext {font-size:16px;}
```

then this markup

```
<p class="largetext">A bit of text</p>
```

displays text 16 pixels high because the second rule's selector states both a tag name and a class name and is therefore more specific— it overrides the more simple rule. This example may seem obvious, but what happens to that bit of markup if you use these styles instead?

```
p {font-size:12px;}

.largetext {font-size:16px;}
```

The answer is that while both these rules match the tag, the class wins, and the text is 16 pixels. Here's why: Class names selectors have a higher specificity than simple tag name selectors. Specificity is determined by the number of tags, classes, and IDs on each selector.

Calculating Specificity

Here's how to calculate the specificity of any selector. There is a simple scoring system for each selector that can calculate a three-value "ICE" formula:

I - C - E

The dashes are separators, not subtraction signs. Here's how the scoring works:

1. Add one to I for each ID in the selector.

2. Add one to C for each class in the selector.

3. Add one to E for each element (tag) name.

4. Read the result as a three-digit number.

So let's look at the specificity of these examples

ICE does not really provide a three-digit number; it's just that in most cases, reading the result as a three-digit number works; the highest number wins. Just understand that you can end up with something like 0-1-12, and 0-2-0 is still more specific.

0 - 0 - 1 specificity=1 ────────┤ P

0 - 1 - 1 specificity=11 ────────┤ p.largetext

1 - 0 - 1 specificity=101 ────────┤ p#largetext

1 - 0 - 2 specificity=102 ────────┤ body p#largetext

1 - 1 - 3 specificity=113 ────────┤ body p#largetext ul.mylist

1 - 1 - 4 specificity=114 ────────┤ body p#largetext ul.mylist li

Each example is a higher specificity than the previous one.

Cascade Rule 4: Sort by order. If two rules that both affect the same property of an element also have exactly the same specificity, the one furthest down the Cascade wins.

And that, dear reader, is the Cascade and, yes, it is somewhat hard to understand, especially if you have not yet had much experience with CSS, but my simplified version of the Cascade rules (see *Charlie's Simple Cascade Summary*) applies in virtually all cases, and is much easier to remember.

Charlie's Simple Cascade Summary

There are just three rules to remember in this simplified version of the Cascade rules, and these rules apply in virtually every case.

Rule 1: Selectors with IDs override selectors with classes, which override selectors with tag names.

Rule 2: If the same property for the same tag is defined in more than one location, inline styles override embedded styles, which override style sheet styles. In style sheets, later styles override earlier styles with the same specificity.

Rule 2 loses out to Rule 1, though—if a selector is more specific, it overrides, wherever it is.

Rule 3: Defined styles override inherited styles, regardless of specificity. A little explanation is required for Rule 3. This markup

```
<div id="cascade_demo">

  <p id="inheritance_fact">Inheritance is <em>weak</em> in the Cascade</p>

</div>
```

and this rule

```
div#cascade_demo p#inheritance_fact {color:blue;}
```

2 - 0 - 2 (high specificity)

results in all the text, including the word "weak, being blue because the em inherits the color from its parent, the p tag.

As soon as we add this rule for the em

```
em {color:red;}
```

0 - 0 - 1 (low specificity)

the em text is red, even though the rule has the lowest possible specificity (0 - 0 - 1). The inherited style for the em is overridden by the defined style for the em, even though the inherited rule has far higher specificity.

Rule Declarations

So far I've focused on how you use CSS rule selectors to target tags, but I haven't yet looked in any detail at the other part of a CSS rule, the declaration. I've used numerous different declarations to illustrate the selector examples but have only explained them minimally. Now it's time to start looking at declarations in detail.

The diagram earlier in this chapter illustrating the structure of a CSS rule (**Figure 2.2**), shows that a declaration is made of two parts: a property and a value. The property states which aspect of the element is affected (its color, its height, and so on) and the value states what that property is set to (green, 12px, and so on).

Every element has a number of properties that can be set using CSS; these differ from element to element. You can set the `font-size` property for text, but not for an image, for example. We will look at the different properties of the various HTML elements as we encounter them in subsequent chapters, but because there are only a few different types of CSS property values, I'll discuss those now.

Values fall into three main types:

Word values. For example, in `font-weight:bold`, `bold` is a word value. Word values are also referred to as keywords.

Numerical values. Numerical values are followed by a unit type, such as inches or points. In the declaration `font-size:12px`, `12` is the numerical value and `px` is the unit type—pixels. Note that if the value is 0, no unit type is required.

Color values. Color values can be written in several formats: RGB (red, green, blue), HSL (Hue, Saturation, and Luminance), and hexadecimal (for example, `color:#336699`).

Let's look in more detail at each of the three types of property values.

Word Values

Words are used for all kinds of CSS property values. For example, the `visibility` property has the values `visible` and `hidden`; `border-style` properties include `solid`, `dashed`, and `inset`.

Except for a couple of examples like this, there's not much I can tell you about word values that would make sense until I start using them in later chapters, because the words used are specific to each property. Numerical and color values, however, can only be expressed in certain ways.

Numerical Values

You use numerical values to describe the length (in CSS, the term "length" is used generically to mean height, width, thickness, and so on) of all kinds of elements. These values fall into two main groups: absolute and relative.

Absolute values (**Table 2.1**) describe a length in the real world (for example, 6 inches), as compared to a relative measurement, which is simply the relationship to some other measurable thing (when you say "twice as long as," that's a measure relative to something else).

TABLE 2.1 Examples of Absolute Values

ABSOLUTE VALUE	UNIT ABBREVIATION	EXAMPLE*
Inches	in	height:6in
Centimeters	cm	height:40cm
Millimeters	mm	height:500mm
Points	pt	height:60pt
Picas	pc	height:90pc
Pixels	px	height:72px

*Examples are not equivalent lengths.

Pixels are the only absolute unit that I use in this book and in my work, except in print style sheets—because paper is measured in inches, it makes sense to design print layouts with the same units.

Although the absolute units are self-explanatory, the relative units (**Table 2.2**) warrant a little more explanation.

Em and ex are both measurements of type size, although in CSS they can be applied to any element property as a unit of length. The em is derived from the width of the M character in a font, so its size varies, depending on which font you are using. ex is the

TABLE 2.2 Examples of Relative Values

RELATIVE VALUE	UNIT ABBREVIATION	EXAMPLE*
Em	em	height:1.2em
Ex	ex	height:6ex
Percentage	%	height:120%

*Examples are not equivalent lengths.

equivalent of the x-height of the given font (so named because it is the height of a lowercase x—in other words, the center bit of the font's letters without the ascenders and descenders that appear on characters such as d and p).

Percentages are useful for setting the width of contained elements, such as divs, to a proportion of the container's width. Using structural HTML elements that are a percentage of the width of the body element is the basis of "liquid" designs that proportionally change their width as the user resizes the browser window, as you will see in Chapter 5.

Color Values

You can use several value types to specify color. You can mix and match these options in the same style sheet, if you wish.

COLOR NAME (E.G., RED)

As you have seen from all the earlier color examples in the selector discussions, you can simply specify a color by name, or keyword to use the official term.

The W3C defines 16 color keywords: aqua, black, blue, fuchsia, gray, green, lime, maroon, navy, olive, purple, red, silver, teal, white, and yellow. See http://www.w3.org/TR/css3-color/#html4 for a list of the names and their respective sRGB color values.

Most modern browsers offer many more colors (the 140 X11 color names), but if you want to specify colors by name, you can only absolutely rely on the 16 stated above. See http://en.wikipedia.org/wiki/X11_color_names for a list of the names and their respective RGB color values.

Generally speaking, keyword colors are useful for specifying black and white, but for serious color work, you need to use one of the following options.

HEXADECIMAL (#RRGGBB AND #RGB)

Most hex colors aren't easy to guess at a glance; for example, #7ca9be is a dusky blue-green color, but how could you know that? Let's look at just the first value in each rgb pair, 7, a, and b in this case. Blue and green are almost equal, and red is not so strong. With this information, it's possible to make an informed guess as to what the color is—green-blue.

If you already know languages like C++, PHP, or JavaScript, then you are familiar with the hexadecimal (hex) notation for color. The format is

`#rrggbb - e.g., #ff8800 - orange`

Don't forget the # (hash) symbol in front of the value!

In this six-character value, the first two characters define red, the next two green, and the next two blue. Computers use units of two to count, rather than base 10 like us mortals, and that's why hex is base 16 (2 to the power of 4), using the 16 numbers/letters 0–9 and a–f. a through f effectively function as 10 through 15. Because each of the rgb colors is represented by a pair of these base 16 numbers, there are 256 (16 × 16) possible values for each, resulting in 16,777,216 combinations (256 × 256 × 256) of colors.

For example, pure red is `#ff0000`, pure green is `#00ff00`, and pure blue is `#0000ff`.

You can also use this shorthand hex format

`#rgb`

The now-obsolete 216-color Web-safe color palette is entirely made up of values with matched pairs like this.

if you use a color where each pair has the same two letters.

Based on the examples above, you can write pure red as `#f00`, pure green as `#0f0`, and pure blue as `#00f`. `#ff3322` (a strong red) could be abbreviated to `#f32`. This is particularly handy for quickly specifying shades of gray; for example, you can use `#000` for black, `#444` for 75% gray, `#888` for 50% gray, `#bbb` for 25% gray, and `#fff` for white.

RGB NUMERICAL (R, G, B)

Each element is defined by a value from 0 to 255. The format is like this:

`rgb(r, g, b)`

For example, the declaration `rgb(0,255,0)` is pure green.

Really, it's the same format as the hex rgb with a different way to state the values; 256 values can be specified for each of the three colors, so the same number of colors can be defined as with the hexadecimal values. The difference here is that we are using familiar base 10 that we were taught in kindergarten, not base 16 that is taught in computer science classes (you did study computer science at school, right?).

RGB PERCENTAGES (R%, G% B%)

This is a notation that uses a percentage of each color like this

```
r%, g%, b%
```

Acceptable values are 0% to 100%. Although this yields only a piddling one million color combinations ($100 \times 100 \times 100$), that's more than enough for most of us. Also, it's much easier to make a guess at the color you want in rgb percentages compared with hex notation.

So, for example, 100%, 0%, 0% is max red, 0%, 100%, 0% is max green, and 46%, 76%, 80% is close to that dusky green-blue color I demonstrated in hexadecimal earlier.

HSL (HUE, SATURATION, AND LUMINANCE)

The format is like this

```
HSL(0,0%,0%)
```

HSL is more intuitive for specifying colors than the variations of rgb you have seen so far, because it is easier to create and read the colors.

The first value in an HSL color definition is hue—which is the actual color, as in red or green. Colors are spread around the circumference of a circle (aka a color wheel) and the hue value represents the number of degrees around the circle.

The numerical values for hue in HSL colors define the position of the color around this color wheel (**Figure 2.20**).

FIGURE 2.20 In the HSL color model, the hue value is defined by the number of degrees around the color wheel.

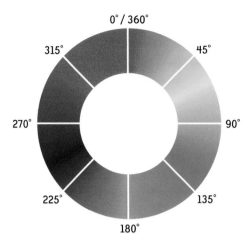

Red is at 0 and 360. Cyan is directly opposite at 180. Here are the approximate hue values for the colors of the rainbow.

Red: 0

Orange: 35

Yellow: 60

Green: 125

Blue: 230

Indigo: 280

Violet: 305

The saturation and luminance settings are quite simple to understand. Saturation sets how much of the color is present; grayish colors have low saturation, intense colors have high saturation. Luminance sets how dark or light the color is; 0% always results in black, 100% always results in white, so you need to be somewhere in between to actually see the hue.

If you keep the above list of the rainbow hue values on hand while you work, you will quickly discover you can create any color very easily. Both RGB and hexadecimal colors require you to mix the color levels in your head to "read" a color, but with HSL you just have one value for the color, and then if you start with both saturation and luminance at 50%, you will be able to dial in the desired shade quickly from there.

ALPHA CHANNELS

Note that both RGB and HSL allow you to specify an alpha channel value that sets the level of opacity of the color (i.e. how much of the background shows through it), using the formats RGBA and HSLA, respectively. In both formats, the A (alpha) value can be set to a value between 1 (opaque) and 0 (transparent). You will learn about using alpha channels in later chapters.

Some Color Resources

http://colrd.com—Colrd is a Pinterest-style site with inspiring graphics and images, and the color palettes derived from them.

http://kuler.com—The Adobe Kuler site offers thousands of color swatches, palette creation tools and listings of popular colors that others are choosing.

Summary

In this chapter, you have learned about CSS rules and how they set the style properties of HTML elements. You have seen the numerous rule selectors that can be combined to enable you to select sets of elements within the markup, and how rule declarations state the new property settings of the selected elements. You have seen how the Cascade, inheritance, and specificity together determine, when more than one style affects an element property, which style is applied to the element. You have also learned about the various numerical and keyword options that can be used to define the values to which properties can be set, and the different color models that can be used to specify colors.

In the next chapter, you will learn how to style and structure the visual hierarchy of your page's text, to make your typography look engaging and professional.

CHAPTER 3

Positioning Elements

IN THIS CHAPTER, YOU WILL LEARN about the *box model*, the position and display properties, and how to float and clear elements. Positioning techniques you will learn in this chapter are central to understanding CSS and will give you the core abilities you need to successfully create CSS page layouts.

The box model describes the rectangular boxes that are generated for every HTML element in your markup. These boxes are laid out on the page according to the visual formatting model. Visual formating is primarily controlled by three properties: the position property, which defines the positional relationship between the elements on the page; the display property, which determines whether elements stack, sit side-by-side, or even display on the page at all; and the float property, which gives additional positioning options and can be used to organize elements into multi-column layouts.

Understanding the Box Model

As you saw in Chapter 1, every element you create in your markup produces a box on the page, so an HTML page is actually an arrangement of boxes.

By default, the border of each box isn't visible and the background of the box is transparent, so the underlying box structure is not immediately apparent. As you have seen, with CSS and tools like the Web Developer Toolbar, it's easy to turn on the borders and color the backgrounds of the boxes. You can then start to see your page structure in a whole new light.

Let's look first at the properties of every element's box. These properties fall into three groups.

- **Border.** You can set the thickness, style, and color of the border.

To learn more about the box model, see http://www.w3.org/TR/REC-CSS2/box.html.

- **Padding.** You can set the distance of a box's content from its border.

- **Margin.** You can set the distance between this box and adjacent elements.

A simple way to think about these properties is that margins push outward from the border and padding pushes inward from the border, as shown in **Figure 3.1**. Because a box has four sides, properties associated with border, padding, and margin each have four settings: top, right, bottom, and left.

FIGURE 3.1 This box model diagram shows the relationship between border, padding, and margins of an HTML element.

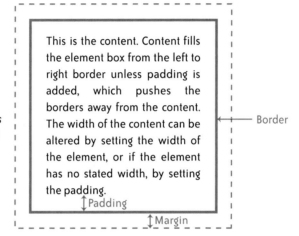

An element box also has a background layer that can be colored and to which images can be added. I'll cover properties relating to an element's background at the end of this chapter.

While you can specify individual values for the border, margin, and width of the four sides of the box individually, CSS offers some convenient shorthand styling options so that you don't have to write as many as 12 declarations for every box you want to display! See the sidebar, *Shorthand Styling,* for details.

Box Border

A fourth border *property,* border-radius, *does not affect the working of the box model and I will cover it in Chapter 7.*

border has three associated properties:

- **Width.** This includes thin, medium, thick, or any width unit except % values and negative values.

- **Style.** Value can be none, hidden, dotted, dashed, solid, double, groove, ridge, inset, or outset.

- **Color.** This includes any color value (for example, RGB, HSL, hexadecimal, or color keyword).

Shorthand Styling

CSS offers some shorthand ways to specify borders, padding, and margins within a single declaration. In these shorthand declarations, the order of the sides of the box is always top, right, bottom, left. You can remember this as TRouBLe, which you will be in if you forget, or you can visualize the order as the hands on a clock going around from 12. To specify margins for an element, instead of writing

```
{margin-top:5px; margin-right:10px; margin-bottom:12px; margin-left:8px;}
```

you can simply write

```
{margin:5px 10px 12px 8px;}
```

Note the space between each of the four values: you don't need a delimiter such as a comma. You don't even have to specify all four values—if you don't provide one, the opposite side's value is used.

```
{margin:12px 10px 6px;}
```

In the preceding example, because the last value, left, is missing, the right value is used and the left margin is also set to 10px. In this next example

```
{margin:12px 10px;}
```

only the first two values, top and right, are specified, so the missing values for bottom and left are set to 12px and 10px, respectively. Finally, if only one value is supplied

```
{margin:12px;}
```

then all four sides are set to this value. Using shorthand, you can't specify only bottom and left without providing values to top and right, even if those values are both zero, but you can write 0 without a value type like this

```
{margin:0 0 2px 4px;}
```

Also, there are three levels of granularity with which you can reference box properties, depending on how specific about which side and which property of the box you want to style. From least to most specific, they are

1. All three properties, all four sides

```
{border:2px dashed red;}
```

2. One property, all four sides

```
{border-style:dashed;}
```

3. One property, one side

```
{border-left-style:dashed;}
```

It's common to mix these three levels of shorthand styling to get the desired result. Let's say I want the box to have a four-pixel, red border top and bottom, a one-pixel red border on the left, and no border on the right.

```
{border:4px solid red;} /* first set all sides the same */
```

```
{border-left-width:1px;} /* changes left border width */
```

```
{border-right:none;} /* removes right border */
```

The same three levels of variations can be used with other properties, such as padding and border-radius.

I showed several simple border-related styles as examples in the sidebar, *Shorthand Styling*, but here are a few slightly more complex examples to consolidate your knowledge.

```
p.warning {border:solid #F33;}
```

With this rule, any paragraph with the "warning" class would have an attention-grabbing, four-pixel-wide solid red line around it, as shown in **Figure 3.2**.

FIGURE 3.2 Here, because I want all four sides to be the same, I can style the border with the shorthand border property.

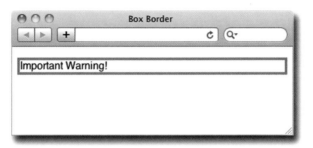

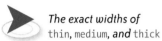 *The exact widths of* thin, medium, *and* thick *lines are not specifically defined in the CSS recommendations, so the weight of lines specified using keyword widths may vary between browsers. The line styles, with the exception of* solid *which is a simple continuous line, are not explicitly defined in the CSS specifications, so a dashed line may have different dash and space lengths from browser to browser.*

Next, let's say I want the border to be solid and red on all four sides, but I want the right and bottom sides thinner for visual interest. I'll use two rules to achieve the desired result: The first rule uses the "all-four-sides-at-once" shorthand border to specify the styling common to all four sides, and the second rule uses border-width to specify the widths of the borders individually.

```
p.warning {border:solid #f33;}
```

```
p.warning {border-width:4px 1px 1px 4px;}
```

This results in **Figure 3.3**.

FIGURE 3.3 By specifying a separate border-width rule, I can provide separate width values for each side of the box.

It can be very helpful to temporarily display the border of a box during development so that you can more clearly see the effects of styles such as margin and padding. By default, styles for element boxes are: `border-width` set to `medium`, `border-style` set to `none`, and `border-color` set to `black`. Because `border-style` is set to `none`, the box doesn't display. To quickly display a paragraph's box, for example, write this

`p {border:solid 1px;}`

This sets `border-style` to a solid line and the box displays. You'll notice I also set the border to 1 pixel to reduce it from the default 3 pixels so it adds only minimally to the width and height of the layout.

Box Padding

Padding adds space between the box's content and the border of the box. **Figure 3.4** shows the text content of an element with a visible box border.

`p {font:16px helvetica, arial, sans-serif; width:220px; border:2px solid red; background-color:#caebff;}`

FIGURE 3.4 Without padding, the content touches the border.

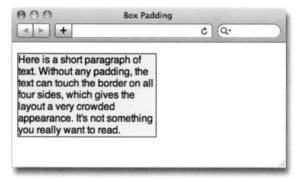

Unless you do something about it, the text of an element always touches the border of the element, which is not a very pleasing look. A little padding makes a big difference, as you can see in **Figure 3.5**.

`p {font:16px helvetica, arial, sans-serif; width:220px; border:2px solid red; background-color:#caebff; padding:10px;}`

As part of the inner area of the box, the padding takes on the color of the box's background. If you compare **Figures 3.4** and **3.5**, you'll observe that the padding adds to the stated width of the box, and

FIGURE 3.5 If you display an element's border, you will almost always add padding to prevent the content from touching it.

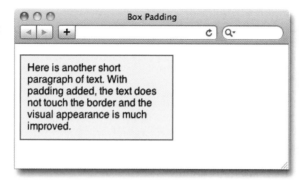

does not squeeze down the content as you might expect—I'll revisit this effect later in the chapter.

Box Margin

The box margin is slightly more complex than borders and padding. In **Figure 3.6**, three sets of one heading and two paragraphs are displayed. The first set shows the heading and two paragraphs as they appear by default. The second set shows the same arrangement of a heading and two paragraphs, but this time their borders

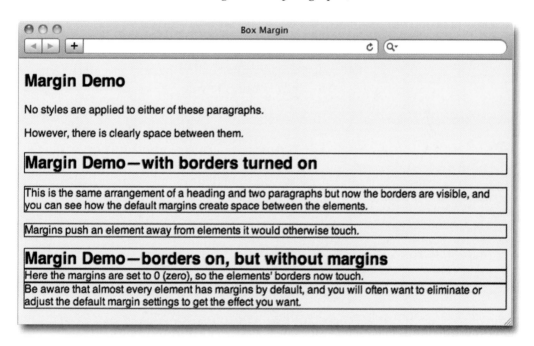

FIGURE 3.6 Learning to control margins around the elements is a key layout skill.

are displayed so you can see that their default margins create space between them. The third set shows what happens when the margins are set to zero—the elements then touch one another.

Collapsing Margins

Vertical margins collapse, and you need to remember this important fact. Let me explain what this means and why it matters. Imagine that you have three paragraphs, one after the other, and each is styled with this rule

font specs omitted for brevity ——| `p {height:50px; border:1px solid #000; background-color:#fff; margin-top:50px; margin-bottom:30px;}`

Although vertical margins collapse, horizontal margins do not. Instead, horizontal margins act as you would expect—margin values are added together to create space between horizontally adjacent elements.

Because the bottom margin of the first paragraph is adjacent to the top margin of the second, you might reasonably assume that there are 80 pixels (50 + 30) between the two paragraphs, but you'd be wrong. The distance between them is actually 50 pixels. When top and bottom margins meet, they overlap until one of the margins touches the border of the other element. In this case, the larger top margin of the lower paragraph touches first, so it determines how far apart the elements are set—50 pixels (**Figure 3.7**). This effect is known as collapsing.

Let me explain the purpose of this collapsing effect. Imagine a sequence of paragraphs that share the same styling. When one of these paragraphs is first or last position in the sequence, the top or

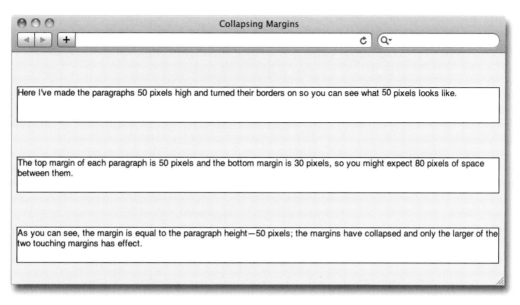

FIGURE 3.7 Vertical margins collapse (that is, they overlap) until the margin of one element touches the border of the other.

bottom margin sets the distance of that element from the top or bottom edge of the containing element. The paragraphs that are in-between do not need both margins; as shown in the preceding figure they simply collapse into each other, and the larger margin sets the distance.

Setting Units for Margins

Often, you will want to mix units when you set margins for text elements. For example, the left and right margins of a paragraph might be set in pixels so that the text remains a fixed distance from the sides of the containing element regardless of the type size, but you might set the top and bottom margins in ems so that the vertical spacing between paragraphs is relative to the size of the paragraphs' text, like this

note the shorthand styling: top and bottom margins are .75 em, left and right margins are 30 pixels.

`p {font-size:1em; margin:.75em 30px;}`

In this example, the vertical space between the paragraphs is always three-quarters of the height of the text (the top and bottom margins, both .75 em, collapse to a total of .75 em). If you or the user increase the text size, not only does the paragraphs' text get bigger, but the space between the paragraphs also increases proportionately, maintaining the overall look of the layout. In this case, the left and right margins, set in pixels, will remain unchanged, as you probably don't want the change in font size to affect the width of the layout.

How Big Is a Box?

The way the W3C box model works is at the heart of some of the most frustrating aspects of CSS for beginner and expert alike. Note in the discussion that follows, I am referring to block-level elements, such as headings, paragraphs, and lists; inline elements behave differently.

Let's review the box model step by step. I'll discuss setting the width of a box here, since managing element width is critical to creating multi-column layouts. First, you will see the effects of adding border, padding, and margins to an element that does not have its width set, and then see the change in behavior that occurs when the width of the element is set in the CSS.

As we move to HTML5, and older non-standard browsers fade away, XHTML doctypes, that state whether the site is to be rendered in strict mode (modern W3C box model behavior) or in quirks mode (with different box model behavior for IE6 and earlier) become unnecessary. If you want to know more about quirks mode, read http://www.quirksmode.org/css/quirksmode.html.

AN UNWIDTHED BOX

"Unwidthed," means the width property of an element is not explicitly set and is a word I made up especially for you, but please, no need to thank me. Also, the words "element" and "box" are used interchangeably from here on, depending on which one I think is clearest at any given moment.

If you don't set the width of a block-level element, then its default width setting is auto, which makes it expand to the width of its parent. Let's look at an element in this default auto state. I'll use some simple markup

```
<body>
  <p>This element's width property is not set…</p>
</body>
```

and start with this CSS

```
body {font-family:helvetica, arial, sans-serif; font-size:1em; margin:0px; background-color:#caebff;}
```

```
p {margin:0; background-color:#fff;}
```

On the containing element, body, I've set the font, set its background color, and removed the default margins, which will remain unchanged through these box width examples. On the paragraph, I've removed its default margins. With the margins removed, the body element entirely fills the browser window and the paragraph entirely fills the body element, as shown in **Figure 3.8**.

FIGURE 3.8 This paragraph has no borders, padding, or margins.

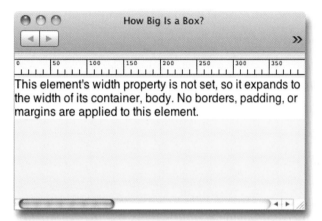

I've added a ruler graphic along the top of the window (code not shown) to help you see exactly what is happening at each step. This also enabled me to accurately drag the window corner to exactly 400 pixels for the purpose of this example.

With no borders, padding, or margins applied, the paragraph element's text also expands to the width of the body element. Now let's add some padding to create some space around the text, as shown in **Figure 3.9**.

font specs omitted for brevity ———┤
```
p {margin:0; background-color:#fff; padding:0 20px;}
```

FIGURE 3.9 The padding makes the text block narrower.

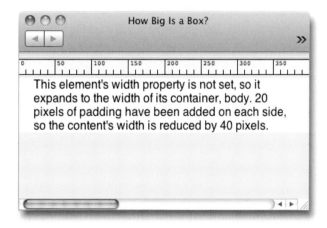

With the padding added, the text block is now 360 pixels wide (20 pixels of padding are added on each side).

Next, as shown in **Figure 3.10**, I'll add 6-pixel left and right borders.

```
p {margin:0; background-color:#fff; padding:0 20px;
border:solid red; border-width:0 6px 0 6px;}
```

FIGURE 3.10 Adding borders
further reduces the width of the
content box.

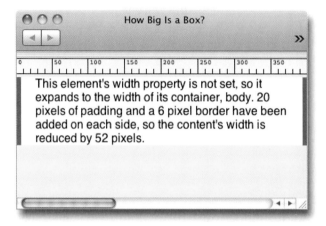

With a 6-pixel border and the 20 pixels of padding on each side, the content is now 348 pixels wide (400 – 52). Finally, let's add a margin to each side of the element (**Figure 3.11**).

```
p {margin:0 30px; background-color:#fff; padding:0 20px;
border:solid red; border-width:0 6px 0 6px;}
```

FIGURE 3.11 With borders, padding, and margins added, the
content is now much narrower.

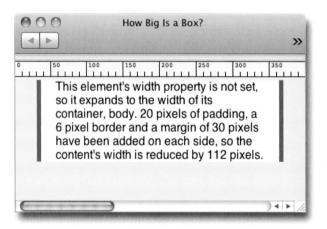

The margins create space between the element box and the window, so the content is now 288 pixels wide (400 − ((20 + 6 + 30) × 2)). The total space claimed by the element, however, remains the same—the width of the parent element, 400 pixels.

Box Model Observation #1: Unwidthed elements (no width set) will always expand to fill the width of their containing element. Adding horizontal borders, padding, and margins causes the content to be reduced in width by the total width of the horizontal borders, padding, and margins.

A WIDTHED BOX

Now let's do this same exercise again, using an element whose width is stated in the CSS, as shown in **Figure 3.12**.

font specs omitted for brevity ⟶ `p {width:400px; background-color:#fff; margin:0;}`

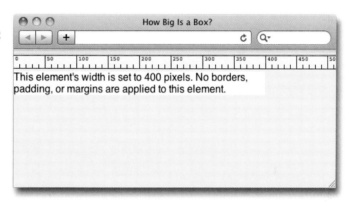

FIGURE 3.12 By setting the width property, this block-level element no longer exhibits the default behavior of expanding to the width of its containing element (in this case, body).

Now the paragraph's width is fixed at 400 pixels. Without any padding, the content is the stated width also, and it touches the sides of the box. Let's add 20 pixels of padding to the element, like this

`p {width:400px; background-color:#fff; margin:0;`
`padding:0 20px;}`

After the previous example, you might reasonably expect that the content within would now get squeezed down to 360 pixels, but you would be wrong. Instead, when the width of the box is set, adding this padding actually makes the element wider by 40 pixels (**Figure 3.13**).

FIGURE 3.13 Adding padding causes the box to get wider.

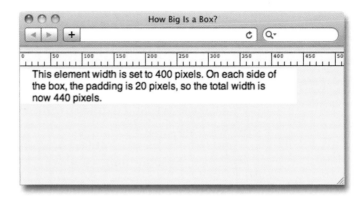

If I then also add the 6-pixel border to the right and left sides of the box (**Figure 3.14**)

```
p {width:400px; background-color:#fff; margin:0;
padding:0 20px; border:solid red; border-width:0 6px 0 6px;}
```

the box grows wider by another 12 pixels. Now the original 400-pixel-wide box is a total of 452 pixels wide (6 + 20 + 400 + 20 + 6 = 452).

FIGURE 3.14 Adding borders causes the box to grow even wider.

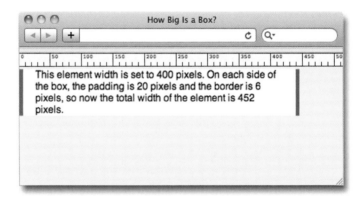

Let's now add right and left margins to create space on each side of the element (**Figure 3.15**).

```
p {width:400px; background-color:#fff; margin:0 30px;
padding:0 20px; border:solid red; border-width:0 6px 0 6px;
}
```

Adding the 30-pixel margins further increases the overall space occupied by the element, and it claims a total of 512 pixels (30 + 6 + 20 + 400 + 20 + 6 + 30 = 512).

FIGURE 3.15 Margins create space around an element. I have set the width of the browser window to indicate the space now occupied by this element.

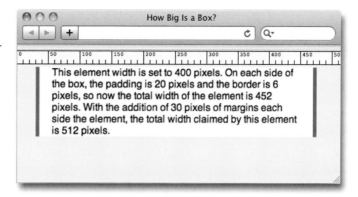

Box Model Observation #2: A box with a specified width expands to claim more horizontal space as borders, padding, and margins are added. Effectively, the width property only sets the width of the box's content, not the horizontal space the box occupies.

> The new CSS3 box-sizing *property allows you to make a widthed box exhibit the default* auto *behavior, but it is only supported by the most recent browsers, so I don't recommend its use at the time of writing this book (Summer 2012).*

I have demonstrated the difference in the behavior of widthed and unwidthed boxes in great detail here for a reason. Their very different behaviors have important implications when you build a layout with multiple columns where the columns must maintain their widths for the layout to work. "Floated layouts," which you will learn about in Chapter 5, can display incorrectly if a column width gets inadvertently increased by changes to the borders, padding, and margins.

The take-away is that when you set an element's width property, it will react differently from its default auto width behavior when borders, padding, and margins are applied.

Now let's look at the other key technique you need to understand when it comes to creating CSS based layouts—floating and clearing.

Floating and Clearing

Another powerful technique you can use to organize your page's layout involves floating and clearing, using the float and clear properties. Floating an element is a way of moving it out of the normal flow of the document, and is a technique that you use not only for its intended purpose of flowing text around images, but also for creating columns and making block-level elements sit side-by-side.

There are many more rules that govern floats, and you can read about them in Eric Meyer's book Cascading Style Sheets 2.0 Programmer's Reference (2006, McGraw-Hill Osborne Media). In short, as Eric writes, "When an element is floated…these (float) rules say 'place the element as high, and as far to one side, as possible'." Even though it was published some time ago, this book is an essential reference for any serious CSS programmer as it contains a level of detail about the inner workings of CSS that is almost impossible to find elsewhere.

The CSS3 Columns Module specifies how columns can be defined using CSS, but at the time of writing, only Opera and IE10 support them, so for the foreseeable future, floats are the best way to create columns.

Elements that follow a floated element will move up next to the floated element if there is room for them to do so.

The `clear` property enables you to stop such elements from moving up next to a floated element. If, for example, you have two paragraphs and only want the first to sit next to the floated element, even though both would fit, you can "clear" the second one so it's positioned under the floated element.

Before I cover both these properties in detail, I'll mention that while floating elements is an essential and very useful CSS technique, floating can cause all kinds of headaches for CSS newbies. This is because floated content is not directly in the document flow, and so affects the layout of elements that enclose or follow it in the markup. I have carefully designed the following floating and clearing examples to give you the knowledge that you need to be successful when working with floats.

The Float Property

The `float` property is primarily used to flow text around images, but it also provides the easiest way to create multi-column layouts.

Let's start with an example of how to flow text around an image.

FLOWING TEXT AROUND AN IMAGE

For the floating effect to work, the markup should state the floated image first, followed by the text that will wrap around it.

```
<img …… />

<p>…the paragraph text…</p>
```

Here's the CSS.

font specs omitted for brevity ——

```
p {margin:0; border:1px solid red;}
```

the margin prevents the text from touching the image

```
img {float:left; margin:0 4px 4px 0;}
```

This CSS floats the image to the left, so that the text wraps around it to its right (**Figure 3.16**).

In short, when you float an image, or any element, you are asking it to be pushed, as far as is possible, up and to one side of its parent element; in this example, that parent element is body. In the example here, the paragraph (with a red border) no longer sees

FIGURE 3.16 A floated image is removed from the document flow. If a text element follows it in the markup, that element's text will wrap around it.

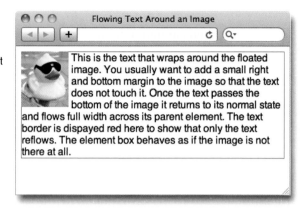

When you float an element, you must also set its width, or some unpredictable results can occur. However, images implicitly have width and so don't need to have a width assigned to them when floated.

the floated element as preceding it in the document flow, so it also takes the top left corner position of the parent; however, its content, the text, wraps itself around the floated image.

From here, it's a simple step to use float to form columns (**Figure 3.17**). I simply set a width on the paragraph and float it, too.

```
p {float:left; margin:0; width:200px; border:1px solid red;}

img {float:left; margin:0 4px 4px 0;}
```

FIGURE 3.17 When the fixed width paragraph is floated next to the floated image, it forms a column and no longer wraps the image.

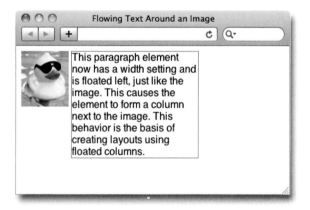

When you float both the image and the "widthed" paragraph like this, the text-wrapping effect stops, and the paragraph also tries to move up and as far to the left as possible also, and in this way forms a column next to the image. This is the principle of creating multi-column layouts using float. If a set of sibling elements have their widths set, are floated, and there is room for them to do so, they line up next to one another.

If you create three floated, fixed-width elements, they will sit next to each other in this way, giving you a layout of three columns that act as containers into which you can put other elements. I will demonstrate floated layouts in depth in Chapter 5.

Let's look at another gotta-understand aspect of floats—floated elements are "out-of-the-flow" and therefore not enclosed by their parent element: This can have a disruptive effect on your layout.

Three Ways to Enclose Floated Elements

Because a floated element is not directly in the document flow, its parent element doesn't see it and so doesn't enclose it. Because this behavior is not always desirable, I teach you three ways to force elements to enclose their floated children. You need to know all three, so you can use the one that is best for a given situation.

To illustrate this float behavior, what it can do to your layout, and the three ways you can fix it, let's start with an image and its text caption enclosed inside a `section` tag. `section` is followed by `footer` to represent, in this example, the full width footer that is commonly found across the bottom of Web pages.

```
<section>

  <img src="images/rubber_duck2.jpg">

  <p>It's fun to float.</p>

</section>

<footer> Here is the footer element that runs across the
bottom of the page.</footer>
```

So that you can clearly see what is happening, I'll display the element boxes of `section` and `footer`, as shown in **Figure 3.18**.

```
section {border:1px solid blue; margin:0 0 10px 0;}
```

removes large top and ——————| `p {margin 0;}`
bottom margins
font specs omitted for brevity —| `footer {border:1px solid red;}`

What you are seeing here is normal document flow; block-level elements enclose any child elements and stack one below the next down the page. Let's say you want the caption to sit to the right of the image, not below it. As you saw in the previous exercise, the easiest way to do this is to float the image. Let's try that.

FIGURE 3.18 Two block-level elements: section, containing an image and a caption, and footer, stack one below the next in the normal document flow.

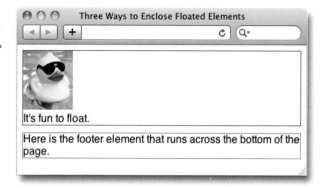

```
section {border:1px solid blue; margin:0 0 10px 0;}

img {float:left;}

footer {border:1px solid red;}
```

Figure 3.19 shows the outcome.

FIGURE 3.19 When the image is floated to move the caption next to the image, the parent section collapses to the height of the non-floated text element.

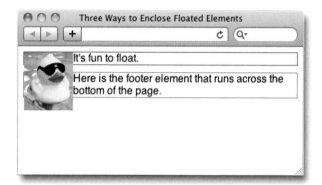

Oops! The caption is now next to the image as I intended, but section no longer encloses the floated element, but the non-floated text element. footer then moves up, right under the preceding block-level element, section, just like it's supposed to. The result, however, is not what I wanted.

METHOD 1—ADD OVERFLOW:HIDDEN TO THE PARENT ELEMENT

There is a simple, if unintuitive, solution to make section enclose the floated element: apply overflow:hidden to the enclosing element to force it to enclose the floated content.

```
section {border:1px solid blue; margin:0 0 10px 0;
overflow:hidden;}
```

```
img {float:left;}
```

```
p {border:1px solid red;}
```

Once the overflow:hidden declaration is applied to the container, the footer returns to the desired position (**Figure 3.20**).

FIGURE 3.20 With the overflow:hidden declaration applied to the container, it now encloses its floated content.

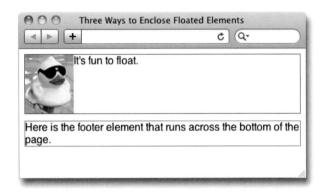

 The true purpose of overflow:hidden *is to prevent oversize content, such as a large image, from forcing the containing element to expand to show the oversized content. Instead, with* overflow:hidden *applied, the container remains at its defined size and the oversize child content is simply cropped by the container. However,* overflow:hidden *also reliably serves this useful second role of forcing elements to enclose their floated content.*

METHOD 2—FLOAT THE PARENT, TOO!

The second way that you can force a parent element to enclose its floated children is by floating the parent element, too.

```
section {border:1px solid blue; float:left; width:100%;}
```

```
img {float:left;}
```

```
footer {border:1px solid red; clear:left;}
```

When floated, section tightly encloses (aka shrink-wraps) its child elements, whether they are floated or not. So, we now need to add width:100% to make section full width again. Also, because section is now floated, footer will try to move up next to it, so we need to force footer to sit under section by adding clear:left to it: A cleared element cannot move up next to a floated element. This code has the same outcome as shown in **Figure 3.20**.

METHOD 3—ADD A NON-FLOATED CLEARING ELEMENT

The third way that you can force a parent element to enclose its floated children is by adding a non-floated element as the last child element and clearing it. Because a containing element always encloses non-floated elements, the containing element encloses this element, and the preceding floated elements. There are two ways to add a clearing element as the last child element.

The first, though not ideal, way to do this is simply to add an HTML element directly into the markup as the last child element and apply the CSS property clear to it; a div is best for this purpose as it has no default styling, and so does not introduce extra space into the layout.

```
<section>

  <img src="images/rubber_duck.jpg">

  <p>It's fun to float.</p>

  <div class="clear_me"></div>

</section>

<footer> Here is the footer element…</footer>
```

Here I add a class to the div so I can clear it in the CSS

```
section {border:1px solid blue;}

img {float:left;}

.clear_me {clear:left;}

footer {border:1px solid red;}
```

The floated elements are now enclosed, as shown in **Figure 3.20**. If you'd rather avoid adding purely presentational elements like this, here's how to add a clearing element using only CSS. I first add a class to section

```
<section class="clearfix">

  <img src="images/rubber_duck.jpg">

  <p>It's fun to float.</p>

</section>

<footer> Here is the footer element…</footer>
```

and use the magical clearfix CSS code!

```
.clearfix:after {

  content:".";

  display:block;

  height:0;
```

This clearfix *code, devised by programmer Tony Aslett, adds a cleared, non-floated element that contains just a period (you have to have some content, and a period is the smallest content available). Some additional declarations ensure that this pseudo-element takes up no height and is not visible on the page.*

The value of both *on the* clear *property means that* section *clears (sits below) elements floated both left and right. I could have used the value* left *in this case, but by using* both*, if I switch the float on the images to* right *later,* clear *still works.*

```
visibility:hidden;

clear:both;

}
```

Again, the floated elements are enclosed as shown in **Figure 3.20**, but this time without an extra element being hard-coded into the markup. You can temporarily remove the height and visibility dec-larations in the clearfix code above to see the period that it adds into the markup.

I use the clearfix CSS to solve float issues like this in just about every site I create, because floating is the only reliable way (until more browsers support the CSS3 Columns Module recommenda-tions) to create columns. I'll explain exactly why in Chapter 5.

To conclude this section of the chapter, there are three ways to force parent elements to enclose their floated children.

- Apply overflow:hidden to the parent.

- Float the parent element.

- Add a non-floated element as the last item within the parent, either by coding that element into the markup, or inserting it adding the clearfix class to the parent. (Of course, you need the related clearfix CSS in your style sheet.)

Which one of these three you use depends on the circumstance: For example, you can't use the overflow:hidden technique on the top-level of a drop-down menu, or the child drop-downs won't display. This is because the drop-downs display outside the area of their parent element, which is exactly what overflow:hidden is intended to prevent. As another example, you can't use the "float-the-parent" technique on an element that has been centered with auto margins, as it then moves to the left or right, depending on the float value applied. So you need all three of these techniques in your bag of tricks to cover all the different situations in which floated elements need to be enclosed.

USING CLEAR WITHOUT A CONTAINING ELEMENT

Sometimes, you will need to clear floated elements when there is no convenient parent wrapper to force around them. The most simple way is to apply the CSS clear:both to the element that is floating up to force it to sit under the floated element. However, when there is room for more than one element to float up, this simple approach may not work and you need to be more creative.

To demonstrate this point, **Figure 3.21** shows a layout with six elements—three images, each with associated descriptive text next to it. This layout is achieved by floating the images, so the text that follows each image in the markup text moves up next to the floated image.

FIGURE 3.21 Because there is room, the third image and its text can float up next to the second image—not the desired effect.

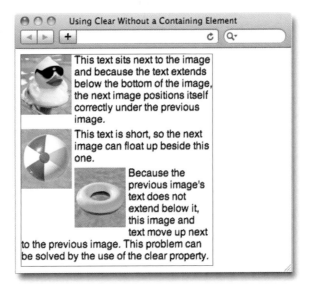

Here's the HTML for the preceding figure (with the text content edited to save space)

```
<section>
  <img src="images/rubber_duck3.jpg">
  <p>This text sits next to the image and because the...</p>
  <img src="images/beach_ball.jpg">
  <p>This text is short, so the next image can float up...</p>
  <img src="images/yellow_float.jpg">
  <p>Because the previous image's text does not...</p>
</section>
```

to which I apply this CSS

```
section {width:300px; border:1px solid red;}
img {float:left; margin:0 4px 4px 0;}
p {margin:0 0 5px 0;}
```

font specs omitted for brevity ——┤

The objective was to have each text block sit next to its image. However, because the second paragraph's text is not long enough to extend below the bottom of the second floated image, the resulting space allows the next image/paragraph pair to float up.

In the preceding example, the layout is technically correct: the third image/paragraph pair has room to sit next to the previous floated element, so they do, because the purpose of floating is to move an element up as high and far to the left or right (depending on the float value) as possible. This result isn't what I want visually.

Because there is no containing element around each image/paragraph pair here, I can't use the "force-the-parent-to-enclose" techniques from the previous example. However, I can still use the clearfix CSS

```
.clearfix:after {

  content:".";

  display:block;

  height:0;

  visibility:hidden;

  clear:both;

  }
```

like this

```
<section>

  <img src="images/rubber_duck3.jpg">

  <p class="clearfix">This text sits next to the image and
  because the...</p>

  <img src="images/beach_ball.jpg">

  <p class="clearfix">This text is short, so the next image
  can float up...</p>

  <img src="images/yellow_float.jpg">
```

```
<p class="clearfix">Because the previous image's text does
not…</p>.

</section>
```

FIGURE 3.22 Now that the clear-fix class adds a clearing element, the layout displays correctly.

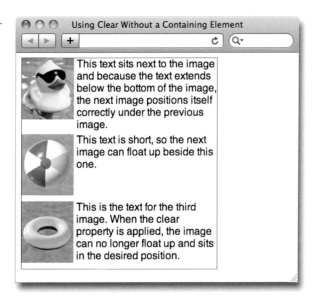

As shown in **Figure 3.22**, "cleared" elements are added into the markup after each of the paragraphs. Because the third image and paragraph follow one of these cleared elements in the markup, they can no longer float up, and the desired layout is achieved. I added clearfix to *all* of the paragraphs, not just the second one that needs it in this example. This is to illustrate what I would do if this were a real site: in the future, if the text of any of the three paragraphs was made shorter than its image, the layout would not break.

Now that you have an understanding of the float and clear properties, let's end this chapter by looking at two other concepts that are key to creating CSS layouts: the position and display properties.

The Position Property

At the heart of all CSS-based layouts is the position property. The position property determines where an element box is positioned in respect to where it would normally appear in the document flow.

There are four values for the position property: static, relative, absolute, and fixed, with static as the default. I'll illustrate each of these terms using markup with four paragraphs.

```
<p>First Paragraph</p>
```

```
<p>Second Paragraph</p>
```

```
<p id="specialpara">Third Paragraph (with ID)</p>
```

```
<p>Fourth Paragraph</p>
```

In each example, I will leave paragraphs one, two, and four in the default static positioning and alter the position value of paragraph three.

I have added an ID named specialpara to the third paragraph so I can change its position property without affecting the other paragraphs.

Static Positioning

First, let's view the four paragraphs with the default position of static (**Figure 3.23**).

FIGURE 3.23 Static positioning causes block-level elements to stack in the default document flow.

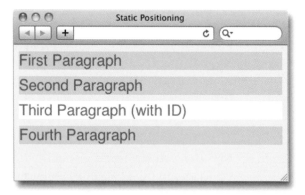

With static positioning, each element appears in the normal document flow—they are block elements so they stack under one another down the page. The unstyled HTML layouts I showed in Chapter 1 also display static document flow.

To break away from this sequential layout of elements provided by the default static positioning, you must change a box's position property to one of the three other possible values.

Relative Positioning

Let's next set the third paragraph's `position` property to `relative`. Doing this alone produces no visible effect, but once an element is relatively positioned, it can be moved with respect to its default position by using the properties `top`, `right`, `bottom`, and `left`. In most cases, providing values for just `top` and `left` produces the result you want. This example

```
p#specialpara {position:relative; top:25px; left:30px;}
```

produces the result shown in **Figure 3.24**.

FIGURE 3.24 Relative positioning allows you to use the `top` and `left` properties to move the element with respect to its normal position in the document flow.

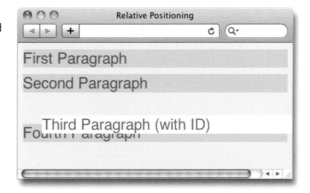

Now the paragraph is moved down by 25 pixels and right by 30 pixels from its normal position in the document flow, which pushes it outside of its containing element, `body`, resulting in part of it being offscreen. However, although the element moves relative to its original position, nothing else changes. The space originally occupied by the element is retained, as is the positioning of the other elements.

> You can also use negative values for top and left to move an element up and to the left.

The take-away here is that if you move an element in this way, you must allow space for it. In the example shown in **Figure 3.24**, you might take the next step of adding a `margin-top` value of 30 pixels or greater to the fourth paragraph to move it down, and so avoid it from being overlapped by the repositioned third paragraph.

Absolute Positioning

Absolute positioning is a whole different animal from `static` and `relative`, as this type of positioning takes an element entirely out of the flow of the document. Let's modify the code used for the relative positioning example by changing `relative` to `absolute`

`p#specialpara {`**`position:absolute;`**` top:25px; left:30px;}`

Figure 3.25 shows the result.

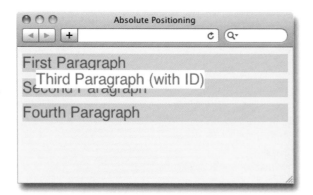

In **Figure 3.25**, you can see that the space previously occupied by the element is gone. The absolutely-positioned element is entirely removed from the document flow, and it is now positioned with respect to the top-level element, body. And this brings us neatly to the important concept of positioning context.

Let's start thinking about this concept by saying that the default positioning context of an absolutely-positioned element is the body element. As **Figure 3.25** shows, the offset provided by the top and left values moves the absolutely positioned element in relation to the body element—the top ancestor container in the markup hierarchy—not in relation to the element's default position in the document flow, as is the case with relative positioning.

Because the absolutely positioned element's positioning context is body, it moves when the page is scrolled to retain its relationship to the body element, which also moves when the page is scrolled.

Before I show you how to use an element other than body as the positioning context for an absolutely positioned element, let me cover the last of the four positioning properties—fixed positioning.

Fixed Positioning

Fixed positioning is similar to absolute positioning, in that the element is entirely removed from the document flow.

```
p#specialpara {position:fixed; top:30px; left:20px;}
```

The difference is that a fixed-position element's positioning context is the viewport (the browser window or the screen of a handheld device, for example), so the element does not move when the page is scrolled. **Figures 3.26** and **3.27** show the effects of fixed positioning.

FIGURE 3.26 Fixed positioning looks a lot like absolute positioning…

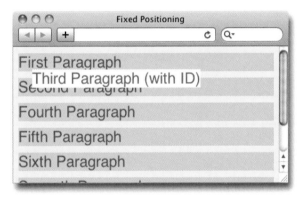

FIGURE 3.27 …until you scroll the page—the fixed element does not move.

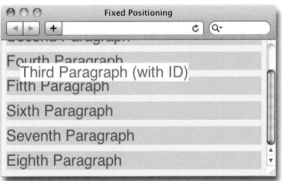

Fixed positioning is not something you will use frequently—its most common application is to create a navigation element that stays in place when the page scrolls.

Now that you understand the difference between the four `position` property values, let's dig a little deeper into the concept of positioning context.

Positioning Context

When you change an element's position property to relative, absolute, or fixed, and you then move the element using the properties top, right, bottom, or left, you are moving that element with respect to another element. That other element is known as its positioning context.

As you saw in *Absolute Positioning* earlier, the default positioning context of an absolutely positioned element is body. This is because body, uniquely, is an ancestor of every element in your markup. However, you can use any ancestor of an absolutely positioned element as its positioning context by setting that ancestor's position value to relative.

Let's look at this markup

```
<body>

  <div id="outer">

    <div id="inner">This is text…</div>

  </div>

</body>
```

Text should be properly marked up in an element such as a paragraph to define it semantically, but for clarity in this example, I have put the text directly into the inner div.

and this CSS

```
div#outer {width:250px; margin:50px 40px; border-top:3px solid red;}

div#inner {top:10px; left:20px; background:#ccc;}
```

Because the top and left of the inner div are defined in this code, you might be wondering: Why in **Figure 3.28**, isn't the inner div 10 pixels down from the top of the outer one and 20 pixels to the left, as specified? Instead the two elements both share the same origin (top left) point. The answer is that the inner (and irrelevantly, the outer) div has the default positioning of static. This means it is in the regular document flow, and because the outer div has no content, the inner div starts in the same place. Only when you set an element to one of the other three positioning options—relative, absolute, or fixed—do the top, right, bottom, and left properties actually have effect. Let's see this in action by setting the inner div's position property to absolute.

FIGURE 3.28 Here are two nested divs. I've added a red border to the top of the outer div and colored the inner div gray. Because the inner div has static (default) positioning, top and left properties are ignored.

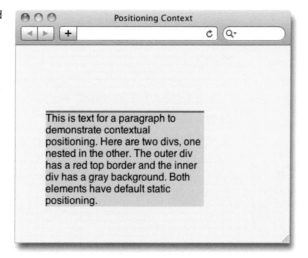

> If you use margins and padding carefully, in most cases, all that you need to organize your page layouts is static positioning. Many beginning CSS designers mistakenly change the position property of almost every element only to find it hard to control all these freed-up elements. Don't change the position property of an element from the default static unless you really need to.

```
div#outer {width:250px; margin:50px 40px; border-top:3px
solid red;}

div#inner {position:absolute; top:10px; left:20px;
background:#ccc;}
```

But absolutely positioned with respect to what? Because there is no relatively positioned element for it to reference, it positions itself by default with respect to the body element. This is because body is the default positioning context. The inner div entirely ignores its parent (outer div) element, and its top and left properties offset it with respect to body, as shown in **Figure 3.29**.

FIGURE 3.29 Although the inner div (gray background) is inside the outer div (indicated by its red top border) in the markup, its absolute display positioning dictates that, without any other relative positioned element to use as a context, it positions itself relative to the body element.

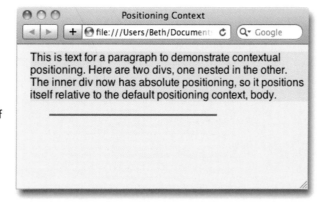

If I now set the `position` property of the outer `div` to `relative`

```
div#outer {position:relative; width:250px; margin:50px 40px;
border-top:3px solid red;}
```

```
div#inner {position:absolute; top:10px; left:20px;
background:#ccc;}
```

the positioning context of the absolutely positioned inner `div` is now the outer `div`, as shown in **Figure 3.30**.

FIGURE 3.30 Once the outer `div` has a relative positioning, absolutely positioned descendants position themselves relative to it, as defined by their top and left attributes.

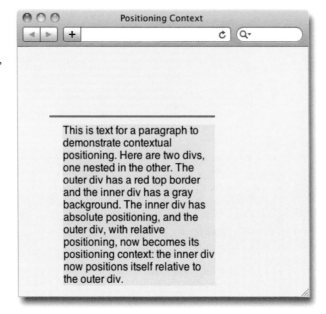

The `top` and `left` properties of the inner `div` now position it with respect to the outer `div`. If you were now to move the outer `div` by setting its `left` and `top` position properties to anything other than zero, the inner `div` would move by the same amount to maintain its positioning relationship to the outer `div`, its positioning context.

The Display Property

Just as every element has a `position` property, every element also has a `display` property. Although there are a number of `display` property values, most elements have a default `display` property value of either `block` or `inline`. In case you slept through class during Chapter 1, the difference between block and inline elements is

* Block elements, such as paragraphs, headings, and lists, sit one above another when displayed in the browser.

* Inline elements, such as `a`, `span`, and `img`, sit side-by-side when they are displayed in the browser and only appear on a new line if there is insufficient room on the previous one.

The ability to change block elements to inline elements, and vice versa, like this

block by default ——————⊣ `p {display:inline;}`

inline by default ——————⊣ `a {display:block;}`

is a powerful capability that allows you, for example, to force an inline element to fill its containing element. I'll do this with links later when I create CSS drop-down menus.

One other value for `display` worth mentioning here is `none`. When an element's `display` property is set to `none`, that element, and any elements nested inside it, are not displayed on the page. Any space that was occupied by the element is removed; it's as if the related markup did not exist. This contrasts with the `visibility` property, whose most useful corresponding values are `visible` (default) or `hidden`. If an element's `visibility` is set to `hidden`, the element is hidden, but the space it occupied remains.

Backgrounds

One final aspect of positioning elements is backgrounds, which provide a means to add color and images into an element's background. If you have worked in graphics programs like Adobe Photoshop or Adobe Fireworks, you will be familiar with the concept of layers. Every element box can be thought of as having two layers. An element's foreground layer is made up of the content of the element (such as text or an image) and the border of the box. The element's background layer can be filled with a solid color, using the `background-color` property, and can also contain any number of images, using the `background-image` property, which stacks the images on top of the background color.

Before CSS3, all you could do with the background layer was set the background color, and add a single background image on top of it. Now, you can add multiple images (and the new CSS3 gradients) into an element's background. Let's now revisit the box model diagram from earlier in the chapter in a three-dimensional view that also illustrates the element's background layer (**Figure 3.31**).

FIGURE 3.31 This box model diagram shows the components of the foreground and background layers of an element.

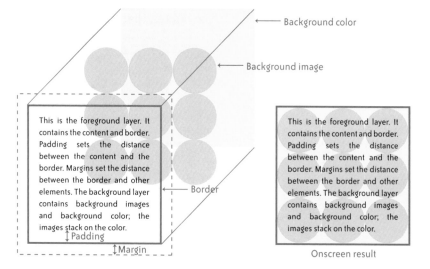

CSS Background Properties

These are the CSS background properties.

- `background-color`
- `background-image`
- `background-repeat`
- `background-position`
- `background-size`
- `background-attachment`
- `background` (shorthand)
- `background-clip`, `background-origin`, `background-break` (not well supported currently)

These properties give you extensive control of background elements. Let's examine them individually.

Background Color

`background-color` is the most simple of the background properties. You set a color using the `background-color` property, and the background is filled with that color, as shown in **Figure 3.32**.

```
body {background-color:#caebff;}
```

```
p {font-family:helvetica, arial, sans-serif; font-size:18px;
width:350px; margin:20px auto; padding:10px;
background-color:#fff; color:#666; border:4px solid;}
```

box layout styles ──────────────

background and foreground styles discussed in this example

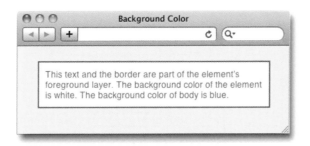

FIGURE 3.32 The body `background-color` is set to blue. The paragraph's `background-color` is set to white, and `color`, the foreground color which affects both the border and the text, is set to gray.

This example, besides showing how to color an element's background, also illustrates that the foreground layer is made up of both the content and the border. If you use the `border-color` property to set an element's border style and width, but not its color, its color is set by the `color` property that also sets the color of the type. The default color is black. If you want the border and text to be different colors, set each individually.

Background Image

Here's a small image of a circle that I will use to illustrate the `background-image` and the `background-repeat` properties (**Figure 3.33**).

FIGURE 3.33 Here I've added a border to a small circle graphic so you can see there is white space around the circle.

I'll start by using the `background-image` property to add this circle image into the background of an element, as shown in **Figure 3.34**.

```
p {font-size:28px; font-family:helvetica, arial, sans-serif;
width:345px; height:110px; margin:20px auto; padding:10px;
color:#000; border:4px solid #aaa; background-color:#fff;
background-image:url(images/blue_circle.png);}
```

FIGURE 3.34 A background image that is smaller than the element repeats horizontally and vertically to fill it.

As the preceding figure shows, by default, the image is repeated across and down the element from its top left corner as many times as is needed to fill it. Because of this top left origin, the circles along the bottom and right are cut off by the width and height of the box.

Note that a background image is specified in a different way from the img tag, using the format

background-image:url(imagePath/imageName)

There is no need to put quotes around the image reference, although you can if you wish.

The default settings of across-and-down repeating and top left origin position can be changed by background-repeat and background-position respectively, so let's now look at these two properties.

Background Repeat

There are four possible values for background-repeat. The default is simply repeat, which, as you saw in the preceding figure, repeats the image horizontally and vertically as many times as is needed to fill the element. The other values are repeat-x for horizontal repeating, repeat-y for vertical repeating, and no-repeat which causes the image to display once only, as illustrated in **Figure 3.35**.

There are all kinds of uses for these repeat options. For example, the repeat-x and repeat-y values allow you to easily add repeating, decorative border graphics to your work, and no-repeat allows you to add a single image as a background. Additional control of the

FIGURE 3.35 The four back-ground-repeat values.

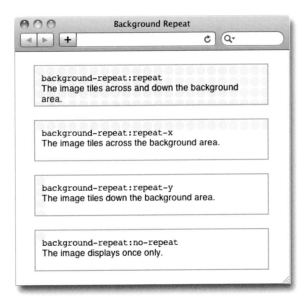

three background properties I have shown so far comes from the `background-position` property which I'll look at next.

One last note—CSS3 offers a couple of as-yet-unsupported ways to make the repeats fill the element an exact number of times.

- `background-repeat:round` rescales the image until the repeats fill an exact number of times.

- `background-repeat:space` adds space between the tiles until they fit the element exactly.

Background Position

`background-position` is probably the most complex of the background properties. The four basic `background-position` settings are the keywords `top`, `left`, `bottom`, `right`, and `center`, and you can specify any two of them in the property values. If you state `top right`, then the top right corner of the image is positioned in the top right corner of the element. If you state `center center`, then the center of the image is positioned in the center of the element. Let me now describe this concept in more detail.

The `background-position` property simultaneously defines the origin point of both the element and the image. That origin point defines the horizontal and vertical coordinates of a point within both the element and the image by which they are aligned. By default, the origin-point values for `background-position` are `top` and `left`. So, if you do not specify a background image's `background-position` property, the top left corner of the image is aligned with the top left corner of the element, and any repeating runs out from that point. You can observe this default top left positioning in the four examples in the preceding figure.

Armed with this knowledge, let's now look at the `background-position` property in action, by looking again at the first of the preceding figure's examples, where the across and down repeating is controlled by the top left defaults of the `background-position` property. Let's then see the difference when I set the `background-position` values to `center center` (**Figure 3.36**).

shorthand for center center ——┤ `p#center {background-position:center;}`

FIGURE 3.36 When the background position is `center center`, the image is centered in the element and tiles out in every direction.

If only one `background-position` keyword is used, as in the code example for this figure, the other value is set to `center`.

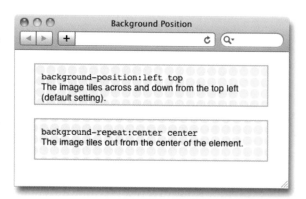

As you can see when you compare the two examples of the preceding figure, in the second example, the image repeats from the center out in all directions.

I'll now position a larger image in the center of the element. This time, I'll use percentages as the positioning values (**Figure 3.37**).

```
div {height:150px; width:250px; border:2px solid #aaa;
margin:20px auto; background-image:url(images/turq_
spiral_150.png); background-repeat:no-repeat; background-
position:50% 50%;}
```

By setting `background-position` to `50% 50%`, and the background-repeat to `no-repeat`, the image is centered in the background.

FIGURE 3.37 A background image is centered in an element using the `background-position` property.

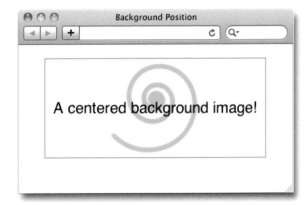

If you are wondering how I vertically centered the text in this element, I simply set the line-height of the text to the height of the element—line height is distributed equally above and below the type. I also set the `text-align` *property of the type to* `center`, *to align it hoziontally, thereby centering the type in both directions, just like the image behind it.*

Background Size

The new but well-supported CSS3 property, `background-size,` gives you control of the size of the background image. The following are examples of values that can be used for the `background-size` property.

Background Position Values

There are three kinds of values you can use to position background images; keywords, percentages, and absolute or relative numerical units such as pixels or percentages. Two values can be supplied for the horizontal and vertical position respectively.

Keywords can be stated in either order: `left bottom` and `bottom left` give the same result. For maximum browser compatibility, it's best not to mix keywords with numerical values.

When you state numerical values, such as 40% 30%, then the first value is the horizonal position and the second is the vertical position. If you only state one value, then that is used as the horizontal value and the vertical value is set to `center`.

If you position with keywords or percentages, the values are applied to both the element and the image; in other words, if you set the values to 33% 33%, then a point 33% into the image horizontally is aligned with a point 33% horizontally across the element. The same would apply vertically. As another example, you saw earlier how `center center` places the center of the image in the center of the element in both directions.

Absolute units like pixels work differently. If you set the position with pixels, then the left and top edges of the image are positioned the stated distance from the top left corner of the element.

You can also set negative distances so that the image's top and/or left corner is outside of the element, and then only part of the image shows within the element. The same result can be achieved by assigning positive values high enough to push part of the image out of the element to the right or bottom. The part of the image outside the element does not display.

- 50%—the image is scaled to fill 50% of the larger dimension of the element.

- 100px 50px—the image is sized to 100 pixels wide and 50 pixels high.

- cover—the image is enlarged until it entirely fills the element.

- contain—the image is sized so it fits inside the element.

Building on the positioning of the preceding figure, where a single repeat of an image is centered in the element, I then apply the values listed above (**Figure 3.38**).

FIGURE 3.38 Various back-
ground-size settings applied to
a non-repeating, centered background image.

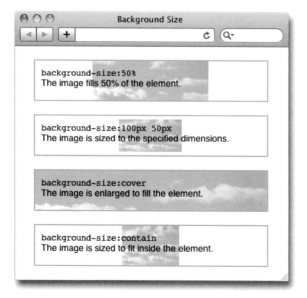

This new property greatly expands the design options for background images. Just be careful not to over enlarge small images as their quality will deteriorate.

Background Attachment

The background-attachment property determines if a background image within a scrolling element moves when the element is scrolled. The default is scroll, and the background image moves with the element. If the value is changed to fixed, then the background image does not move when the element is scrolled.

A common application of `background-attachment:fixed` is adding a faded, watermark image that is centered in the `body` element, so that the page scrolls over the unmoving image.

A CSS rule to achieve this effect could be written like this

```
body {
    background-image:url(images/watermark.png);
    background-position:center;
    background-color:#fff;
    background-repeat:no-repeat;
    background-size:contain;
    background-attachment:fixed;
}
```

As you can see, rules for background images can get pretty long, but you can use the shorthand `background` property to state all these values in a single rule.

Background Shorthand

The `background` property is a shorthand that allows you to put all the properties of the background element into one rule. The preceding `background-attachment` example could be written using the `background` shorthand like this

```
body {background:url(images/watermark.png) center #fff
no-repeat contain fixed;}
```

If I leave a property value out (say here I had omitted `no-repeat`), the default value (`repeat`) would be used in its place.

Other CSS3 Background Properties

Modernizr is a JavaScript library that detects HTML5 and CSS3 features in the user's browser. Learn more at http://modernizr.com.

CSS3 has added some new `background` properties that I will mention briefly. Their implementation is patchy, so if you use them, be sure to check what your page looks like without them, or use Modernizr to detect their support and provide alternative CSS for non-supporting browsers.

Learn more about these new properties at http://www.w3.org/TR/2001/ WD-css3-background-20010924.

- `background-clip` controls where the image displays—only under the content and not under the padding, for example. By default, the background extends under the border.

- `background-origin` sets the origin point to locations other than the top left of the element box—the top left of the content, for example.

- `background-break` allows you to control the display of split elements (such as inline boxes that go across multiple lines).

Multiple Background Images

CSS3 lets us add multiple background images into the background of the element, which I will do using the `background` shorthand, as shown in **Figure 3.39**.

```
p {height:150px; width:348px; border:2px solid #aaa;
margin:20px auto; font:24px/150px helvetica, arial, sans-
serif; text-align:center; background:
url(images/turq_spiral.png) 30px -10px no-repeat,
url(images/pink_spiral.png) 145px 0px no-repeat,
url(images/gray_spiral.png) 140px -30px no-repeat, #ffbd75;}
```

FIGURE 3.39 Multiple images can be stacked in the background. The first image listed in the CSS appears on top.

In the CSS, I put each image on a separate line to help you see that each background image and its positioning and repeat values is separated by a comma. Also I added the `background-color` value last (highlighted in the code) to act as a fallback so the background of the element is not left in its default transparent state if the images fail to load. Note that the first stated image will display at the top of the stacking order, that is, closest to the foreground.

Vendor Specific Prefixes (VSPs)

In order to encourage browser vendors to adopt the W3C's CSS3 recommendations quickly, the concept of vendor specific prefixes came into being.

These prefixes, prepended to CSS property names, allow vendors to experiment with W3C working drafts of new CSS properties. The browser vendors can quickly add new properties to the browser while indicating that they are interim, partial, or experimental implementations of the recommendation—caveat emptor.

Here's an example that illustrates the W3C-recommended syntax for the CSS3 `transform` property:

```
transform: skewX(-45deg);
```

However, `transform` is a CSS3 feature that is still in development, and to ensure it works with the largest number of browsers and their experimental implementations, you would also add all the different VSPs for the browsers you want to support. The browser simply uses whichever one it understands.

```
-moz-transform:skewX(-45deg);      /* Firefox */
-webkit-transform:skewX(-45deg);   /* Chrome and Safari */
-ms-transform:skewX(-45deg);       /* Microsoft Internet Explorer */
-o-transform:skewX(-45deg);        /* Opera */
transform:skewX(-45deg);           /* add regular W3C declaration last */
```

As you can see, VSPs always start with a hyphen, followed by the prefix name and another hyphen; then comes the actual W3C property name. Note also that, as illustrated above, the regular W3C version of the property should always be included after any VSPs, so that it will set the property at a time in the future when the property is implemented in a final, non-prefixed version. As you can see, the `-webkit-` prefix is used by both Safari and Chrome, because both are powered by the Webkit rendering engine.

These CSS3 properties require VSPs:

`border-image`	`translate`
`linear-gradient`	`transition`
`radial-gradient`	`background*`
`transform`	`background-image*`
`transform-origin`	

* for multiple background images or gradients

To save space in this book, I will not always add a full set of VSPs for every example that might use them, and will simply indicate that they are required. As browsers evolve, the need for VSPs changes. Check *http://caniuse.com* for the latest information on CSS3 and VSPs. To add VSPs automatically, use the -prefix-free polyfill—see the Appendix for details.

Background Gradients

A gradient, or blend, is a color fill that transitions between two or more colors across its length. Before CSS3, gradients had to be created in a graphics program such as Adobe Photoshop and added as a background image, but now gradients can be created programmatically with CSS.

There are two types of gradients, linear and radial. Linear gradients extend from one side of an element to the other, while radial gradients spread outwards from a point within the element to its edges.

Let's start with some simple linear gradients.

Here's the HTML

```
<div class="gradient1"></div>
<div class="gradient2"></div>
<div class="gradient3"></div>
```

and this is the CSS

styles the element box ———

```
div {height:150px; width:200px; border:1px solid #ccc;
float:left; margin:16px;}
```

top to bottom by default ———

```
.gradient1 {background:linear-gradient(#e86a43, #fff);}
```

left to right ———

```
.gradient2 {background:linear-gradient(left, #64d1dd,
#fff);}
```

top-left to bottom-right ———

```
.gradient3 {background:linear-gradient(-45deg, #e86a43,
#fff);}
```

FIGURE 3.40 Three simple linear gradients.

Figure 3.40 shows three simple examples of linear gradients. **Example 1** states a start and end color with the gradient moving smoothly from one color to the other across its length in the default direction, which is top to bottom. **Example 2** states the origin key-

word left, so its gradient starts at the left and extends to the opposite side. The origin value for **Example 3** states -45deg (degrees) which moves the start point from the default top center to top-left.

STOP POINTS

Stop points are points along a gradient where a particular color and opacity are defined. The gradient of the transition is created by the change required to get the stated color value of the next stop point. You can add as many stop points as you wish. The location of a stop point is usually expressed as a percentage of the distance across the gradient. **Figure 3.41** shows four gradients that use stop points.

single stop point at 50% ─────── ┤
```
.gradient1 {background:linear-gradient(#64d1dd, #fff 50%,
#64d1dd);}
```

gradient begins at 20% and ─────── ┤ ends at 80%
```
.gradient2 {background:linear-gradient(#e86a43 20%, #fff
50%, #e86a43 80%);}
```

three stop points: 25%, 50%, 75% ─┤
```
.gradient3 {background:linear-gradient(#64d1dd, #fff 25%,
#64d1dd 50%, #fff 75%, #64d1dd);}
```

double stop points produce ─────── ┤ sharp transitions
```
.gradient4 {background:linear-gradient(#e86a43, #fff 25%,
#64d1dd 25%, #64d1dd 75%, #fff 75%, #e86a43);}
```

FIGURE 3.41 Linear gradients with stop points.

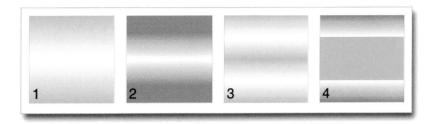

Figure 3.41, Example 1 shows a single stop point at 50% so the color transitions smoothly from the start to the stated stop point color (white), and then transitions smoothly from that point to the end color. Note that the first and last point positions default to 0 and 100% if not stated.

When the locations of the stop points are not defined with percentages or other values, the colors are distributed evenly along the gradient; in this case 0%, 50%, and 100%.

Example 2 shows what happens when the start and end points are stated at points other than 0% and 100%. Up to the position of the first stop point (20%), the color is solid in the color of that first stated stop point, and then transitions to the color of the next stop point. The same effect can be seen at the last stop point at 80%: that stop point's color then extends solid to the end of the element.

Example 3 simply shows multiple stop points transitioning back and forth between the same two colors, while **Example 4** shows that by stating two colors at the same stop point, a hard transition can be achieved.

RADIAL GRADIENTS

Radial gradients are a little more complex than linear gradients as there are more control options available. If you are a programmer, you might have noticed from their parentheses that gradient properties are functions; that is, the property accepts a number of values known as arguments that are used in generating the gradient. When creating radial gradients, you can use arguments for shape, positioning, size, color, and opacity.

In these examples, each gradient has three defined colors.

I'm only stating the -webkit- VSP here. See the sidebar, Vendor Specific Prefixes, for the other required VSPs.

```
.gradient1 {background: -webkit-radial-gradient(#fff,
#64d1dd, #70aa25);}
```

```
.gradient2 {background: -webkit-radial-gradient(circle,
#fff, #64d1dd, #e86a43);}
```

```
.gradient3 {background: -webkit-radial-gradient(50px 30px,
circle, #fff, #64d1dd, #4947ba);}
```

FIGURE 3.42 Three three-color radial gradients. The first is the default "fit-to-shape" gradient, the second is a circular gradient, and the third is a positioned circular gradient.

In **Figure 3.42**, **Example 1** shows the default shape behavior where the blend fits the element, in this case a rectangle. If the element was square, the gradient would be circular.

In **Example 2**, the shape keyword circle causes the blend to extend out evenly and reach its final stop shade at the nearest edge, for a circular gradient. The remaining distance on the longer axis is filled with the end color. In **Example 3**, the position arguments, 50px 30px, place the circular fill near the top-left corner.

This give you a basic grounding in how gradients work and I'll show more examples when I use them in various design applications in later chapters.

You can get more detail on these examples and on the positioning of radial fills in my eBook, *Visual Stylin' with CSS*, published by Peachpit Press 2012.

Summary

In this chapter, you have learned about the workings of the box model and how to set margins, padding, and borders. You have seen how floating enables you to wrap text around images and make block elements sit next to each other, and how to clear floated elements and force containing elements to enclose floated child elements. You have learned about the position and display properties, and the control they give you when organizing elements on the page. Finally, you have seen how you can use the background layer of an element to add color, images, and gradients behind an element's content.

Now I'll move on to CSS fonts and text, and show you techniques to create professional-looking typography.

CHAPTER 4

Stylin' Fonts and Text

Much of Web design deals with text, in paragraphs, headings, lists, menus, and forms, so understanding the CSS properties in this chapter is essential to making a site that looks professional. Almost more than any other factor, type makes the clearest visual statement about the quality of your site's offerings. Graphics are the icing on the cake; typography is where good design begins.

In this chapter, you'll learn about fonts and text, and the respective CSS properties you can use to style them. I'll also introduce you to the wonderful world of Web fonts, which download to your user along with your pages. Now you no longer have to rely on the user having your font choices installed on his device, and you can be confident that every user will see your typography in the way you intend.

Let's start with fonts.

Fonts

The fonts you specify in your Web pages can come from three sources.

- The fonts that are installed on the user's device. (Until recently, these have been the only fonts reliably available to your Web pages.)

- Fonts that are hosted on third-party sites, most notably Typekit and Google, and linked to your page using the link tag.

- Fonts that are hosted on your Web server and served to the user's browser along with the page, using the @font-face rule.

In the font property descriptions that follow, the examples will show the first of these sources: the fonts that are installed on the user's computer. See *Web Fonts Demystified* later in this chapter for a discussion of the other two sources.

Aren't Fonts and Text the Same Thing?

The answer is "No," and here's why.

Fonts are the different kinds of typefaces. Each font is a set of letters, numbers, and symbols with a unique visual appearance. Fonts are categorized into *collections,* based on their general look, such as serif, sans-serif, or mono-space. Fonts are made up of *families,* with names such as Times and Helvetica. A font family in turn can be broken down into font *faces,* which are variations on the basic design of the font, such as Times Roman, Times Bold, Helvetica Condensed, and Bodoni Italic.

Text simply describes words and characters, like this sentence or the heading of a chapter, regardless of the font in which it is set.

CSS has a set of properties relating to fonts and a set of properties relating to text. *Font properties* relate to the size and appearance of collections of type. What is its family (Times or Helvetica, for example)? What size is it? Is it bold or italic? *Text properties* relate to the font's treatment. What is its line height and letter spacing? Is it underlined or indented? And so on.

Here's a way I think about this perhaps seemingly subtle distinction. You can apply font styles, such as bold and italic, to a single character, but text properties, such as line height and text indent, only really make sense in the context of a block of text, such as a headline or a paragraph.

Now let's look at the six properties that relate to font styling:

- `font-family`
- `font-size`
- `font-style`
- `font-weight`
- `font-variant`
- `font` (shorthand)

Font-Family Property

Example: `h2 {font-family:times, serif;}`

`font-family` determines the font in which an element is displayed. Typically, you set a primary font for the entire page, and then only add `font-family` styles to elements that you want to display in a different font. To specify the font for the entire page, you set the `font-family` of the `body` element:

`body {font-family:verdana, sans-serif;}`

From my own testing I've observed that font-family *names are not case sensitive, but do not alter the case of a font name generated by Google or another hosted font service or your font may not display.*

font-family is an inherited property, so its value is passed to all its descendants, which in the case of body is all the other elements in the markup.

Because fonts must either be on the user's computer, or delivered over the Web, there is always a possibility that a particular font you specify might not be available to a page. For this reason, fonts are always specified in lists called font stacks.

SPECIFYING INSTALLED FONTS USING FONT STACKS

Fonts are installed in the operating system of a device, which allows all resident applications to share them. Only a limited set of fonts come installed in the typical operating system, and fonts can be added and removed by the user, so you can never be absolutely certain what fonts will be available to display your pages. Because of this, when stating the font in which you want text to display, you must also list additional "fallback" fonts in case your first choice isn't available on the user's system. This list of choices is called a font stack.

In short, font stacks ensure that the user sees your page text in the intended font if it is installed on her device, and if it is not, then in a font that you specify as an acceptable substitute.

```
body {font-family:"trebuchet ms", tahoma, sans-serif;}
```

Because the font name, Trebuchet MS, is more than one word, it has to be in quotes.

This font stack effectively tells the browser "Display this document in Trebuchet MS, and if the system doesn't have it, use Tahoma, and if neither is installed, use whatever generic sans-serif font is available." It is very important to make the last item of a font-family declaration a generic declaration, typically "serif" or "sans-serif", as a final fallback.

There are five generic font-family names:

Serif—serif fonts have small details at the terminals (tips) of the characters (like this text)

Sans-serif—sans-serif fonts have no details at the terminals (like the headings of this book)

Monospace—every monospace font character occupies the same amount of horizontal space (like the code examples in this book)

Cursive—cursive fonts look like handwriting (like the headline of *The Hound of the Baskervilles* example later in this chapter).

Fantasy—fonts that don't fit the other categories (typically the strange and bizarre)

The purpose of these generic fonts is to ensure, that if none of your choices are available that, at a minimum, your document displays in the right *type* (no pun intended) of font.

It's worth taking some care when selecting the fonts that you put in a font stack. For example, Dreamweaver offers a list of selectable font stacks that pop up every time you type `font-family:` in your CSS file, but these fonts are not ideal substitutes for one another. For example, here is a font stack that Dreamweaver offers:

```
verdana, arial, helvetica, sans-serif;
```

> *x-height is the main area of the letters, excluding the ascenders and descenders of letters like d and p, which the letter x does not have, hence the name.*

Verdana is a bulky font that has a much larger x-height than Arial, so if a user does not have Verdana installed, your page will be displayed in Arial, a font that is smaller than the one you intended. More words will fit on each line, and the vertical height of text blocks may be shorter.

A good test is to view your pages with each font in the stack as the first choice so that you can see how the layout changes if it displays in one of the fallback fonts.

A better fallback for Verdana might be Tahoma, which has the same large x-height.

```
verdana, tahoma, sans-serif
```

> *You can learn more about selecting fonts for your font stacks at http://unitinteractive.com/blog/2008/06/26/better-css-font-stacks.*

For a stack of lighter sans-serif fonts, you might use

```
helvetica, arial, sans-serif
```

Here's a stack of serif fonts starting with a font that the user may not have.

```
{font-family:"hoefler text", georgia, times, serif;}
```

In a case like this, always complete the stack with fonts that are supplied with most computer's operating systems, here Georgia and Times, and end with the generic, serif.

So, Which Fonts Are Available to All Users' Browsers?

That is a common question which has no definitive answer but you have a high probability that any Mac or PC will have these fonts installed:

Serif	Sans-serif	Monospace
Georgia	Arial	Courier New
Palatino/Book Antiqua	Arial Black	Lucida Console/Monaco
Times New Roman	Arial Narrow	
	Tahoma	**Cursive**
	Trebuchet MS	Comic Sans MS
	Verdana	
		Fantasy
		Impact

Because of the often obscure fonts on today's phones and tablets, it is more important than ever to include fallback generic font families in your font stacks. If you want to specify a specific font, use a hosted Web font or one that is downloaded from your Web server—see *Web Fonts Demystified*, later in the chapter.

Font-Size Property

Example: h2 {font-size:18px;}

Every HTML text element has a default font-size set by the browser style sheet, so when you set an element's font-size, you are changing its font size from that default. Font sizing can appear to act unpredictably if you don't understand how the inheritance of font sizes down the hierarchy is affected by which font size units you use. There are two types of units that you can use to set the font-size: absolute units, such as pixels or points, and relative units, such as percentages or ems. Let me explain the difference between them.

font-size is an inherited property, so a change to the font size of an element will result in a proportional change of size in the font sizes of its descendant elements. This means that if you set the font-size of the body element to 200%, then the text of all the elements on your page will double in size.

This effect occurs because in the browser style sheet, all element font sizes are set in the relative unit, em. For example, the h1 element is 2em, the h2 element is 1.5em, and p (paragraph) is 1em. By default, 1em is equivalent to 16 pixels—this is known as the font-size baseline. So by default, h1 is 32 pixels (16 × 2em = 32 pixels), h2 is 24 pixels, and p is 16 pixels.

If you set the body text to 20px, you are resetting the baseline, so now h1 would be 40px (20 pixels × 2em = 40 pixels), h2 would be 30 pixels, and p would be 20 pixels. However, font-size inheritance will not occur in descendant elements that have been sized with absolute units such as pixels—these elements will always display at their specified size.

Let's learn more about font sizing by looking at each method of sizing fonts in turn.

ABSOLUTE FONT SIZING

Fonts can also be sized using keywords such as x-small, medium, and x-large. Medium is equal to the baseline size and the other keywords produce smaller or larger text. Because keywords produce a limited set of sizes, they are not widely used, but you can learn more about them at http://css-discuss.incutio.com/wiki/Using_Keywords.

Sizing text with absolute units such as pixels, picas, or inches is simple; when you set the size of an element using absolute units, it stays that size no matter what font sizing is applied to its ancestors. The downside of absolute sizing is that if you decide to proportionally change the overall size of the text on your page, you have to change every absolute font-size in the style sheet; an absolutely-sized page requires more effort to fine tune.

In short, if you change the size of the body tag's font, any absolutely-sized elements do not change size, but elements that have not been sized in your CSS will change proportionally to the size stated on body.

RELATIVE FONT SIZING

Sizing text with relative units such as percentages, ems, or rems is slightly more complex; when you set the size of an element using relative units, the size of the text is set relative to the size of the nearest "sized" ancestor.

Let's consider this simple markup

```
<body>
    <p>This is <strong>very important!</strong></p>
</body>
```

If you want to use ems but also need to set specific pixels sizes, a good trick is to set body's font-size to 62.5%. By doing this, the baseline size is changed from 16 to 10 pixels (16 × 62.5% = 10). Now it's simple to translate ems to pixels: 1em equals 10px, 1.5em equals 15px, 2em equals 20px, and so on.

Set your font sizes working down the hierarchy when using relative sizes.

and this CSS

```
p {font-size:.75em;}

strong {font-size:.75em;}
```

In this example, the p tag text would be 12 pixels (the body tag's 16 pixel baseline × .75 = 12). Because strong is a child of p, its point size would be 9 points. What you see is that relative sizes compound down through the hierarchy—strong is 16 pixels × .75 × .75 = 9 pixels. Relative units can take practice to master, as unlike absolute sizes, changing the relative font size of an element also changes all the child elements by the same proportion.

However, with relative sizing, you have the ability to tweak the size of all elements proportionally by resizing body, or a number of elements by changing a shared ancestor element. This can be time saving as you experiment with your layout, but it also takes planning for the same reason; a change to an element's font-size affects all its descendant elements, too.

You cannot tweak font sizes like this if you work in absolute font-size units—each absolutely-sized element must be resized individually. Of course, if you do size in absolute units, you can size an element without getting the often-unwanted "knock-on" effect of a change of size in its ancestors.

However, with today's wide range of screen sizes, from massive monitors to tiny phones, the need for text that can be easily scaled makes relative sizing the preferred approach.

A NOTE ON REM UNITS

IE9 and earlier will only scale text set in relative units (not absolute units such as pixels) when the user changes the text size of the layout using the browser's View > Text Size menu. This means that the minor downside of using rems is that if IE7 and IE6 users want larger type, they have to use View > Zoom and increase the text size of the entire page. Just another reason for them to upgrade to a modern browser.

The new relative rem (root em) unit is a CSS3 addition that is generating a lot of excitement in the Web community. When you size an element in rems, the size is relative, but only to the root HTML element. This gives you the best of both relative and absolute worlds; you can use relative sizing to proportionally change the overall font size by changing the font size of the HTML element, but unlike ems, font sizes are not compounded down through the hierarchy. Rems are supported by all the current browsers, but not by IE8 and earlier. The fallback is simple, however, and that is to provide absolute pixel sizing to browsers that don't understand, and therefore ignore, rem declarations, like this

IE8 and earlier use 14px ⎯⎯⎯⎯⎯| `p {font-size:14px; font-size:.875rem;}`

Let's now look at the other font-related CSS properties.

Font-Style Property

Values: `italic, oblique, normal`

Example: `h2 {font-style:italic;}`

`font-style` determines whether a font is italicized or not. You can also write `oblique` instead of `italic`—the result is the same.

There are only two useful settings for the `font-style` property: `italic` to make regular text italicized, and `normal` to make a section within italicized type regular "upright" text. In this example

```
p {font-style:italic;}

span {font-style:normal;}

<p>This is italicized text with <span>a piece of non-italic
text</span> in the middle.</p>
```

the code produces the result in **Figure 4.1**.

FIGURE 4.1 The `normal` value for the `font-style` property causes a specified section of text to appear normal within a bit of italicized text.

> *This is italicized text with* a piece of non-italic text *in the middle.*

Note that the main purpose of italic text is to indicate emphasis, as in "It's *very* hot today!" If you want to indicate emphasis, use the `em` tag, which styles the text as italic by default.

The Normal Value

`normal` causes any of the possible effects of a property not to be applied. Why might you want to do this?

The reason this option is available is so you can selectively override a default or a global property you have set. Headlines `h1` through `h6` are bold by default, so if you want to unbold the `h3` element, for example, you need to write `h3 {font-weight:normal;}`. If your style sheet states `a {font-variant:small-caps;}` so that all links are in small caps, and you want one special set of links to be in regular upper- and lowercase type, you might write a declaration such as `a.speciallink {font-variant:normal;}`.

Font-Weight Property

Possible values: 100, 200, and so on to 900, or lighter, normal, bold, and bolder.

Example: a {font-weight:bold;}

Despite all the numerical options listed here, browsers only display two visual results for all font-weight values—bold or normal. Because interpretation of the numerical values differs among browsers, you'll see the switch from normal to bold at various values—typically around 400. It's best to avoid using all values except bold and normal, as illustrated in **Figure 4.2**.

```
p.shows_weight {font-weight:bold;}

p.shows_weight span {font-weight:normal;}

<p class="shows_weight">This is bolded text with <span>a
piece of non-bolded text</span> in the middle.</p>
```

FIGURE 4.2 The normal value for the font-weight property causes a specified section of text to appear normal within the bolded text.

This is bolded text with a piece of non-bolded text in the middle.

Note that the primary purpose of bold text is to indicate importance, as in "**Danger!**" Mark up important text with the strong tag, which styles the text as bold by default.

Font-Variant Property

Values: small-caps, normal

Example: blockquote {font-variant:small-caps;}

This property accepts just one value (besides normal), and that is small-caps. This causes all lowercase letters to be set in small caps, like this:

```
h3 {font-variant:small-caps;}
```

The code above produces the result in **Figure 4.3**.

FIGURE 4.3 Here is a heading styled in small caps. Note the first letter of this text is in uppercase in the markup and remains unchanged.

THIS TEXT SHOWS THE FONT-VARIANT VALUE SMALL-CAPS.

I often use `small-caps` with the `::first-line` pseudo-element as I demonstrate in *The Hound of the Baskervilles* example at the end of this chapter. Use this styling sparingly because text in all uppercase is harder to read as it lacks the visual cues provided by the ascenders and descenders of lowercase type.

Font Property

Example: `p {font: bold italic small-caps .9em helvetica, arial, sans-serif;}`

`<p>Here's a piece of text loaded up with every possible font property.</p>`

The code above produces the result in **Figure 4.4**.

FIGURE 4.4 Bolded, italicized, small-capped, sized, and `font-family` specified—all in a single CSS rule.

HERE'S A PIECE OF TEXT LOADED UP WITH EVERY POSSIBLE FONT PROPERTY.

Jumping ahead in this chapter somewhat, you can write the `font-size` property to also include the `line-height` property (which is a text property rather than a font property) by writing the size as `12px/1.5` or similar. You'll learn more about the `line-height` property in the "Text Properties" section next.

The `font` property is a shorthand styling that lets you apply all of the font properties in a single declaration, reducing the amount of CSS you have to write. You must follow two rules, however, so that the browser can interpret the properties correctly.

Rule 1: Values for `font-size` and `font-family` must always be declared.

Rule 2: The sequence for the values is as follows:

1. `font-weight`, `font-style`, `font-variant`, in any order, then
2. `font-size`, then
3. `font-family`

Text Properties

Now that you've looked at how to style font properties, it's time to look at how to style text properties. If you want to indent a paragraph, create a superscript such as the 6 in 10^6, create more space between each letter of a headline, and many other type formatting tasks, you will use the CSS text properties.

Here are the most useful text-related CSS properties:

- `text-indent`
- `letter-spacing`
- `word-spacing`
- `text-decoration`
- `text-align`
- `line-height`
- `text-transform`
- `vertical-align`

Text-Indent Property

Values: any length value (positive or negative)

Example: p `{text-indent:3em;}`

This property sets the start position of the text box in relation to the containing element. By default, that is the top-left corner of the container.

If you set a positive value to the `text-indent`, then the text moves to the right, creating an indented paragraph (**Figure 4.5, example 1**).

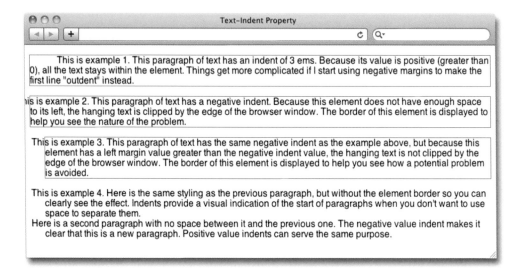

FIGURE 4.5 These four examples illustrate the `text-indent` property.

Inherited Values are Computed Values

One more important note here: `text-indent` is inherited by child elements. For example, if you set a `text-indent` on a `div`, all the paragraphs inside the `div` will have that `text-indent` value. However, **as with all inherited CSS values**, it's not the defined value that's passed down but the computed value. Here's an example that explains the implications of this fact.

Let's say you have a `div` containing text that's 400 pixels wide with a 5 percent text indent. In this case, the indent for that text is 20 pixels (5 percent of 400). Within the `div` is a paragraph that's 200 pixels wide. As a child element, the paragraph inherits any `text-indent` value, so it is indented too, but the value it inherits is the result of the calculation made on the parent, that is, 20 pixels, not the defined 5 percent. As a result, it too has a 20 pixel indent even though it's half the width of the parent element. This ensures that all the paragraphs have nice matching indents, regardless of their widths. Of course, you can override this behavior by explicitly setting a different `text-indent` for child elements.

However, if you set a negative value for `text-indent`, the first line hangs out to the left of the containing element, so make sure that there is a place for it to go. If there's an element to the left, the hanging text can overlap it, or if it's close to the edge of the browser window, it is clipped (**Figure 4.5, example 2**). The way to avoid this problem is always to specify a positive left margin value greater than the specified negative indent. In **Figure 4.5 example 2**, the negative indent is –1.5 ems, but in **Figure 4.5, example 3**, there is also a left margin value of 2 ems. Here is how this is written.

```
p {text-indent:-1.5em; margin-left:2em; border:1px solid
red;}
```

Indents can help give text a professionally-styled look and also give the reader clear visual entry points into the text blocks. Remember to set indents and related margins in ems, as I have done here, so that the indent remains proportional to the line length if the user (or you) changes the font size.

Letter-Spacing Property

Values: any length values (positive or negative)

Example: p `{letter-spacing:.2em;}`

Positive `letter-spacing` values increase the overall space between letters, while negative values decrease it. Always use relative values such as ems for letter spacing, even if you are setting the font size in pixels, so that the spacing remains proportional if the font size

Meet the Text Snake

A very important concept of how CSS manages text is that CSS puts an invisible box around the text inside an element. For example, if you put a block of text in a paragraph p element, CSS sees the actual text as a long line of text, even if it gets broken across multiple lines in order to fit in the container. To make this clear, in **Figure 4.6**, the border of the containing element (the paragraph) is in red, and the border of the text box is in green. Text properties are applied to the green text box.

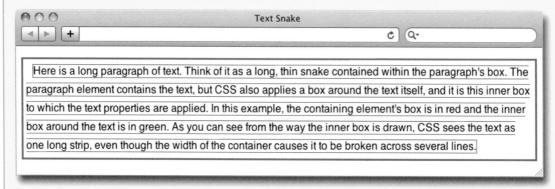

FIGURE 4.6 Text is contained within a long, skinny box that is often broken across multiple lines.

In this example, I mark up the text like this

```
<p><span>Here is a long paragraph…</span></p>
```

and apply the following styles

```
p {border:3px solid red;}
span {border:1px solid green;}
```

Note that the text box is broken across the lines and is only closed at the beginning of the first line and the end of the last line. Knowing this can help you get things looking the way you want faster. For example, if you want to indent the first line of a paragraph, you can use the text property text-indent, as I do in **Figure 4.5**, and then you are moving the start position of the text box. Subsequent lines are not indented because to CSS, it's just one long piece of text.

If you want the whole paragraph indented, then you need to set the margin-left property of the paragraph; in other words, you have to push the whole container to the right. All you need to remember is that text properties are applied to the long, thin, snake-like inner text box, not the box of the containing element.

changes. Examples are shown in **Figure 4.7**. `letter-spacing` controls tracking, which is the typographical term for the letter spacing applied to all characters in a block of text. This contrasts with kerning, which is the term for adjusting the space between two specific characters.

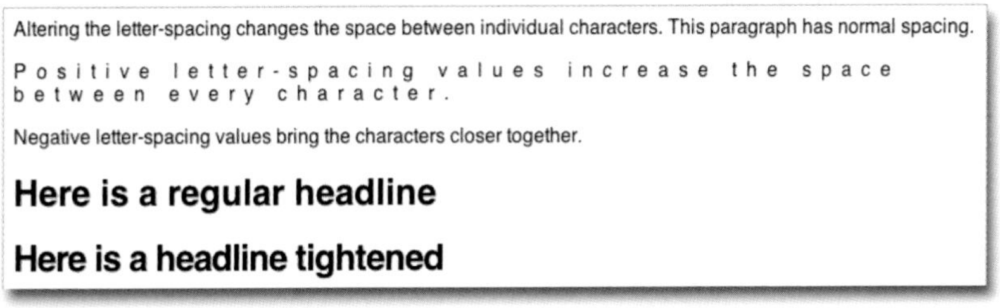

FIGURE 4.7 You can see how changing the `letter-spacing` value changes the look of your text.

> Altering the letter-spacing changes the space between individual characters. This paragraph has normal spacing.
>
> Positive letter-spacing values increase the space between every character.
>
> Negative letter-spacing values bring the characters closer together.
>
> **Here is a regular headline**
>
> **Here is a headline tightened**

The default letter spacing of a font appears looser as the text gets larger, so tightening the letter spacing of a headline adds refinement to your Web page. Note the text and headline I tightened in **Figure 4.7** only have .05 em (a twentieth of an em) of letter spacing removed from between each character; much more and the letters would start to merge into each other.

Word-Spacing Property

If you use wide letter spacing, then the spaces between the words aren't as easy to differentiate, so that's a good time to add in a little word spacing, too.

Values: any length values (positive or negative)

Example: `p {word-spacing:.2em;}`

Word spacing is very similar to letter spacing except, as you might imagine, the space changes between each word rather than between each letter. CSS treats any character or group of characters with white space around them as a word. Second, even more than letter spacing, word spacing can easily be overdone and result in some very hard-to-read text (**Figure 4.8**).

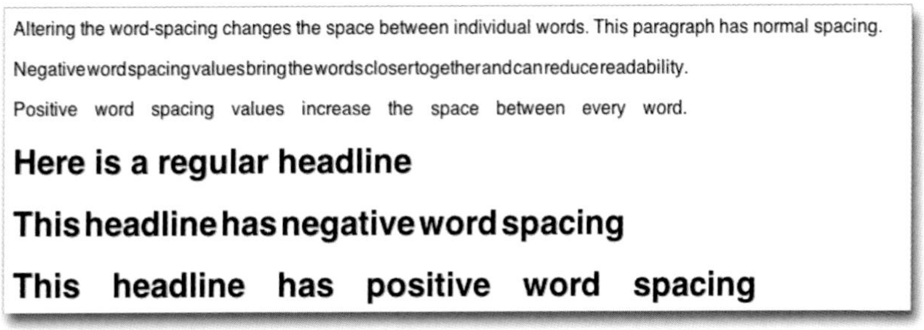

FIGURE 4.8 Paragraphs and headlines with normal, negative, and positive word spacing.

> Altering the word-spacing changes the space between individual words. This paragraph has normal spacing.
>
> Negativewordspacingvaluesbringthewordsclosertogetherandcanreducereadability.
>
> Positive word spacing values increase the space between every word.
>
> **Here is a regular headline**
>
> **This headline has negative word spacing**
>
> **This   headline   has   positive   word   spacing**

Text-Decoration Property

Values: underline, overline, line-through, blink, none

Example: .retailprice {text-decoration:line-through;}

These values, with the exception of blink, are displayed in **Figure 4.9**. blink, which makes text flash on and off, is truly annoying, and should be used sparingly, or better yet, not at all.

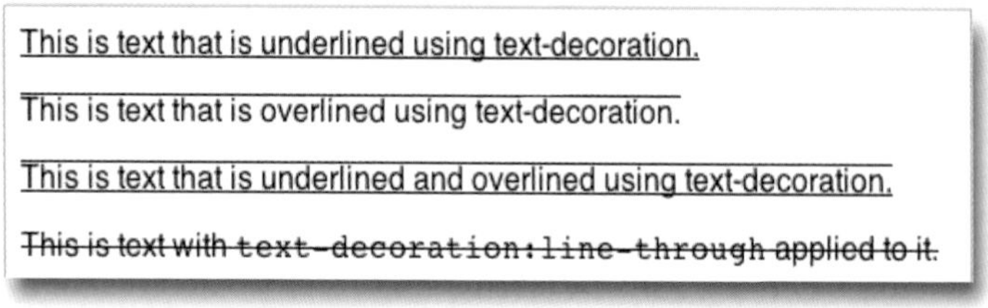

FIGURE 4.9 These are the various text-decoration values, but the most useful application is the control of underlining on links.

> This is text that is underlined using text-decoration.
> This is text that is overlined using text-decoration.
> This is text that is underlined and overlined using text-decoration.
> This is text with text-decoration:line-through applied to it.

Note that Web users are so used to underlining as the visual cue for links that you are setting them up for frustration and a lot of useless clicking if you underline text that is not in fact a link.

The primary application of text decoration is controlling the underlining of links. Here's an example that removes the underlining of links in a navigation bar, where the text is obviously clickable and underlining is just clutter, but adds it back when the user rolls over a link, providing a little tactile feedback.

nav a {text-decoration:none;}

a:hover {text-decoration:underline;}

Text-Align Property

Values: left, right, center, justify

Example: p {text-align:right;}

There are only four values for this property: left, right, center, and justify. The text aligns horizontally within the element. Note that center will also center a smaller fixed-width element or image horizontally within a larger element. **Figure 4.10** shows the four possible text-align values in action.

FIGURE 4.10 The four text-align values.

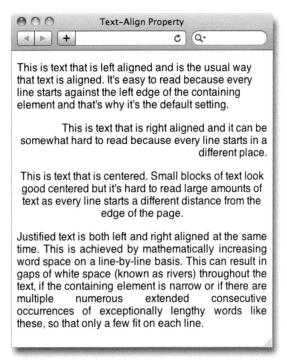

Line-Height Property

Values: any numerical value (value type is optional)

Example: p {line-height:1.5;}

In case you're wondering where the term "leading" comes from, in the early days of printing, a strip of lead was used to space the lines of type.

line-height is the CSS equivalent of *leading* (pronounced like the metal) in the world of print. Leading creates space between the lines of a block of text.

Line height is distributed above and below the text. For example, if you have a font size of 12 pixels and you set the line height to 20 pixels, the browser adds 4 pixels of space above and 4 pixels of space below to achieve the 20 pixel line height.

On a single line of text like a headline, line-height acts like another margin, and large headlines (h1 and h2, for example) have a significant amount of default line height. This is worth remembering, because sometimes you will find that even after removing margins and padding, you still can't eliminate all the space above and below a headline. To do this you need to reduce the line height also, sometimes to a height less than that of the text, i.e., less than 1.

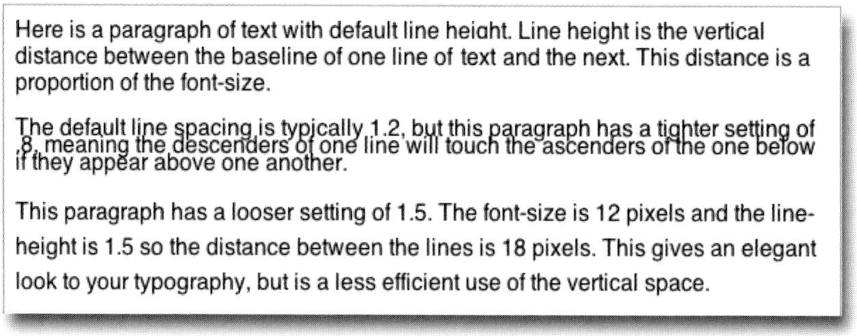

FIGURE 4.11 A variation of the standard line height is a simple way to give a distinctive look to your pages.

> Here is a paragraph of text with default line height. Line height is the vertical distance between the baseline of one line of text and the next. This distance is a proportion of the font-size.
>
> The default line spacing is typically 1.2, but this paragraph has a tighter setting of .8, meaning the descenders of one line will touch the ascenders of the one below if they appear above one another.
>
> This paragraph has a looser setting of 1.5. The font-size is 12 pixels and the line-height is 1.5 so the distance between the lines is 18 pixels. This gives an elegant look to your typography, but is a less efficient use of the vertical space.

As shown in **Figure 4.11**, the simplest way to change this default line height is to use the `font` shorthand property and write a compound value for both `font-size` and `line-height` in one. For example:

```
div#intro {font:1.2em/1.4 helvetica, arial, sans-serif;}
```

In this case, the leading is 1.4 times the font size of 1.2 ems. Note that you don't need any units, such as ems or pixels, specified for the `line-height` part of the value, just a number. In this case, CSS simply takes the calculated size of whatever number of onscreen pixels 1.2 ems works out to be and multiplies it by 1.4 to arrive at the line height. If you later increase the font size to 1.5 ems, the line height (leading) is still 1.4 times the calculated amount of 1.5 ems. Note if you specify a line height in a fixed unit, such as pixels, and you increase the font size, then the lines of text may start to overlap one another.

Text-Transform Property

Values: `none`, `uppercase`, `lowercase`, `capitalize`

Example: `p {text-transform:capitalize;}`

`text-transform` changes the capitalization of text within an element. You can force a line of text to have initial letters capitalized, all text uppercase, or all text lowercase. **Figure 4.12** illustrates these options.

If you want large and small caps, then you need `font-variant:capitalize`.

`capitalize` capitalizes the first letter of every word. This emulates the style of many headlines in ads, newspapers, and magazines, except that a human applying such styling tends to leave the capitalization off minor words such as "of," "as," and "and," as in "Tom and Jerry Go to Vegas." CSS capitalization simply produces "Tom And Jerry Go To Vegas."

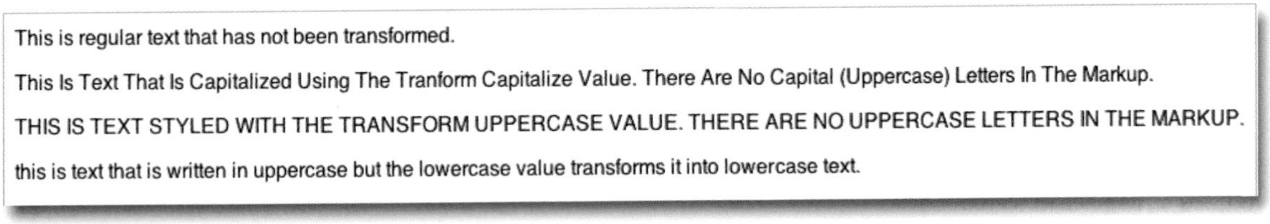

This is regular text that has not been transformed.

This Is Text That Is Capitalized Using The Tranform Capitalize Value. There Are No Capital (Uppercase) Letters In The Markup.

THIS IS TEXT STYLED WITH THE TRANSFORM UPPERCASE VALUE. THERE ARE NO UPPERCASE LETTERS IN THE MARKUP.

this is text that is written in uppercase but the lowercase value transforms it into lowercase text.

FIGURE 4.12 `text-transform` lets you add newspaper-style headline formatting to text.

Vertical-Align Property

Values: any length `value`, `sub`, `sup`, `top`, `middle`, `bottom`

Example: `span {vertical-align:60%;}`

`vertical-align` moves text up or down with respect to the baseline, but note that it only affects inline elements. If you want to vertically align a block-level element, you must also set its display property to `inline`. One of the most common uses is for superscript and subscript numbers in formulas and mathematical expressions, such as x^4–y^{-5} or N_3O. It's also the correct way to style asterisks and other markers within text to indicate footnotes. I don't like the way most browsers style sub- and superscripts by default—the font size is too large and too high (or low, for subscript) for my liking. A little styling can render better, and more consistent cross-browser, proportions.

Here's the HTML for this example

```
<h4>Default <code>sub</code> and <code>sup</code> styles</
h4>

<p>Enjoy mountain spring H<sub>2</sub>O. It's 10<sup>5</sup>
times better than tap<sup>&dagger;</sup> water!</p>

<p class="customsmall"><sup>&dagger;</sup><em>This means
water provided through a municipal distribution system</
em></p>

<h4>Custom <code>sub</code> and <code>sup</code> styles</h4>
```

```
<p class="custom">Enjoy mountain spring H<sub>2</sub>O.
It's 10<sup>5</sup> times better than tap<sup>&dagger;</sup>
water!</p>

<p class="customsmall"><sup>&dagger;</sup><em>This means
water provided through a municipal distribution system</
em></p>
```

and the CSS

```
p.custom sub {font-size:60%; vertical-align:-.4em;}

p.custom sup {font-size:65%; vertical-align:.65em;}

p.customsmall {font-size:.8em; vertical-align:1em;}
```

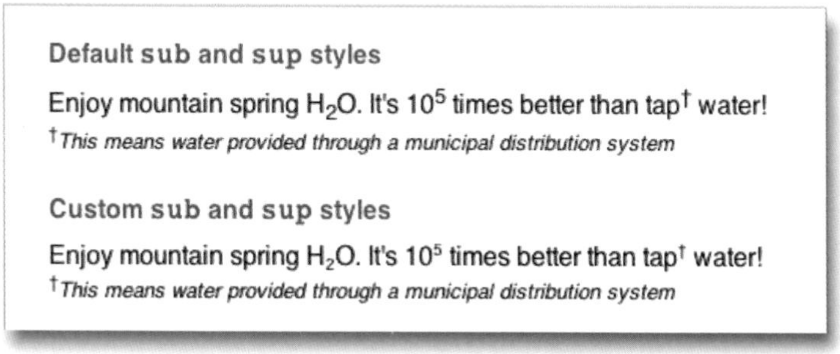

FIGURE 4.13 Superscripting and subscripting vary the vertical position and size of text.

While the HTML tags sup and sub create superscript or subscript text automatically, it's worth using vertical-align and font-size in combination to produce a more pleasing result (**Figure 4.13**). This covers the font and text properties of CSS. Now let's look at how fonts can be downloaded into your Web pages.

Web Fonts Demystified

A now widely implemented CSS feature is the capability to embed downloadable fonts into your pages, using the @font-face rule.

@font-face gives designers greatly expanded font options beyond the basic system fonts. Now you can ensure that the fonts you specify are available to your user's browser because they are downloaded to the browser from a Web server and you no longer have to rely on your font choices being installed on the user's device.

There are three ways to specify Web fonts:

- Use a hosted font library that delivers fonts to your Web pages, such as Google Web Fonts or Adobe's Typekit

- Use a pre-packaged @font-face kit

- Generate an @font-face kit from one of your own fonts using Font Squirrel

Let's start with the easiest method—accessing a hosted font library.

Hosted Font Libraries

The two largest hosted font libraries are Google Web Fonts, which offers free use of their 500-plus font collection, and Adobe's Typekit, which offers subscription-based access to their collection of 739 font families. Both have easy-to-use interfaces.

Here's how the process works on Google Web Fonts. Go to http://www.google.com/webfonts, find the font you want, click the *Add to Collection* button, then click *Use* at the bottom of the page (**Figure 4.14**). Google then generates a link tag with a reference to your selected fonts that you paste into the head of your HTML file.

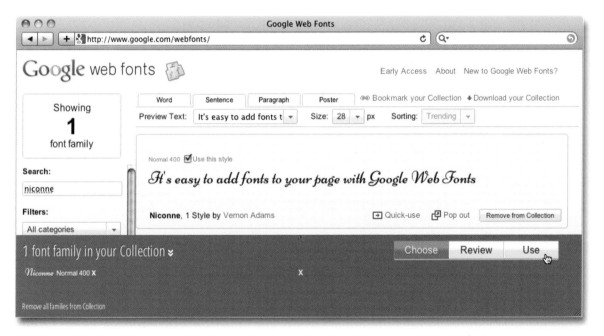

FIGURE 4.14 The font, Niconne, is added to my collection so Google will generate a link to this font.

Multiple fonts can be linked in a single line of code. This `link` tag references the Anton, Niconne, and Prata fonts.

```
<link href='http://fonts.googleapis.com/css?
family=Anton|Niconne|Prata' rel='stylesheet' type='text/css'>
```

Once you have added the link in the `head` of the page, you can then use the fonts in the same way as you would use any other font. When your page is viewed, the font is served into your user's page directly from Google. For example

```
h3 {font: 20px "Prata", serif;}
```

displays as shown in **Figure 4.15**.

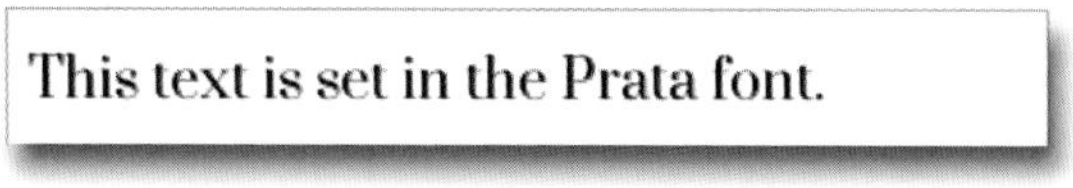

FIGURE 4.15 Your users now see the headline in Prata.

This text is set in the Prata font.

Using a hosted font library offers a quick and reliable way to extend the otherwise limited palette of system fonts. You can add Google fonts to your pages in minutes, and by using them in your designs you can be virtually certain that your users will view your pages in the font that you intended.

Packaged @font-face Kit

The second method of embedding fonts in your pages uses the `@font-face` rule, which requires that the fonts are accessible from your site's, or a third-party, Web server. Fonts served in this way download to the browser when the first page that uses each font loads; after that, they are cached in the user's browser and don't have to download again. Note that the user can't use the font for any purpose except to display Web pages that include that font.

The `@font-face` approach involves more effort, but offers the possibility to use virtually any font you wish. Because of licensing restrictions, you must either purchase a font, or use a royalty-free font, that is licensed for embedding.

One issue with using `@font-face` is that different browsers require different font formats. The Firefox browser, and Webkit browsers such as Safari, Chrome, and mobile Safari iOS since v4.1, use OpenType (OTF) or TrueType (TTF) font formats. Internet Explorer uses the Embedded OpenType (EOT) format, and some other browsers, such as mobile Safari pre-iOS 4.1, use the Scalable Vector Graphics (SVG) format. However, the different font formats are available in ready-to-use kits, or can be readily generated from a font on your computer (again, ensure you have a license to use the font in this way).

Font Squirrel (www.fontsquirrel.com) offers an extensive library of fonts in ready-to-use "font kits." Each font kit includes the font in all the required font formats, and the related CSS code to ensure that each browser is served the correct format. FontSquirrel also has a converter that allows you to upload and convert any font into a font kit.

Here is an example of Font Squirrel's @font-face CSS code for the font Ubuntu Titling Bold, but this format will work for fonts from other sources, too.

```
@font-face {
    font-family: 'UbuntuTitlingBold';
    src: url('UbuntuTitling-Bold-webfont.eot');
    src: url('UbuntuTitling-Bold-webfont.eot?#iefix')
        format('embedded-opentype'),
        url('UbuntuTitling-Bold-webfont.woff')
        format('woff'),
        url('UbuntuTitling-Bold-webfont.ttf')
        format('truetype'),
        url('UbuntuTitling-Bold-webfont.
        svg#UbuntuTitlingBold') format('svg');
    font-weight: normal;
    font-style: normal;
}
```

this is the font name that you reference in your font stack

There is also the interesting "smiley face" variation of cross-browser @font-face code devised by Web maven, Paul Irish, which further ensures that in the unlikely event that a font with the same name is already installed on a user's computer, it won't be confused with the one you want that user to see (http://paulirish.com/2009/bulletproof-font-face-implementation-syntax).

Once this code is added to the page you can reference it with a font-family rule in the normal way, using the font-family name that is stated in the font-family value of the @font-face rule.

If you want to gain a greater understanding of @font-face, I recommend you read Tim Brown's blog article How to Use CSS @font-face (http://nicewebtype.com/ notes/2009/10/30/how-to-use-css-font-face).

Generated @font-face Kit

Sometimes, you need to use a specific font in your design—a typical situation is that a client has a corporate font that you must use in the Web site you are designing. Today, as long as you have licensing rights to use that font as a Web font (check the font's license agreement or check with the company that manufactured the font), you can convert that font into an @font-face kit at Font Squirrel (http://www.fontsquirrel.com/fontface/generator). Just follow the simple steps and in a few minutes, you will have downloaded an @font-face kit that is ready to go onto your server.

Before I move on to some examples of designing with type, I'll make a couple of observations on embedded fonts. Until the day that all browsers manufacturers settle on one font format (which probably should be OpenType), you will have to deal with the complexities of multiple font formats. You can learn all about the preceding multi-font @font-face syntax, and how it ensures Internet Explorer gets the required .eot format font, at Fontspring's Blog (http://www.fontspring.com/blog/fixing-ie9-font-face-problems). Fontspring also sells fonts that are licensed for use with @font-face.

Since the inception of the Web, designers have been limited, except with great effort, to fonts that are generally available on the PC and Mac operating systems. The long-awaited implementation of @font-face in all modern browsers, including IE9 and later, finally gives Web designers the access to the same smorgasbord of fonts available to their print brethren. The fallback for older browsers that don't support @font-face is simple: Those users simply get the next font listed in the font stack, so be sure to list other more common fonts that are found on users' systems after your preferred embedded ones.

Stylin' Text

It's time to put all your new-found knowledge about fonts and text into practice. I'm going to conclude this chapter with three examples of how you can create good-looking typography, from the quick and simple to the considered and sophisticated.

There is the notion of rhythm in typography, that defines the regular flow of the type down the page, generally achieved by working to an underlying grid. Good rhythm helps the eye move smoothly over the page.

Let's start with some quick and basic text styling, and rather than use an underlying grid to organize our type, simply space each element proportionately to its type size. This exercise will allow you to see how to get a result fast if that's what's needed.

Basic Text Layout

As you saw in Chapter 1, the default browser stylings for headings, paragraphs, lists, and other text elements have a very wide range of sizes, and the vertical margins between them are too big. To illustrate how to style these defaults into a more pleasing presentation, here's markup with some commonly used text elements.

```
<article>

  <h1>CSS</h1>

  <p>CSS stands for Cascading Style Sheets. CSS controls the
presentational aspects of your Web pages.</p>

  <h2>Block-Level Elements</h2>

  <p>Block-level elements stack down the page. They
include:</p>

  <ul>

    <li><code>header</code></li>

    <li><code>section</code></li>

    <li><code>h1, h2, etc.</code></li>

  </ul>

  <h2>Inline Elements</h2>

  <p>Inline elements sit next to each other, if there is
room. They include:</p>

  <ul>

    <li><code>img</code></li>

    <li><code>a</code></li>
```

```
    <li><code>em</code></li>

  </ul>

  <blockquote>

    <q>Typography maketh the Web site.</q><cite>CWS</cite>

  </blockquote>

</article>
```

Figure 4.16 shows this markup displayed in a browser.

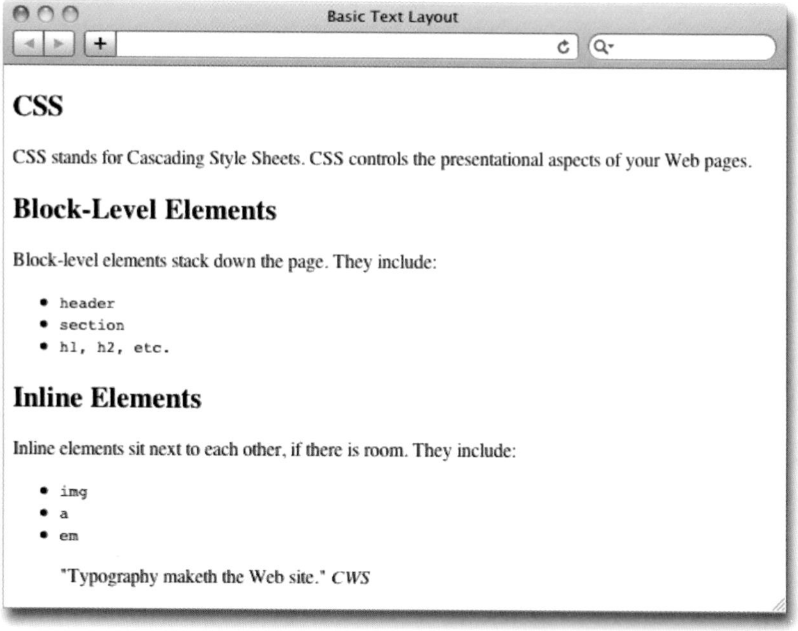

FIGURE 4.16 Unstyled markup is not very attractive.

The font-size *of 1em simply states the default size, and doesn't change anything yet, but I have to state a font size along with the font family in the* font *shorthand property. Also, because I am setting the type in a relative size, ems, if I later want to change the size of all the type on the page, I can make a single adjustment here.*

Here are some steps to quickly style this markup into a more pleasing layout. First, let's remove the margins that are creating all the space between the elements, set the overall font, and style the article tag that encloses all the text elements into a visual container that surrounds the text and centers it on the page.

remove all margins ————— `* {margin:0; padding:0;}`

set overall font size and family ——— `body {font:1.0em helvetica, arial, sans-serif;}`

a centered box ————— `article {width:500px; margin:20px auto; padding:20px; border:2px solid #999;}`

Figure 4.17 shows the displayed result in the browser.

FIGURE 4.17 Removing the default margins greatly reduces the vertical height of the content.

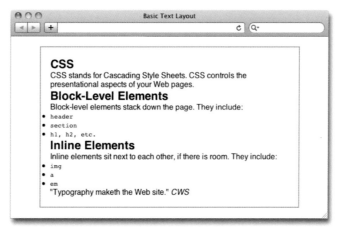

Next, there needs to be some strategically-placed vertical space between the elements. Also, with the margins gone, the list bullets hang into the margin so I'll fix that, too.

space around headings ——— h1, h2, h3, h4, h5, h6 {line-height:1.15em; margin-bottom:.1em;}

space around other text elements ⊣ p, ul, blockquote {line-height:1.15em; margin-bottom:.75em;}

indent on lists ——————— ul {margin-left:32px;}

FIGURE 4.18 Space has been added after the paragraphs.

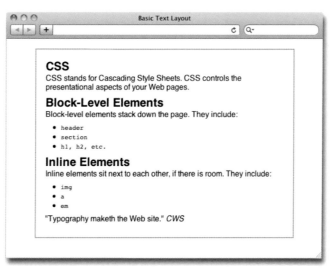

As you can see in **Figure 4.18**, I have tightened up the line-height of all the elements, making each element's line-height only slightly larger than the height of the text. This is because line-height is added equally above and below the text and I only want to add space *below* each element, which I do by applying margins. However, I have to leave *some* line-height or the adjacent lines of the paragraph text (and the headings if they run over to a second line) will touch.

Note there are only two settings for the margins, the exact amount of space of which is relative to each element's font size. I give the headings very small bottom margins (equal to 15% of each one's font size) so they sit close above elements that follow them. I give all the other text elements a larger bottom margin (equal to 75% of each one's font size) to create white space after them in the layout.

As a final step, I want to get a better balance between the headings, so that the bigger headings stand out and the smallest ones don't get lost, and also increase the size of the inline code elements.

```
size heading text ─────────── h1    {font-size:1.9em;}

                              h2    {font-size:1.6em;}

                              h3    {font-size:1.4em;}

                              h4    {font-size:1.2em;}

                              h5    {font-size:1em;}

                              h6    {font-size:.9em;}

size paragraph text ───────── p     {font-size:.9em;}

size code text (too small by ── code {font-size:1.3em;}
default)
```

While this example is quick and basic, it shows that some minimal text styling can greatly improve the appearance of the page and readability of the content (**Figure 4.19**). Let's now look at how to achieve a more sophisticated look through the use of grids.

FIGURE 4.19 Now with larger heading and code text, the page is more visually pleasing and helps the viewer understand the hierarchy of the information.

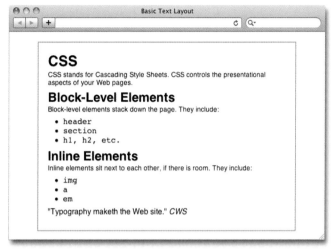

Stylin' Text on a Grid

Using a grid to lay out your type provides a rhythm and visual flow to the page. Because I am looking at type in this chapter, I'll focus on using a grid to create the *vertical* flow of text.

In this example, I'll create a layout based on a vertical 18-pixel grid and every element will align with it. Because a graphic can be added into the background of an element, in this case body, I can temporarily add a simple spacing guide into the page.

Here I use Adobe Fireworks (you can use the graphics program of your choice) to make a white rectangle 100 by 18 pixels and add a 1 pixel gray line along the bottom. I save it in .png format (.jpg or .gif work just fine, too) with the name *grid_18px.png*. **Figure 4.20** shows how it looks (shown on a pale blue background for clarity).

FIGURE 4.20 The tile that I will use in the background of the page. A thin gray line runs along its bottom edge.

I add this image into the background of the body element

add the grid lines ⎯⎯⎯⎯⎯⎯⎯ `body {background-image:url(images/grid_18px.png);}`

and it tiles itself across and down the page (**Figure 4.21**).

FIGURE 4.21 A tiled image added to the body element creates a ruled background on which type can be vertically aligned

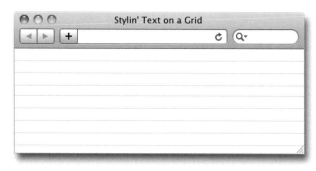

With the horizontal lines of the grid in the background, I now start positioning the text elements, using the grid as a guide.

For this example, I use just a few common text elements but it's easy, once you get the hang of how this works, to build a text style sheet with a full set of "grid-aligned" HTML text elements that you can use as the basis for all your sites.

I'll start with a simple paragraph

```
<p>In traditional typography, text is composed…</p>
```

and this CSS

remove padding and margins off all elements

```
* {margin:0; padding:0;}
body {
```

add the grid lines

```
  background-image:url(images/grid_18px.png);
```

set the font

```
  font:100% helvetica, arial, sans-serif;
```

large left and right margins create a crude column for this demo

```
  margin:0 40px 0;
}
p {
```

set the font size

```
  font-size:13px;
```

set line-height equal to grid distance

```
  line-height:18px;
}
```

Note that I match the text's line-height to the grid distance: 18 pixels. With all default margins and padding removed, I now know every line will be 18 pixels apart (**Figure 4.22**).

FIGURE 4.22 The 18-pixel line height causes the spacing of the lines to match the grid distance.

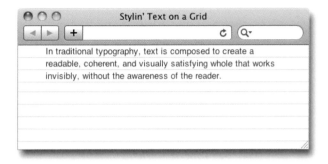

Next I add 4 pixels of padding to the container, body, to push this element down and align the baseline of its text with the grid. Once this first element aligns to the grid, it will be easy to get the elements that follow it to do the same. Actually, I'll add 22 pixels (4 + 18) to also give an empty line of breathing space at the top, by adding this declaration to body.

```
padding-top:22px;
```

While I'm at it, I'll add this declaration onto the paragraph:

```
p {
    font-size:13px;
    line-height:18px;
    margin-bottom:18px;
}
```

set the font size ─────────────┤ `font-size:13px;`

set line-height = to grid height ─┤ `line-height:18px;`

This will create exactly one empty grid line between each paragraph. Adding another paragraph will help show the effect of these two changes (**Figure 4.23**).

FIGURE 4.23 With padding added to body, the text now aligns perfectly with the grid.

Now that the text and grid are aligned, and the paragraphs are correctly spaced, I'll set font sizes for the other text elements. I start with the h3 tag, which I set at 18 pixels. Of course, it too will have a line-height of 18 pixels so that it occupies exactly one line of the grid. To test its spacing, I'll insert it in the markup between the two paragraphs.

```
<p>In traditional typography, text is composed…</p>

<h3>Type for Every Use</h3>

<p>The ubiquity of type has led typographers…</p>
```

Here's the CSS for the new heading:

```
h3 {font-size:18px; line-height:18px;}
```

FIGURE 4.24 The baseline of the h3 element's text sits slightly below the grid line.

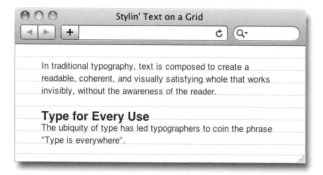

As you can see, the headline sits a couple of pixels below the baseline but, surprisingly, does not push the following paragraph down by the same amount (**Figure 4.24**). The reason is, that while the headline's line-height is correct, at this size and with this font the text is slightly offset within it. Here's how to correct this.

FIGURE 4.25 A small negative top margin and an equal positive bottom margin pulls the headline up into perfect alignment on the grid.

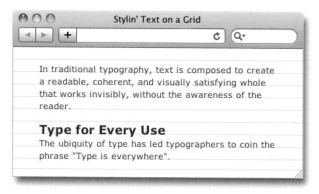

```
h3 {font-size:18px; line-height:18px; margin-top:-2px;
margin-bottom:2px;}
```

The negative top margin pulls the type up, and the same amount of positive bottom margin offsets this change to keep the element that follows exactly where it was (**Figure 4.25**).

A second and similar alignment technique is needed for those elements, usually headings, that are larger than the grid distance. To illustrate, I'll next add a 24 pixel h1 headline. Obviously, 24-pixel text is going to occupy more than one line of the grid, so in this case I'll set the line-height to span two lines—36 pixels. I'll put the h1 element where it usually appears—the first element on the page.

```
<h1>Typography</h1>

<p>In traditional typography…</p>
```

Let's start with this CSS:

```
h1 {font-size:24px; line-height:36px;}
```

FIGURE 4.26 Because the line-height is equal to two lines of the grid, the type does not sit on a grid line.

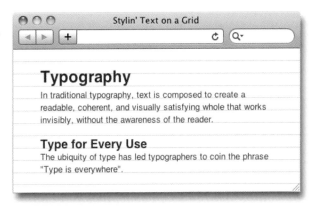

This big headline sits uncomfortably between two lines (**Figure 4.26**). Its descenders will touch the paragraph text if I move it down onto the nearest line, so I'll move it up instead. With a little trial and error, I determine this distance to be 13 pixels.

An alternative approach here would to be to exactly position the baseline of this headline halfway between two grid lines. It can be a nice change of pace to do this, but be sure the next element is aligned to the grid again.

```
h1 {font-size:24px; line-height:36px; margin-top:-13px;
margin-bottom:13px;}
```

This h1 now has some white space below it to set it off from the text (**Figure 4.27**). I could do this with the smaller headline too, but I think it looks better close to the element that follows it.

STYLIN' WITH CSS - CHAPTER 4

FIGURE 4.27 The h1 headline
now sits correctly on a grid line.

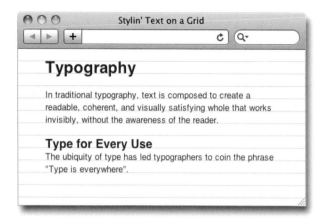

You can see the HTML
for this exercise in the
download code at http://www.
stylinwithcss.com.

To finish this exercise, I'll add some different sized headings, an
unordered list, and a blockquote to show what a more complete
page looks like once the grid is removed.

```
* {margin:0; padding:0;}

body {font:100% helvetica, arial, sans-serif; background-
image:url(images/grid_18px.png); margin:0 20px 0;
padding:21px;}

p {font-size:14px; line-height:18px; margin-bottom:18px;}

h1 {font-size:24px; line-height:36px; margin-top:-13px;
margin-bottom:13px;}

h2 {font-size:18px; line-height:18px; margin-top:-2px;
margin-bottom:2px;}

h3 {font-size:16px; line-height:18px; margin-top:-2px;
margin-bottom:2px;}

ul {margin-bottom:18px;}

li {font-size:13px; list-style-type:none; padding:0 20px;
line-height:18px;}

a {color:#777; text-decoration:none;}

blockquote {font-size:12px; line-height:18px; padding-
top:2px; margin-bottom:16px;}
```

FIGURE 4.28 A page layout based on an 18-pixel grid.

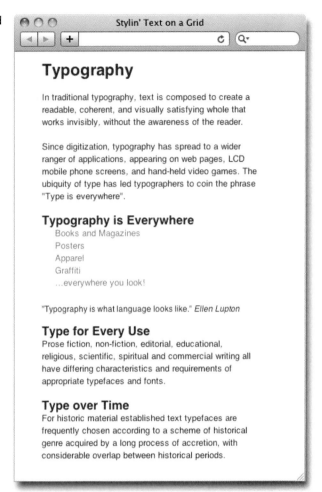

As you can see in **Figure 4.28**, there's something pleasing about a page that's laid out on a grid. From a technical perspective, if you style your type on a grid-based layout for a site where the content will be managed by others, then the page will always lay out nicely, regardless of the order of the elements.

An Exercise in Classic Typography

To end this chapter, I'll lay out a small excerpt of *The Hound of the Baskervilles* (edited for the purpose of this example), using many of the font and text properties you have seen in this chapter. You'll see a number of techniques to achieve high-quality typography, including the use of HTML entities, letter and word spacing, drop caps, a vertical grid (this time 24 pixels), and downloaded fonts.

The markup is quite simple: two headings, a number of paragraphs, and a blockquote.

```
<h2>an excerpt from</h2>

<h1>The Hound of the Baskervilles</h1>

  <p>Holmes stretched out his hand for the manuscript and
flattened it upon his knee. &ldquo;You will observe, Watson,
the alternative use of the long s and the short. It is
one of several indications which enabled me to fix the
date.&rdquo; At the head was written: &ldquo;Baskerville
Hall,&rdquo; and below in large, scrawling figures:
&ldquo;1742.&rdquo;</p>

  <p>&ldquo;It appears to be a statement of some
sort.&rdquo;</p>

  <p>&ldquo;Yes&mdash;it is a statement of a certain legend
which runs in the Baskerville family.&rdquo;</p>

  <blockquote>

  <q>Of the origin of the Hound of the Baskervilles there
have been many statements, yet as I come in a direct line
from Hugo Baskerville, and as I had the story from my
father&hellip;</q>

  </blockquote>

  <p>When Dr. Mortimer had finished reading this singular
narrative he pushed his spectacles up on his forehead and
stared across at Mr. Sherlock Holmes.</p>
```

You can see in this markup that I have highlighted instances of the four different HTML entities that I am using for the punctuation, specifically left double-quote (“) to open dialogue, right double-quote (”) to close dialogue, ellipsis (…) for omission, and em dash (—) for the long dashes that indicate pauses or as a replacement for parentheses.

STEP 1—SETTING THE FONTS AND THE UNDERLYING GRID

I'm using the FontSquirrel font Crimson Roman for the overall text in this example. I downloaded the font kit, put it on my Web server

HTML Entity Reference

These Web sites provide tables that list the HTML entities.

http://htmlhelp.com/reference/html40/entities/special.html

http://code.stephenmorley.org/html-and-css/character-entity-references-cheat-sheet

The first URL above includes both HTML entity values, and the hex values that you need when adding entities as content in the ::before and ::after pseudo-elements. For example, a hex code shown in the table as “ (left double-quote) needs to be modified for pseudo-element content, like this

```
e::before {content:"\201C";}
```

Note the backslash in front of the number. The hex value for the right double-quote is \201D.

Within the text of your HTML content, you must **always** replace all ampersands and all < (less-than) symbols with their HTML entities, which are & and > respectively. This is because "&" is reserved for the first character of HTML entities, and "<" is reserved for the first character of HTML tags. That's what browsers expect to see when they encounter these characters.

(and also stored it locally for development), and I added the provided @font-face rule to my style sheet. I can then specify it in a font-family rule.

```
@font-face {

    font-family:'CrimsonRoman';

    src: url('fonts/Crimson-fontfacekit/Crimson-Roman-webfont.
    eot');

    src: url('fonts/Crimson-fontfacekit/Crimson-Roman-webfont.
        eot?#iefix') format('embedded-opentype'),

        url('fonts/Crimson-fontfacekit/Crimson-Roman-webfont.
        woff') format('woff'),

        url('fonts/Crimson-fontfacekit/Crimson-Roman-webfont.
        ttf') format('truetype'),

        url('fonts/Crimson-fontfacekit/Crimson-Roman-webfont.
        svg#CrimsonRoman') format('svg');

    font-weight: normal;

    font-style: normal;}

* {margin:0; padding:0;}
```

```
body {font-family:"CrimsonRoman", georgia, times, serif;
background-color:#fff;

margin:0 10% 0; background-image:url(grid_24px.png);}
```

I follow my standard procedure of removing all margins and padding, assigning the primary font, and adding left and right margins; I also add the temporary grid for aligning the type, as shown in **Figure 4.29**.

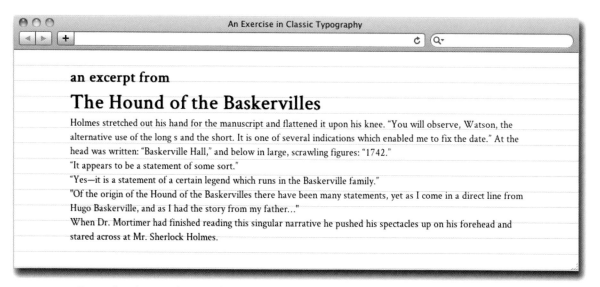

FIGURE 4.29 Text and grid are in place, ready to be aligned.

STEP 2—STYLING THE HEADINGS

I now work my way, element by element, down the page, aligning each element with the grid as I go. I want the first, minor headline to contrast with the main heading, which I plan to style in a large cursive font, so I'll style this smaller heading in widely-spaced small capital letters.

```
body {font-family:"CrimsonRoman", georgia, times, serif;
background-color:#fff; margin:29px 10% 0; background-
image:url(grid_24px.png);}
```

```
h2 {font-size:18px; line-height:24px; font-weight:bold;
text-align:center; font-variant:small-caps; word-
spacing:.5em; letter-spacing:.6em;}
```

Typography Resources

http://ilovetypography.com On this site you can follow the typographic musings of designer John Boardley and enjoy the unique typographic treatments on each page.

http://www.thinkingwithtype.com This is the Web site for the book, *Thinking with Type* by Ellen Lupton. The site features beautiful and classic typographic examples along with information on letterforms and type families.

http://webtypography.net This site calls itself *The Elements of Typographic Style Applied to the Web—A practical guide to web typography*. It is neatly organized by a Table of Contents that lists common typographic considerations and tips.

For this heading I first use the font-variant property to convert the text to small caps and then apply the word-spacing and letter-spacing properties to get the look I want (**Figure 4.30**).

FIGURE 4.30 The small heading is now aligned with the grid and styled with a mix of font and text properties.

Next, I go to Google Web Fonts, where I find a cursive font called Pinyon that has a styling compatible with my subject matter. I copy the link tag generated by Google Web Fonts into the head of my HTML document so I can now reference the font in a font-family declaration. I again need my little negative/positive margin trick that I first showed in **Figure 4.25** to pull the type into exact alignment with the grid. **Figure 4.31** shows the result.

Note the line-height is set to a four-times multiple of the grid distance.

```
<link href='http://fonts.googleapis.com/
css?family=Pinyon+Script' rel='stylesheet' type='text/css'>

h1 {font-size:60px; line-height:96px; font-family:"Pinyon
Script", cursive; margin:4px 0 -4px; text-align:center;
font-weight:normal; position:relative;}
```

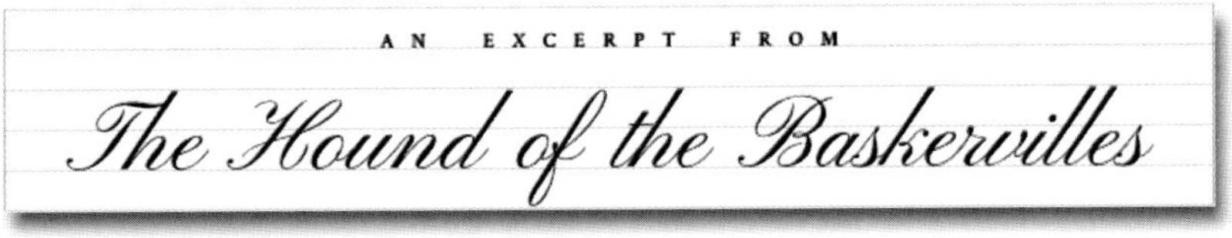

FIGURE 4.31 The large headline is now styled and aligned with the grid.

STEP 3—STYLING THE PARAGRAPH AND THE BLOCKQUOTE

The first paragraph is sitting a little high, so let's set its font size, and most importantly, its line height.

```
p {font-size:18px; line-height:24px;}
```

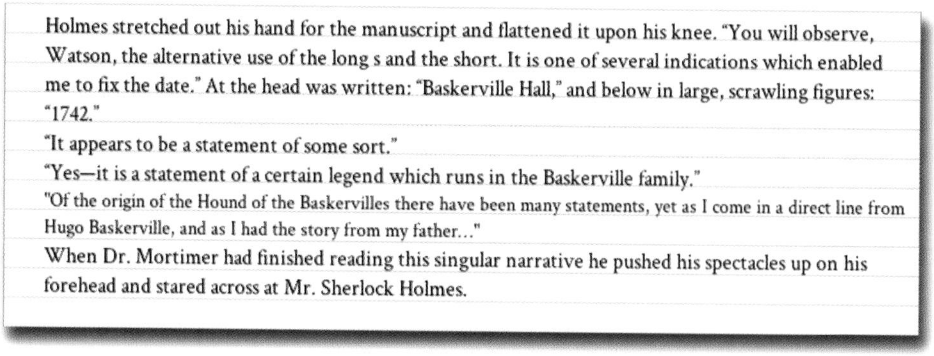

Holmes stretched out his hand for the manuscript and flattened it upon his knee. "You will observe, Watson, the alternative use of the long s and the short. It is one of several indications which enabled me to fix the date." At the head was written: "Baskerville Hall," and below in large, scrawling figures: "1742."

"It appears to be a statement of some sort."

"Yes—it is a statement of a certain legend which runs in the Baskerville family."

"Of the origin of the Hound of the Baskervilles there have been many statements, yet as I come in a direct line from Hugo Baskerville, and as I had the story from my father..."

When Dr. Mortimer had finished reading this singular narrative he pushed his spectacles up on his forehead and stared across at Mr. Sherlock Holmes.

FIGURE 4.32 Setting the paragraph `line-height` aligns it with the grid.

While the first three paragraphs are now aligned with the grid, the subsequent paragraphs are not, because the line height of the block quote that follows the first paragraph also needs to be aligned (**Figure 4.32**). The blockquote text is wrapped in an inline q (quote) tag, which by default, adds quote marks at its beginning and end. I'll indent the containing blockquote, but I'll set the font size and line height on the child quote element, because it contains the text.

```
blockquote {margin:0px 20%;}
```

```
q {font-size:18px; font-style:italic; line-height:24px;}
```

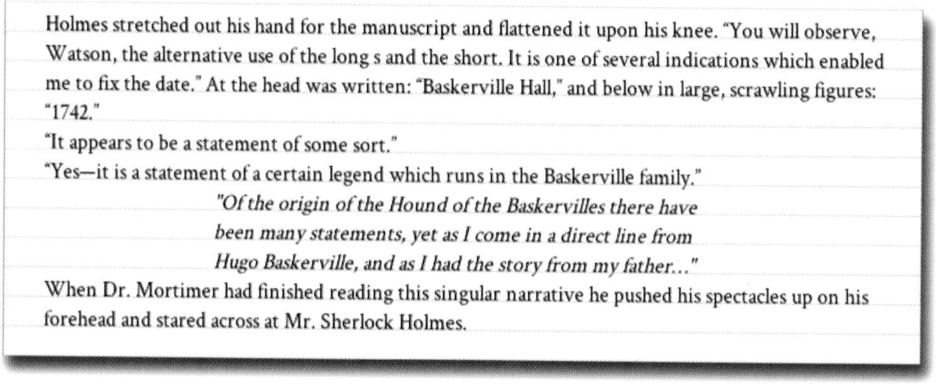

Holmes stretched out his hand for the manuscript and flattened it upon his knee. "You will observe, Watson, the alternative use of the long s and the short. It is one of several indications which enabled me to fix the date." At the head was written: "Baskerville Hall," and below in large, scrawling figures: "1742."

"It appears to be a statement of some sort."

"Yes—it is a statement of a certain legend which runs in the Baskerville family."

"Of the origin of the Hound of the Baskervilles there have been many statements, yet as I come in a direct line from Hugo Baskerville, and as I had the story from my father..."

When Dr. Mortimer had finished reading this singular narrative he pushed his spectacles up on his forehead and stared across at Mr. Sherlock Holmes.

FIGURE 4.33 The block quote is now aligned with the grid.

Indenting and italicizing the quotation adds variation to the page. Notice that with the `blockquote` correctly positioned, the subsequent paragraphs fall into place, too (**Figure 4.33**).

STEP 4—ADDING A DROP CAP

Next, I'll add a distinctive drop cap on the first character of the first paragraph. A drop cap is a large letter that starts a paragraph. There are a number of variations on drop caps, but in this case, I'll align its top edge with the top of the first line of the paragraph and its bottom edge with the baseline of the third line.

Typically, when you see this technique, the first letter is wrapped in a `span`, but this is not feasible or reliable in a site where text is supplied from a content management system. The technique I show here requires no modification to the markup.

I need to select the first letter of the first paragraph that follows the `h1` headline. I do this with a combination of two selectors: the `::first-letter` pseudo-element in combination with a sibling `+` selector. Once selected, that character can be enlarged and floated into position.

```
h1 + p::first-letter {font-family:times, serif; font-
size:90px; float:left; border:1px solid;}
```

FIGURE 4.34 The border is turned on to show that the drop cap's `line-height` is being inherited from the smaller `line-height` of the paragraph text.

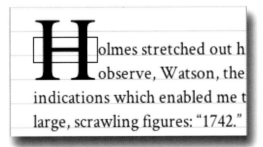

I set `line-height` to less than 1 so that the drop cap is tightly enclosed by its line height and will not force the fourth line of the paragraph to wrap.

The first letter is now enlarged, but is not where I want it to be positioned (**Figure 4.34**). I've turned on the pseudo-element's border as a guide, because what I really need to size and position is its box. The border shows me that this box is only large enough to force two lines of the paragraph to wrap around it because the box is inheriting its size and alignment from the paragraph. I need to set the pseudo-element's `line-height` so its box encloses the drop cap.

```
h1 + p::first-letter {font-family:times, serif; font-
size:90px; float:left; line-height:.65; border:1px solid;}
```

FIGURE 4.35 The element box now tightly surrounds the drop cap.

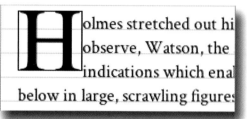

With the box `line-height` increased, the third line now also wraps (**Figure 4.35**). All that is left to do is add a little padding to the top of the element to push it down and align the bottom edge of the letter with the baseline of the paragraph's third line.

```
h1 + p::first-letter {font-family:times, serif; font-size:-
90px; float:left; line-height:.65; padding:.085em 3px 0 0;}
```

Note that I also add 3 pixels of right padding to give visual space between the drop cap and the paragraph text. Also, I no longer need the border so I remove it (**Figure 4.36**).

FIGURE 4.36 The drop cap is now complete.

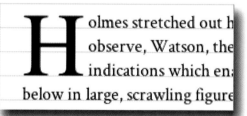

STEP 5—STYLING THE FIRST LINE

The drop cap is now in place, but I'd like to see a visual transition between the large drop cap and the small paragraph text, so I'll add a small cap style to the entire first line of the paragraph text.

```
h1 + p::first-line {font-variant:small-caps; letter-
spacing:.15em;}
```

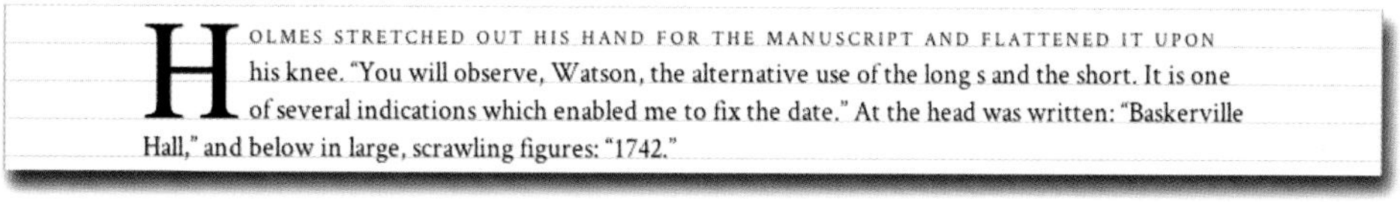

> **H**OLMES STRETCHED OUT HIS HAND FOR THE MANUSCRIPT AND FLATTENED IT UPON his knee. "You will observe, Watson, the alternative use of the long s and the short. It is one of several indications which enabled me to fix the date." At the head was written: "Baskerville Hall," and below in large, scrawling figures: "1742."

FIGURE 4.37 The first line of the paragraph is now set in small caps.

I again use the sibling selector, this time in combination with the `::first-line` pseudo-element to set the first line of the paragraph in small caps. By using the pseudo-element, rather than just typing the first few words in capital letters, the capitalization will adjust if the line length changes. You can see how nicely this styling connects the drop cap with the rest of the paragraph in **Figure 4.37**.

STEP 6—FINISHING TOUCHES

Without some space between the paragraphs, it's hard to see where each one starts. In keeping with convention in books, rather than space the paragraphs apart, I'll instead add a small indent to every paragraph that follows a paragraph; a paragraph that starts a sequence of paragraphs doesn't need the indent. Also, I don't like the anemic quotation marks around the quote, so I will update the default `::before` and `::after` pseudo-elements of the `q` tag and insert nicer ones from the Crimson font. Finally, I am done with the grid so I'll remove that from the `body` tag (not shown).

indent any paragraph that follows a paragraph ———— `p + p {text-indent:14px;}`

quotation marks before quote ———— `q::before {content:"\201C"}`

quotation marks after quote ———— `q::after {content:"\201D"}`

Both these small changes are worth comment. The indents are achieved with the sibling selector, which cause only paragraphs that follow a paragraph to be indented. The paragraph that begins "When Dr. Mortimer..." follows the `blockquote`, not a paragraph, and so does not get the indent, giving a solid lead off to that paragraph by aligning it with the margin (**Figure 4.38**).

The quotation marks added by the `::before` and `::after` pseudo-elements have to be defined with hex entities. I cannot use the normal HTML entities in the content value, as they don't work in this situation; only hex entities work here, and only in a slightly modified state. See the sidebar, *HTML Entity Reference*, earlier in this chapter, for details.

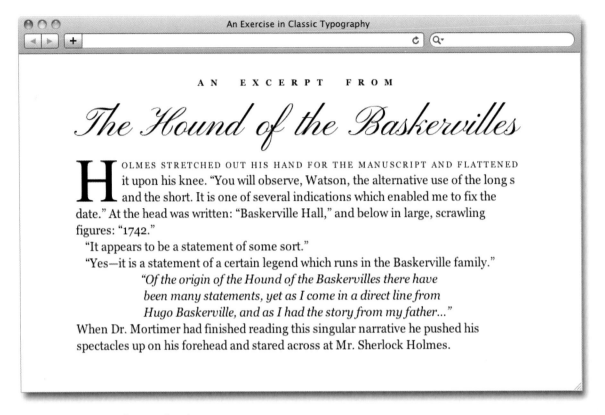

FIGURE 4.38 Here is the completed page.

With these final touches, the layout is complete. It may seem like a lot of work for a small excerpt like this, but of course, these styles could easily be applied to the entire book.

Summary

In this chapter, you have seen the many CSS properties associated with fonts and text, seen the different ways that fonts can be specified for your pages, and looked at various approaches to styling text. Next, I will expand the text layouts you have just seen, and look at techniques to create multi-column page layouts.

CHAPTER 5

Page Layouts

IN THIS CHAPTER, I WILL SHOW YOU how to create multi-column page layouts. Most Web sites use columns to maximize the amount of information that is "above-the-fold," an old newspaper term that on the Web means "without scrolling the page." Typical layouts use two or three columns but four columns is not unusual. Whatever the number of columns in a page's layout, there are some key techniques and ideas that go into every page's creation, and I will cover these in this chapter.

I'll show you several options to create layouts for your pages. You will learn the "floated columns with inner `divs`" method of creating multi-column layouts that has been a common approach for many years. I will also demonstrate some new techniques that are now viable for even the largest sites as CSS3 becomes more widely supported and non-CSS3-capable browsers fade away. Now you can use the `box-sizing` property instead of inner `divs`, and you can use the CSS3 `display` properties that make elements behave like tables (without having to add tables into your HTML!) to easily create fluid layouts with full-length columns.

I will discuss the pros and cons of these and other new techniques, and the polyfills or fallbacks needed to make them work in older browsers (by which I mostly mean IE8 and earlier), so that you can decide which ones you want to incorporate in your designs. Let's start with some basic layout concepts.

Basic Layout Concepts

There are three basic behavior options for multi-column layouts: fixed-width, fluid, and elastic.

- **Fixed-width** layouts do not change size as the user changes the width of the browser window, and are typically around 900 to 1100 pixels wide. 960 pixels is a very popular width for fixed-width layouts as it fits on all modern monitors and the number

The popular CSS layout framework 960 Grid www.960.gs is, as its name suggests, based on a 960-pixel-wide grid.

960 is readily divisible by 16, 12, 10, 8, 6, 5, 4, and 3, making calculations of equal-width columns and other math come out to nice round numbers of pixels.

- **Fluid** layouts change their width as the user adjusts the width of the browser window. While this allows the layout to better scale on large monitors, you give up exact control of the layout when you use a fluid layout, as line lengths change and the relationship of page elements can change as the layout width is adjusted. Amazon.com has a fluid center on their pages, adding white space around content elements to center them when the columns are widened, and currently the navigation sidebar snaps shut into a drop-down menu to create space for the content if the layout is sized below a specific width.

  With today's browser support of CSS media queries, which allow you to serve up CSS based on the user's browser width, fluid layouts are being superseded by layouts that can fix their width at various defined sizes based on the width of the user's display. Creating sites that can adapt to the largest and smallest of screens in this way is known as responsive design, and I will cover responsive design CSS techniques in Chapter 8.

- **Elastic** layouts are similar to fluid layouts, and not only increase the width of the layout when the browser window is widened, but also change the size of all the content elements, too, producing a zooming effect where everything gets bigger. I have not seen many well-executed elastic layouts, and they are complex to manage, so I won't cover them here; my focus in this chapter will be on fixed-width and fluid layouts.

Next, let's look at the difference between a page's height and width.

Layout Height and Layout Width

Before I start to show how to create page layouts, I want to comment on how you need to think about a layout's height and width, because they need to be managed very differently.

LAYOUT HEIGHT

In most cases, you don't need to set the height of the structural elements of the layout, or of any elements, for that matter. In fact, I'll go so far as to say you should actually avoid setting the height of elements. If you do set an element's height, be sure you have a good reason for doing so, such as creating an absolutely-positioned element on your page.

The reason that you typically want to leave an element in its default auto height state is that it can then expand vertically to accommodate whatever amount of content is placed in it. An element that expands in this way can then push down the elements that sit below it and your layout can "breathe" vertically as the quantity of content changes over time. If you explicitly set an element's height, excessive content will either be clipped or flood out of the container, dependant on the setting of the element's overflow property.

LAYOUT WIDTH

In contrast to height, the width of your layout needs to be carefully controlled, so that the layout fits within the width of a reasonably-sized browser window, and text line lengths don't get too long or short. The indiscriminate addition of padding, borders, and large elements can cause floated elements to "slip under" one another if their width is forced wider than the wrapper element that sets the layout's size.

However, while you want to set the width of columns, you don't want to set the width of the content elements within them, but simply let the content elements expand to fill the width of the column—as you well know by now, block-level elements do this by default. Simply let the width of the columns set the width of the content within them.

All this will become easier to understand as I demonstrate how to create the layouts, but for now, just understand that the general strategy is to control the layout's width, but let the content set the layout's height.

Creating Columns

In this section, I'll show you how to create a three-column layout. Once you understand these concepts, you will be able to create layouts with as many columns as you want. I am going to use colored backgrounds for each of the columns of these layouts so you can see exactly what's going on as the focus of this chapter is on page structure.

Let's start simply, with a single fixed-width column centered in the page. I have done some simple styling to the text to improve the look of these layouts. The CSS to style the text is not included here to save space, and that code does not have any impact on the techniques I am showing here. The markup is a `wrapper` to set the width of the layout, with a container for the column inside it.

```
<div id="wrapper">

  <article>

    <! -- some text elements here -->

  </article>

</div>
```

Here's the CSS

```
#wrapper {width:960px; margin:0 auto; border:1px solid;}

article {background:#ffed53;}
```

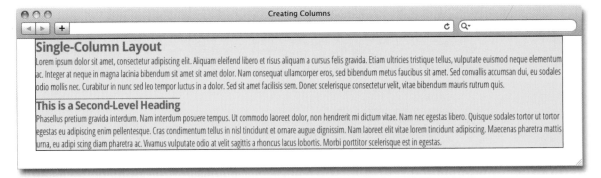

FIGURE 5.1 The background of `article` is colored and has a border to clearly show the centered, single column.

By fixing the width of the `wrapper` and applying `auto` horizontal margins to it, as shown in **Figure 5.1**, the layout is centered in the window. Its height can increase freely as more content is added to it. The `article` element within simply behaves like any unwidthed block-level element and expands horizontally to fill the wrapper. Next, I'll add a navigation element in a second column.

```
<div id="wrapper">

  <nav>

    <!-- an unordered list -->

  </nav>

  <article>

    <! -- some text -->

  </article>

</div>
```

I need to float both containers to get them to sit side by side, a technique I introduced in Chapter 4.

```
#wrapper {width:960px; margin:0 auto; border:1px solid;}

nav {

  width:150px;

  float:left;

  }

nav li {

  list-style-type:none;

  }

article {

  width:810px;

  float:left;

  background:#ffed53;

  }
```

removes bullets from list ──────┤

See The Faux Columns Technique *section later in this chapter to learn how to create a full-height column effect.*

As **Figure 5.2** shows, by making the width of the two containers total the width of the wrapper (150 + 810 = 960), and floating them, they sit side by side to form two columns. Each column is as long as its content. It's easy to add a third column (or as many as you want) in this way.

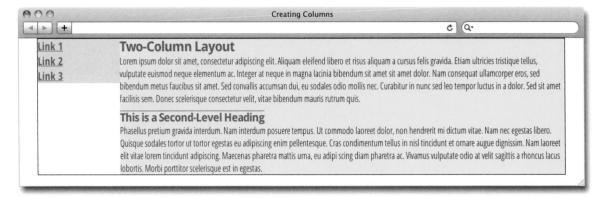

FIGURE 5.2 A second column is added.

```
<div id="wrapper">

  <nav>

    <!-- an unordered list -->

  </nav>

  <article>

    <! -- some text -->

  </article>

  <aside>

    <! -- some text -->

  </aside>

</div>
```

I'll adjust the width of the article column to make room for the new column.

```
#wrapper {width:960px; margin:0 auto; border:1px solid;}

nav {

  width:150px;

  float:left;

  background:#dcd9c0;

  }
```

```
nav li {

  list-style-type:none;

  }

article {

  width:600px;

  float:left;

  background:#ffed53;

  }

aside {

  width:210px;

  float:left;

  background:#3f7ccf;

  }
```

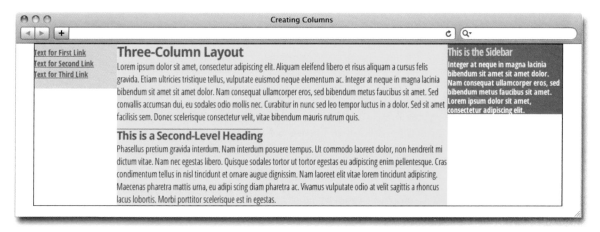

FIGURE 5.3 The layout now has three floated columns.

By simply floating the three containers and setting their widths so they total the width of the wrapper (150 + 600 + 210 = 960), I now have the framework of a three-column layout (**Figure 5.3**). I can add as many columns as I wish in this way, as long as their total width is equal to the wrapper width. Multi-column layouts typically have a full-width header and footer, so let's add those next.

```
<div id="wrapper">

  <header>

    <!-- a text heading -->

  </header>

  <nav>

    <!-- an unordered list -->

  </nav>

  <article>

    <! -- some text -->

  </article>

  <aside>

    <! -- some text -->

  </aside>

  <footer>

    <!-- some text -->

  </footer>

</div>
```

I want the header and footer to be full width, which they are by default, so, as **Figure 5.4** shows, I simply color their backgrounds so I can see exactly where they are in the layout.

```
header {background:#f00;}

footer {background:#000;}
```

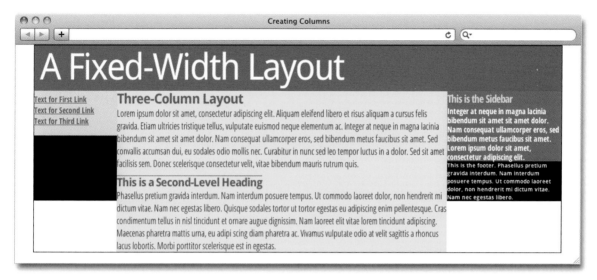

FIGURE 5.4 The header looks good, but the footer has moved up behind the floated columns.

The header is full width and the height of its content and looks good, but the footer follows floated elements so it moves up as high as it can. The fix for this problem is simple (**Figure 5.5**).

```
footer {clear:both;}
```

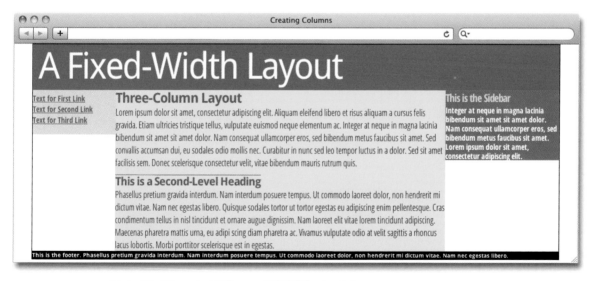

FIGURE 5.5 With clearing applied, the footer positions itself under the longest column.

Adding `clear:both` to the footer (and `clear:left` would work equally well, as there are only left floated elements in this case), prevents the footer from moving up above the bottom of the floated elements. This simple addition ensures that the footer will now always sit under whichever column is longest.

Here's the CSS so far (less the text styles) for the preceding HTML markup.

```
* {margin:0; padding:0;}

#wrapper {width:960px; margin:0 auto; border:1px solid;}

header {background:#f00;}

nav {

  width:150px;

  float:left;

  background:#dcd9c0;

  }

nav li {

  list-style-type:none;

  }

article {

  width:600px;

  float:left;

  background:#ffed53;

  }

aside {

  width:210px;

  float:left;

  background:#3f7ccf;

  }

footer {clear:both; background:#000;}
```

Next, I'll focus on two obvious issues with this layout. First, the content is jammed against the edges of the columns. Second, the columns are only as tall as their content and the layout would look better if they were all full height. Let's start by creating some space around the content. As you will see, this is not as simple as it might seem.

Setting Padding and Borders on Columns

When you start to work with the content inside the columns, the layout can become wider than its container, and the right column slips under the left. There are two ways that this problem typically happens.

- Adding horizontal margins and padding to the columns to move their content away from the sides, or adding margins to the columns to create space between them (and you almost always want to do one or both of these two things as you start to style your layout) increases the width of the layout, and causes "float-slip," where the floated right column no longer has room to sit next to the others, and slips down under the left column.

- Adding large images, or long sequences of characters with no spaces such as URLs, can force the column width to exceed the layout width. Again, this can force the right column to slip under the left one.

Let's see what happens when I add some padding to move the content away from the sides of one of the columns; I'll do this on the center column.

```
article {

  width:600px;

  float:left;

  background:#ffed53;

  padding:10px 20px;

}
```

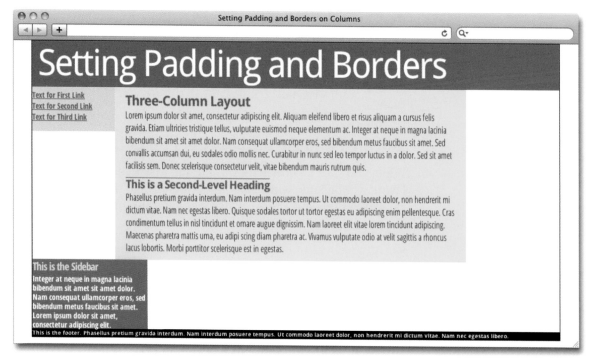

FIGURE 5.6 The content in the center column now no longer touches the edge of the container, but its increased width forces the right column down and under the left column.

The content in the center column, as shown in **Figure 5.6**, is now nicely padded so that it no longer touches the sides. However, its expanded width means the right column no longer has room to sit in its correct position, and it moves down under the left column.

As you will remember from the box model overview in Chapter 3, the addition of any horizontal margins, borders, or padding to a fixed-width element makes that element wider. Adding width to floated columns in this way almost always causes the "float-slip" problem illustrated in **Figure 5.6**, but there are three approaches you can take to prevent it.

- Reduce the stated width of the element by the total of the horizontal margins, borders, and padding that are added to it.

- Apply the padding or margins to elements inside the container instead.

- Switch the way box sizing works by using the CSS3 `box-sizing` property, like this: `section {box-sizing:border-box;}`.

By applying `box-sizing`, the width of the `section` element would be unchanged when borders and padding are added to it, and the content gets narrower instead.

Let's look at each of these options in turn.

1. RESET THE WIDTH TO OFFSET THE PADDING AND BORDERS

Let's say I add 20 pixels of padding to each side of a 600-pixel-wide column. To compensate for the added padding, I could set the column width 40 pixels narrower at 560 pixels, and the right column would move back into position. However, resetting the width of the layout every time I adjust the margins or padding gets very tedious, and while it works, is not an ideal solution. It's too easy to accidently break the layout when adjusting the padding and borders.

2. APPLY PADDING AND BORDERS TO ELEMENTS INSIDE THE CONTAINER

Applying margins or padding to the content elements *does* work. As long as those elements don't have a stated width, their content will simply get narrower as margins or padding are added to them: as the box model states, an unwidthed element fills its parent element horizontally, and its content is reduced in width as margins, borders, and padding are added.

However, a large number of different content elements can be present within a column. If you later decide to change the distance of the content from the edge of the container, you have to adjust that distance on every content element, which is tedious and invites errors. Also, if you want to style the column border, which would also add to its width, you can't do that by styling the individual content elements within it.

So rather than add margins to each element in the container, the best approach is to add an unwidthed `div` inside the column that encloses all the content elements, and apply the borders and padding to that element instead. This allows you to move all the content elements the same distance away from the edge of the column with a single setting on this inner `div` that can easily be adjusted later if needed. Any new content element that is added will be widthed by this inner `div`.

A Note on Presentational Markup

The purpose of HTML is semantic—it gives meaning to content—and CSS exists to separate out the presentational styling, and for good reason. However, some presentational markup is harmful, and some is of no consequence. Creating multi-column layouts with tables, or using `<br />` tags to create line-breaks between paragraphs instead of correctly using `p` tags is very poor practice, because that kind of markup affects the portabilty of the content. For example, once content is in a three-cell table-based layout, it will display that way everywhere, even on a smartphone where such a layout might be entirely inappropriate. When you add presentational markup that creates a specific presentation that cannot be changed with CSS, or that is forced on the user when CSS is not present, then you are misusing HTML. However, adding neutral elements like `div` or `span`, that have no default styles and therefore no effect unless explicitly styled with CSS is, I think, a perfectly acceptable approach to achieving a specific presentational effect.

The only potential problem here, besides having several extra `divs` to work with in your markup, is criticism from the purists who don't think that markup should ever be added for purely presentation purposes. You can read my thoughts on that in the sidebar, *A Note on Presentational Markup*, and read about a code alternative to inner `divs` in the sidebar, *The Child-Star Selector*.

I'll show you how the inner `div` technique works by using it to fix the problem illustrated by **Figure 5.6**.

```
<article>

  <div class="inner">

    <!-- some text -->

  </div>

</article>
```

Now I remove the problem padding from the column, and just to show how well this technique works, I'll apply not only padding but also margins and a border to the new inner `div` element.

```
article {

  width:600px;

  float:left;

  padding:10px 20px;

  background:#ffed53;

  }
```

```
article .inner {

  margin:10px;

  border:2px solid red;

  padding:20px;

}
```

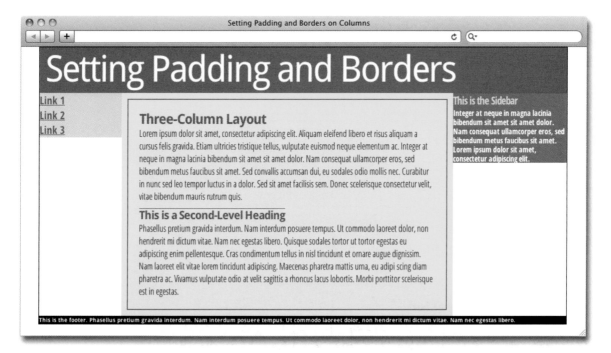

FIGURE 5.7 By applying the margins, border, and padding to the unwidthed inner `div`, the center column width is unchanged, and the right column remains in place.

As **Figure 5.7** shows, this results in the column width being unchanged, while the content width is reduced by the total width of the added margins, border, and padding applied to the inner `div`. The take-away here is once you have the column elements widthed and floated, don't touch 'em! Position the content with an inner `div` instead.

Since I've made my point, I'll remove the margins, padding, and border on the center column. I'll now add inner `div`s to the other two columns and simply put padding on all three columns.

```
<div id="wrapper">
```

```
<header>
  <!-- header text -->
</header>
<nav>
  <div class="inner">
    <ul>
      <!-- link content -->
    </ul>
  </div>
</nav>
<article>
  <div class="inner">
    <!-- text content -->
  </div>
</article>
```

The Child-Star Selector

No, not a Hollywood agent for kids, but a selector combination to set margins on all the elements in a column without using inner `div`s.

The star selector mean "all elements", so If I write a selector followed by the star (asterisk), like this `someSelector *` then I will select all the descendant elements of `someSelector`. The child selector `>` means "child of." So when I add the child selector before the star, like this `someSelector > *` then I will select all the immediate child elements, but no other descendants. This is exactly what I want to do in order to push all the top-level elements inside a container away from the edge. For example, for the section column, write `section > * {margin:0 10px;}`. This declaration adds 10-pixel left and right margins to every child element, but not to other descendant elements. There are two considerations when using the child-star selector. The first is that you must use `margin-top` and `margin-bottom` when setting the vertical space between the child elements—you can't use the `margin` shorthand or it cancels the horizontal margins added to these elements by child-star settings. If you want to indent the content of one of the child elements further, apply padding to the child.

Second, there is a potential performance hit from child-star, as the whole DOM has to be traversed to determine all potential matches. I have found this to be so small an issue as to be immaterial. If you have an absolutely massive page with thousands and thousands of elements, you might want to check the effect child-star has on page rendering speed using ySlow or some other performance measurement tool.

```
<aside>

  <div class="inner">

    <!-- text content -->

  </div>

</aside>

<footer>

  <!-- text content -->

</footer>

</div>
```

Now I use the `divs` to create space around the content in all three columns. I also center the text in the `footer`.

```
nav .inner {padding:10px;}

article .inner {padding:10px 20px;}

aside .inner {padding:10px;}

footer {text-align:center}
```

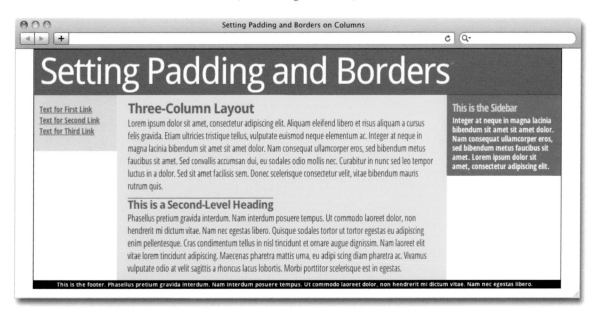

FIGURE 5.8 With padding applied to the inner `div` elements, the layout does not change width.

The padding added to the three columns adds some much-needed space around their text, as you can see in **Figure 5.8**. I've also centered the text in the footer.

These changes make a definite improvement from the appearance of the layout shown in **Figure 5.5**—a few simple touches can give a more designed look to any layout. The key to working with columns and their inner divs is to float and set the width of the columns, but not set the width on any of the content elements within. Let them expand to fill their parent inner div, and then you can move them, and the content within them, away from the edge of the columns by simply setting the margins or padding on the inner divs.

Note that top and bottom margins on the inner div collapse unless the container's top and bottom borders are visible. If you encounter this issue, simply set vertical padding on the container itself. Just be careful not to add horizontal padding at the same time—do something like this article {padding:20px 0;}, which only sets the top and bottom padding.

3. USING BOX-SIZING:BORDER-BOX

This technique could not be more simple. I add the declaration box-sizing:border-box to the CSS of each of the three floated columns, and I can then add padding and margins to the box without having to adjust the width of the columns to compensate, or having to add inner divs. Now, when I add padding and margins, the box remains the same size, and the content is squeezed down instead. Here's the nice, clean, no-inner-divs markup.

```
<div id="wrapper">

    <header>

      <!-- header text -->

    </header>

    <nav>

      <ul>

        <!-- link content -->

      </ul>

    </nav>
```

```
<article>

  <!-- text content -->

</article>

<aside>

  <!-- text content -->

</aside>

<footer>

  <!-- text content -->

</footer>

</div>
```

And here's the CSS.

```
* {margin:0; padding:0;}

#wrapper {width:960px; margin:0 auto; border:1px solid #000;
overflow:hidden;}

header {background:#f00;}

nav {box-sizing:border-box;

  width:150px;

  float:left;

  background:#dcd9c0;

  padding:10px 10px;

  }

nav li {list-style-type:none;}

article {box-sizing:border-box;

  width:600px;

  float:left;

  background:#ffed53;

  padding:10px 20px;

  }
```

removes bullets from list ————┤ `nav li {list-style-type:none;}`

```
aside {box-sizing:border-box;
  width:210px;
  float:left;
  background:#3f7ccf;
  padding:10px 10px;
  }
footer {clear:both; background:#000;}
```

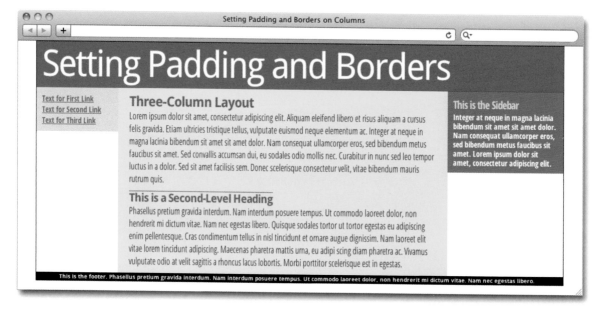

FIGURE 5.9 Using the box-sizing property allows the padding to be applied directly to the column itself.

You can read about polyfills and why they are needed in the Appendix.

Figure 5.9 shows that the addition of padding directly to the columns makes the content narrower and does not adversely affect the layout. As is often the case with solutions that sounds so easy, there's a "but," and the "but" is that IE6 and IE7 don't understand the box-sizing property. However, there's a polyfill for that! It's called borderBoxModel.js and you can add it to your page in conditional comments (then only IE6 and IE7 load it) after all your content HTML and right before the closing body tag, so that the DOM is loaded before it executes, like this.

```
<body>
<!--all my content HTML-->
```

Protecting Against Oversized Elements

Designing dynamic sites that others will update in the future requires an extra level of planning, and the addition of oversized elements is one of the problems you have to anticipate. If an image is added that is wider than a floated column, this can enlarge the layout and cause the right column to slip under. A simple fix is to add `.inner img {max-width:100%;}` to limit the width of images to the width of their parent, in this case, the inner `div`.

An alternative approach is adding `overflow:hidden` to each of the columns, or the inner `div`s if you use them. This will not size down the image to fit, but instead simply crop it (or any oversized element) at the edge of the container.

A second potential problem in dynamic sites is that HTML wraps lines only at the spaces between words. Long URLs, or even long words if the columns are narrow, can therefore cause the column width to increase, so you might also want to add `word-wrap:break-word` to the wrapper around the columns so that all the columns and their content inherit this setting. This allows the browser to break overly long words to a new line. Be aware that `word-wrap` is entirely arbitrary in where it breaks words and doesn't hyphenate. It only kicks in when needed and can protect your layout from being super-sized by a long URL! It's well worth testing your layout with long URLs, large images, and excessive amounts of content in each column to test its resilience, and expose the places where you need to take steps to protect it from the future.

```
<!-- only loads if IE version is less than 8 -->
<!--[if lt IE 8 ]>
    <script src="helpers/borderBoxModel.js"></script>
<![endif]-->
</body>
```

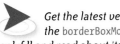 *Get the latest verion of the* `borderBoxModel.js` *polyfill and read about its use and limitations at https://github.com/albertogasparin/borderBoxModel, and read the author's article on* `box-sizing` *at http://albertogasparin.it/articles/2012/02/start-using-css-box-sizing-today.*

Now IE6 and IE7 correctly size the columns according to the `border-box` behavior. After relying on inner `div`s to pad content for years, I am starting to experiment, so far successfully, with applying this alternative box sizing not just to floated columns but to all elements, by adding this into my CSS.

```
* {box-sizing:border-box}
```

Now I can work with a more logical box model where the width property defines the unchanging width of the element box, not the width of its content. I am following in the well-researched footsteps of Web luminaries like Paul Irish when I do this, and you can read his article on this topic at http://paulirish.com/2012/box-sizing-border-box-ftw. Read the comments also, as some interesting issues are raised; like all changes, not everyone is sold on this idea.

Let's now look at a couple of ways to make a fluid layout.

Three-Column, Fluid Center Layouts

There are two ways to achieve a fluid center column: use negative margins to position the right column as the center changes size, or make the column containers behave like table cells using CSS3. The negative margins work well on older browsers, but the CSS3 `table` properties method is more simple. I'll show both these methods.

A Three-Column, Fluid Center Layout with Negative Margins

The issue with creating a three-column layout where the center content area is fluid is managing the right column, and controlling its relationship to the layout as the center content area resizes.

The solution, devised by Web programmer Ryan Brill, manipulates the margins of two `wrapper` elements: the first one around all three columns, and a second one around just the left and center columns. The markup is similar to the CSS for the fixed-width layouts you have already seen, so I won't do a step-by-step on this example, but here's the code with the two `wrappers` highlighted, a couple of screenshots (**Figure 5.10a** and **b**), and a brief explanation.

```
<div id="main_wrapper">

  <header>

    <!-- header content-->

  </header>

  <div id="threecolwrap">          ← encloses the three columns

    <div id="twocolwrap">          ← encloses the left and center columns

      <nav>                        ← the left column

        <!-- nav content -->

      </nav>

      <article>                    ← the center column

        <!-- section content-->

      </article>
```

end of twocolwrap ——————⊣
```
    </div>
```

the right column ——————⊣
```
    <aside>

      <!--sidebar content-->

    </aside>
```

end of threecolwrap ——————⊣
```
  </div>

  <footer>

    <!-- footer content -->

  </footer>

</div>
```

And here's the CSS.

```
* {margin:0; padding:0;}

body {font:1em helvetica, arial, sans-serif;}

div#main_wrapper{
```

centers layout when wider than ⊣
max width
```
  min-width:600px; max-width:1100px;

  margin:0 auto;
```

background graphic aligned ——————
left by default
```
  background:url(images/bg_tile_150pxw.png) repeat-y #eee;

  }

header {

  padding:5px 10px;

  background:#3f7ccf;

  }

div#threecolwrap {
```

floated to force it to enclose the ⊣
floated column
```
  float:left;

  width:100%;
```

background graphic aligned ——————
right
```
  background:url(images/bg_tile_210pxw.png)
  top right repeat-y;

  }

div#twocolwrap {
```

floated to force it to enclose the ⊣
floated column

```
float:left;

width:100%;
```

pulls right column into space ⟶⊣
created by section margin

```
margin-right:-210px;

}

nav {
```

*The code download
includes several lines of
CSS with comments that reference bug fixes for IE6 and 7.*

```
float:left;

width:150px;

background:#f00;

padding:20px 0;

}
```

moves child elements from ⟶⊣
column sides

```
nav > * {margin:0 10px;}

article {

width:auto;

margin-left:150px;
```

adds space to right of fluid ⟶⊣
center column

```
margin-right:210px;

background:#eee;

padding:20px 0;

}
```

moves child elements from ⟶⊣
column sides

```
article > * {margin:0 20px;}

aside {

float:left;

width:210px;

background:#ffed53;

padding:20px 0;

}
```

moves child elements from ⟶⊣
column sides

```
aside > * {margin:0 10px;}

footer {

clear:both;
```

```
width:100%;

text-align:center;

background:#000;

}
```

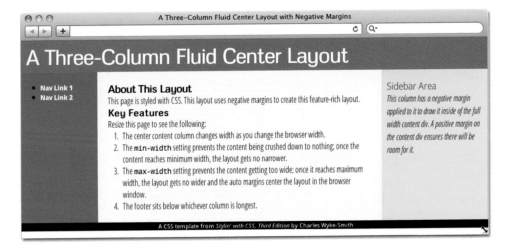

FIGURES 5.10A AND 5.10B As I drag the corner of the window, the center column changes width but the side columns do not, as these two screenshots illustrate.

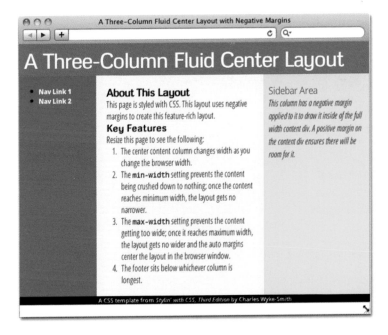

Figures 5.10a and **b** illustrate the fluid center of this layout. Here's how it works. The right column is 210 pixels wide. There is a right margin of 210 pixels on the center column `article` element to create space for the right column, although doing this pushes the right column 210 pixels away. So a negative right margin of 210 pixels, applied to the two-column wrapper around the left and center columns, pulls the right column into this space created by the right margin on the `article`. The `article` center column, sized at 100%, still claims 100% of the space that remains after the left column is floated into position, but its right margin leaves space for the right column to be pulled into position by the negative margin on the inner wrapper. It's a thing of beauty.

THE FAUX COLUMNS TECHNIQUE

A bonus chapter on full height columns with jQuery and faux columns with gradients is available at http://www.stylinwithcss.com.

And if you are wondering how the columns are now all full height, the answer is they are not! What I have done is used a technique know as faux columns to make the columns appear to be the same height. This technique involves adding background graphic elements that are the same width and background color as the columns into the page's wrapper elements behind the columns. The wrapper elements, unlike the columns themselves, are the full height of the content area, so by repeating the background graphics vertically, they visually extend the columns down the page. Here I use separate graphics for the left and right columns, and color the background of the fluid center column (**Figure 5.11**). The left and right column graphics look like this.

FIGURE 5.11 Separate graphics for the left and right columns are needed in the fluid layout.

As you can see highlighted in the preceding CSS, I use the `main_wrapper` div for the left column's graphic and the `threecolwrap` div for the right graphic, and I position it to the div's right edge. I also color the background of `main_wrapper` the color of the center column. This background color fills the background of the entire layout, but the graphics on the side columns, and the header and footer, overlay `main_wrapper` (child elements overlay parent elements), so you only see its color in the center area.

Another aspect of this page layout is that I add horizontal margins to the content elements using the child-star selector, e.g., `nav > * {margin:0 10px;}`, instead of adding this padding to the inner divs, so that you can see this technique in action. See *The Child-Star Selector* sidebar earlier in this chapter for details on this technique.

A Three-Column, Fluid Center Layout with CSS3 Table Properties

While it is undesirable to add HTML table markup to create multi-column layouts, using CSS to make your layout behave as a table is absolutely acceptable. This approach does not cause a permanent table-based presentation that cannot be restyled for, say, presentation in a single-column layout on a handheld device. Tables actually behave in very desirable ways when it comes to creating layouts, as I'll now explain.

Tables are, in their most basic form, three elements: a table wrapper `<table>` containing row wrappers `<tr>` for each row of table data cells `<td>`, like this.

```
<table>
  <tr> <td>Cell 1</td><td>Cell 2</td><td>Cell 3</td> </tr>
  <tr> <td>Cell 1</td><td>Cell 2</td><td>Cell 3</td> </tr>
</table>
```

The CSS `display` property of an HTML element can be changed to `table`, `table-row`, or `table-cell` and it will then simulate the behavior of its HTML equivalent. The big advantages of marking up the CSS columns as table cells are

- Table cells sit side-by-side like columns without floating, so padding can be added directly to them without breaking the layout.

- All table cells in a row are the same height by default so no faux column effects are needed.

- Any column that is not explicitly widthed is fluid.

These three behaviors solve the problems of the layouts that you have been learning about in this chapter. However (there had to be a catch, right?), CSS3 table behaviors are not supported by IE7 and below and there is no graceful fallback, but if you (and your clients) are willing to drop support for IE7, this is a simple, robust, and complete solution, which I would recommend over the others I have shown.

Note that you don't even need `div` wrappers to act as the `table` and `tr` table row elements—you just have to set the `display` property of the three columns to `table-cell`. Browser rendering engines automatically add a table row element around a contiguous set of table cells if the table row is missing, and wrap a table element around table rows if the table element is missing, so you don't need any extra markup—just set each column's `display` property to `table-cell`, and the browser takes care of the rest.

So, all you have to do to get a three-column layout with a fluid center is this

```
<nav><!-- some content --></nav>

<article><!-- some content --></article>

<aside><!-- some content --></aside>
```

and then add this CSS

```
nav {display:table-cell; width:150px; padding:10px;
background:#dcd9c0;}

article {display:table-cell; padding:10px 20px;
background:#ffed53;}

aside {display:table-cell; width:210px; padding:10px;
background:#3f7ccf;}
```

Here I have taken the fixed-width layout shown back at **Figure 5.5**, before I added the inner `div`s to it, and as shown in the preceding CSS, replaced `float:left` with `display:table-cell` on each column, and removed the `width` setting from the center column. Lo and behold, a fluid-center layout with full-height columns to which you can add paddings and borders to your heart's content (**Figure 5.12**)!

Note that this easy, feature-rich layout has no robust polyfill solution for IE7 and IE6, or even an acceptable fallback. The columns sit one above the other in these browsers, so unless you are going to abandon support for older IE versions, you need to use the other layouts I show in this chapter until these browsers are out of the picture.

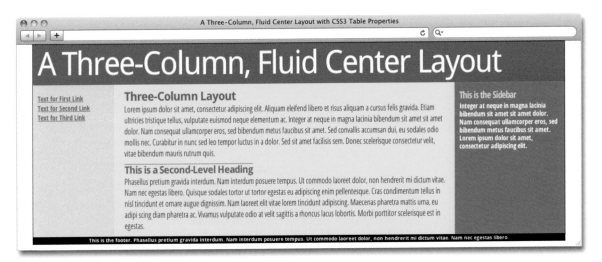

FIGURE 5.12 This fluid layout uses the CSS3 `display:table-cell` declaration to make the columns behave like a row of table cells.

To sum up the layouts you have seen so far, a floated fixed-width layout with inner `div`s is the safest way to go, and works with browsers old and new, but it is also the most work. Using `box-sizing:border-box` (with a polyfill for IE7 and IE6) provides a more intuitive box model and means you don't have to use inner `div`s. Finally, using `display:table-cell` is a simple-to-implement and full-featured option (fluid, if you want, with full-height columns and no inner `div`s needed) but only if your site will no longer support IE6 and IE7.

The layouts I've shown so far all simply have a header and footer with three columns in between. I'll end this chapter with a slightly more complex example that builds on these multi-column techniques.

A Multi-Row, Multi-Column Layout

In this final part of the chapter, and in preparation for styling a complete Web page in Chapter 7, I want to further build your skills from the techniques I have shown in the preceding three-column layouts. Next, I'm going to show a more complex, more real-world page framework; a layout that might be used as the basis of a WordPress template or a corporate Web site.

The layouts you've seen so far have contained only one `article` tag, one `nav` tag, etc., so selecting these elements is easy—you merely use the tag name. As you create more complex pages, you will write multiple instances of such tags in a page. You will then need to use contextual selectors to differentiate them. So I'll use this example to show you the right way to add a minimal number of classes and IDs into your markup to enable you to accurately select any element.

Also, as I showed earlier in the chapter, the use of inner `div`s to pad content can now be achieved using various CSS3-based properties such as `box-sizing:border-box`. However, inner elements, whether `div`s or other types of tags, can also be used for a variety of stylistic purposes, and I will also illustrate that idea as I show this example.

This layout, as illustrated in **Figure 5.13**, is made up of six full-width rows; you can see that the fourth row has three columns and the fifth row has four columns.

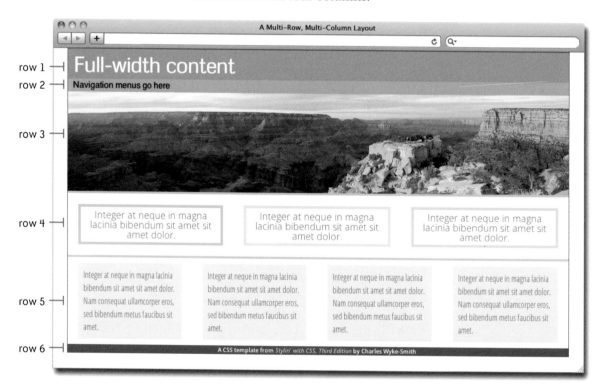

FIGURE 5.13 A layout with six full-width rows and two different sets of columns.

Here's the markup.

```html
<div id="wrapper">
  <header>
    <h1>Full-width content</h1>
  </header>
  <nav>
    <p>Navigation menus go here</p>
  </nav>
  <section id="branding">
    <img src="images/grand_canyon.jpg" alt="Grand Canyon" />
  </section><!--end branding area -->
  <section id="feature_area">
    <article>
      <div class="inner">
        <p>Lorem Ipsum text</p>
      </div>
    </article>
    <!-- repeat article element two more times -->
  </section><!--end feature_area -->
  <section id="promo_area">
    <article>
      <div class="inner">
        <p>Lorem Ipsum text</p>
      </div>
    </article>
    <!-- repeat article element three more times -->
  </section><!--end promo_area -->
  <footer>
```

```
<p>A CSS template from <a href="http://www.stylinwithcss.
com"><em>Stylin' with CSS, Third Edition</em></a> by
Charles Wyke-Smith</p>

   </footer>

</div>
```

You have already seen most of the techniques that style this code into the layout just shown: the full-width "row" elements that simply expand by default to fill the wrapper, the floated elements that form the columns, and the inner divs that get the horizontal padding instead of the containers, to prevent the "slip-under" problem caused by the layout getting wider. So instead of filling a couple of pages with CSS that you have already seen, let's focus on just a few specific CSS fragments, while I show you some strategies to make CSS selections in more complex markup that might contain hundreds of HTML elements.

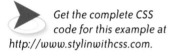

Get the complete CSS code for this example at http://www.stylinwithcss.com.

Real-World CSS Selectors

You may want to refer back to Chapter 2 to review the various CSS selector options.

As your page layouts get more complex, the same HTML element types (section, article, nav, etc.) are used in many places—for example, the preceding layout has seven article elements in it. You need a way to differentiate these identically named tags in order to select the one you want. The wrong solution to this challenge is to label these seven article tags with seven different class names, which is a common approach used by CSS newbies. Not only is it an inappropriate uses of classes—they are intended to identify elements with common characteristics—but this approach clutters your markup, and makes the CSS hard to read because you have to constantly reference the HTML to remind yourself where each class name is located.

The coder's slang term, hook, is a uniquely referenceable location in your code that allows other code to connect with it.

A much better approach is to add IDs to the top level of each main section of your markup (this is a correct use of IDs, which are intended to identify unique elements on the page). These IDs then act as your means to hook into the HTML when used at the start of the contextual selectors that define the path to the descendants you want to select. This approach minimizes the class and ID attributes on your markup, and the resultant contextual selectors state a clear path to the element(s) that they reference, making your CSS more readable.

Take a look at the preceding HTML markup. The three IDs I have added are the only hooks I need to precisely target any element— and I may not need any more, or very few, as content elements are added to the layout. Let me now demonstrate this idea in action by showing how I styled row 4 with the three colored-border boxes.

The top-level element of this markup is `section id="feature_ area"`, which is the row container for the three `article` elements that are styled into the columns. Let's look at the CSS for that row.

styles for the four article ⎯⎯⎯⎯⎮
columns
```css
section#feature_area article {

    float:left;

    width:320px;
```
you can only add vertical ⎯⎯⎯⎮
padding to the column containers
```css
    padding:10px 0;

    background:#fff;

    border-top:4px solid #f7be84;

}
```
styles common to all content ⎯⎯⎮
boxes
```css
section#feature_area article .inner {

    margin:10px 20px;

    padding:5px;

    background:#fff;

    border:5px solid;

}

section#feature_area article:nth-child(1) .inner {

    border-color:#d7dd6f;

}

section#feature_area article:nth-child(2) .inner {

    border-color:#f6dec5;
```
styles for the individual ⎯⎯⎮
content boxes
```css
}

section#feature_area article:nth-child(3) .inner {

    border-color:#d1d8e4;

}
```

I use `section#feature_area article` to select all three boxes, and then use one rule stating the styles common to these elements— width, padding, and the thickness of their borders. I now only have to manage one set of declarations for all three boxes.

I then write three rules for the differences between the boxes. Here's the rule that selects the middle inner `div`:

```
section#feature_area article:nth-child(2) .inner {
border:5px solid #f6dec5;}
```

Reading backwards, this selector states: Find the element with the class `inner` that is the second `article` child of the `section` element with the ID `feature_area`, and color its border pale orange.

You can see that with just the one ID on the top-level element as the hook, I can select any of its descendant elements (even the content elements I'll later add within them), and equally importantly, avoid inadvertently styling any other part of the markup. If you only add a class or ID to your markup when no other means of selecting an element is available, you will end up with HTML that is clean and uncluttered, and CSS that is easier to read and maintain.

Inner Divs in Action

This layout is also a good opportunity to review how inner `divs` provide both positioning and styling options. In this layout, the inner `divs` not only allow horizontal padding to be added without breaking the layout, but also have an important visual function, as they are each styled to provide a colored border around the content blocks. Their parent `article` elements are not visible, but I'll temporarily color the center one so you can see where they are (**Figure 5.14**).

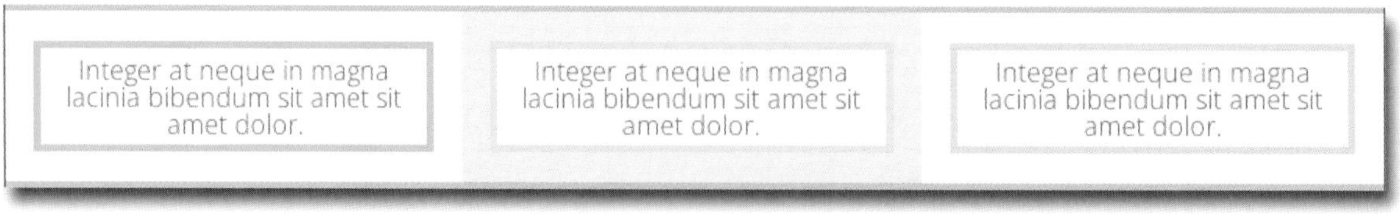

Integer at neque in magna lacinia bibendum sit amet sit amet dolor.

Integer at neque in magna lacinia bibendum sit amet sit amet dolor.

Integer at neque in magna lacinia bibendum sit amet sit amet dolor.

FIGURE 5.14 The center `article` element is colored gray.

Coloring the center element of the three `article` elements shows that they fill the `section` row container and touch edge to edge.

Note exactly how I styled the space around the inner divs. The horizontal space is created by left and right margins that push the divs away from the sides of their parent article element (I can't add horizontal padding to the parent without breaking the layout). The vertical space is created by padding on the parent, because, as you saw earlier, any vertical margins on the child simply collapse when there are no top and bottom borders drawn on the parent.

That concludes my discussion of this layout and I hope you now have a deeper understanding of the use of contextual selectors in your code. I'll style a variation on this layout more fully in Chapter 7.

Summary

In this chapter, you have seen that multi-columns layouts can be created by floating widthed elements, and by using table behaviors. You have seen how layouts can be fixed and centered on the page, or fluid with minimum and maximum width settings. You've learned how to use inner divs to create space in floated layouts without changing the layout's overall width, and how to create faux columns. You've also learned how to minimize the IDs and classes in your markup by thinking of them as contextual hooks rather than as labels on the elements. In Chapter 7, you will see how the layouts you just learned to create form the framework of a complete Web page, as I combine them with interface components, such as menus, forms, and popups, all of which you will learn about in the next chapter.

Interface Components

INTERFACE COMPONENTS IS MY TERM for the common user interface (UI) elements that HTML provides, such as lists and forms. Other common UI components include drop-down menus and popup overlays, and while HTML does not provide specific elements for them, I'll demonstrate how to mark up and style them, too.

A bonus chapter on tables and lists basics, complete with sample code, is available for download at www. stylinwithcss.com.

I'll also show you how to write these components in a reusable way so that you don't have to code them from scratch every time, and can add them to a library of style sheets that you can easily fine tune for each project.

Every site needs navigation. Let's start by seeing how HTML lists can be styled into attractive and functional navigation menus.

Creating Navigation Menus

A menu is a set of links. An HTML list logically groups the links, and causes them to display appropriately even if CSS is not present to style them. By default, because list items are block-level elements, lists stack vertically.

A Vertical Menu

Let's start with a very simple example to show you the key techniques you need to style lists into menus.

```
<nav class="list1">

  <ul>

    <li><a href="#">Alternative</a></li>

    <li><a href="#">Country</a></li>

    <li><a href="#">Jazz</a></li>
```

```
<li><a href="#">Rock</a></li>

</ul>

</nav>
```

In this markup, I added a link around the text of each list item to make the text clickable. (Each link has a # URL placeholder that can later be replaced with a real URL.)

I'll start by coding this first example to show some problems you can run into when you first try to style navigation links, and how to fix them. Here's some code that produces a clean, simple styling (**Figure 6.1**).

remove default padding and margins ——— `* {margin:0; padding:0;}`

positions menu on page for this example ——— `nav {margin:50px; width:150px;}`

box around menu ——— `.list1 ul {border:1px solid #f00; border-radius:3px; padding:5px 10px 3px;}`

removes bullets around menu and creates space around links ——— `.list1 li {list-style-type:none; padding:3px 10px;}`

"not-first-child" selector ——— `.list1 li + li {border-top:1px solid #f00;}`

styling of links ——— `.list1 a {text-decoration:none; font:20px Exo, helvetica, arial, sans-serif; font-weight:400; color:#000; background:#ffed53;}`

hover highlight ——— `.list1 a:hover {color:#069;}`

FIGURE 6.1 Here is a styled unordered list. As the arrow cursor indicates, the non-text areas of the list items are not clickable.

The styling is quite simple (**Figure 6.1**). The new HTML5 nav element gives me a semantically appropriate container to which I can add a class as context for styling the steps of the example.

USING THE "NOT-FIRST-CHILD" SELECTOR

There are two interesting aspects of the preceding code. First, the highlighted li + li selector means "any li that follows an li."

In any contiguous sequence of elements such as I have here (`li`), this will select all of these elements except the first. This selection enables me to add a top border to all the list elements except the first one, thereby creating dividing lines between them. If I simply added the top border in the `li` declaration, I would also get a line above the first item, which I don't want. I call this the "not-first-child" selector, and it is very useful when working with lists. An alternative way to achieve this result is

sets top border on every li ⎯⎯⎯ `li {border-top:1px solid #f00;}`

removes border off first li in ⎯⎯⎯ `li:first-child {border-top:none;}`
group

THE RIGHT WAY TO MAKE LIST ITEMS HOT

In **Figures 6.2a** and **b**, I have colored the background of each link to show you the link's hot (clickable) area. As you can see, only the text itself is hot, because links are inline elements that shrink-wrap their content. It would be better user experience if the entire area between the lines was also hot. I demonstrate this problem because it goes unfixed on many sites, and it means the user can click on the link area and nothing happens because the click was not on the text itself.

Also, there are 3 pixels of top and bottom padding to the `li` elements to create space between the links and the lines, but this causes the cursor to flicker between the "over-the-link" finger pointer and the arrow cursor states as it moves from the links onto the small slivers of `li` between them.

FIGURE 6.2A AND B A temporary yellow background on the `a` links show the limited "hot" click-able areas. The cursor flickers between states as it crosses the small gaps between the links.

Let's fix both these problems by moving the padding and the divid-ing lines from the `li` elements to the links within, and making the links completely fill the list items.

`* {margin:0; padding:0;}`

`nav {margin:50px; width:150px;}`

```
.list2 ul {border:1px solid #f00; border-radius:3px;
padding:5px 10px 3px;}

.list2 li {list-style-type:none; padding:3px 10px;}

.list2 li + li a {border-top:1px solid #f00;}

.list2 a {display:block; padding:3px 10px; text-
decoration:none; font:20px Exo, helvetica, arial, sans-
serif; font-weight:400; color:#000; background:#ffed53;}

.list2 a:hover {color:#069;}
```

By modifying the `li + li` selector to `li + li a`, I am now adding top borders to *the links inside* list items that follow a list item (still with me?). I also move the padding from the list items to the links within. Now the links touch vertically, with no space between them, so the cursor no longer flickers between states as it moves from one link to the next. Finally, by setting each link's `display` property to `block`, the link's element box no longer shrink-wraps its content but instead expands to fill its parent, expanding the hot area. **Figures 6.3a** and **b** clearly illustrate these improvements.

FIGURE 6.3A AND B Each link now fills the entire area of the list item, so the whole area is clickable. This area is temporarily highlighted in yellow in Figure 6.3a. Figure 6.3b on the right, shows the finished state with the yellow testing background removed.

A Horizontal Menu

By default, list items stack vertically, but it's easy to make them sit side-by-side to form horizontal menus. The way to do this is to float the list elements. Here's a simple list

```
<nav class="list1">

  <ul>

    <li><a href="#">Shirts</a></li>

    <li><a href="#">Pants</a></li>

    <li><a href="#">Dresses</a></li>
```

```
        <li><a href="#">Shoes</a></li>
        <li><a href="#">Accessories</a></li>
    </ul>
</nav>
```

and some CSS that is very similar to the CSS for the vertical links

```
.list1 ul {
```

forces ul to enclose floated li — overflow:hidden;
elements

```
}
.list1 li {
```

makes list horizontal —————— float:left;

removes bullets —————— list-style-type:none;

```
}
.list1 a {
```

makes links fill li elements —— display:block;

```
    padding:0 16px;
```

removes underlining from links — text-decoration:none;

```
    color:#999;
}
.list1 li + li a {border-left:1px solid #aaa;}
```

left border on all links but first — .list1 a:hover {color:#555;}
link

FIGURE 6.4 A simple styling of a
horizontal menu.

| Shirts | Pants | Dresses | **Shoes** | Accessories |

Figure 6.4 illustrates a modern look that is common on fashion and retail sites. Of note in this code: the floating of the li elements to make the list horizontal instead of vertical, and the display:block declaration on the links, which makes the links fill the li elements so the entire element is hot. As you saw in **Figure 6.1**, the li + li a selector enables me to add vertical lines on the left side of

every link except the first to create the dividers. Let's now take this styling a step further.

Drop-Down Menus

I get more email about drop-down menus than any other subject so I'm going to explain them here in detail. Let's take a good look at what they are, how they are created, and the variations that you might need. A drop-down menu, which is based on a set of nested lists, combines the vertical and horizontal styling techniques you have just learned (**Figure 6.5**).

FIGURE 6.5 A three-level drop-down menu.

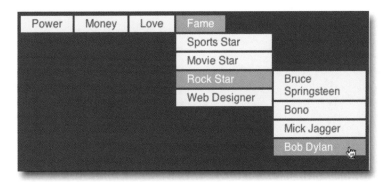

To style this menu I will simply apply the class `multi_drop_menu` to the list's container, typically a `nav` element. Every style in this menu's CSS begins with `.multi_drop_menu`, to ensure that these styles are only applied to lists that are in a container with this class.

The markup builds on the markup for the previous menu examples. Here's the markup, which may look intimidating, but is really just three nested lists.

```
<nav class="multi_drop_menu">
```
level 1 ────────────────┤
```
  <ul>
    <li><a href="#">Power</a></li>
    <li><a href="#">Money</a></li>
    <li><a href="#">Love</a></li>
    <li><a href="#">Fame</a>
```
level 2 ────────────────┤
```
      <ul>
```

```
              <li><a href="#">Sports Star</a></li>
              <li><a href="#">Movie Star</a></li>
              <li><a href="#">Rock Star</a>
```

level 3 ──────────────┤
```
                <ul>
                  <li><a href="#">Bruce Springsteen</a></li>
                  <li><a href="#">Bono</a></li>
                  <li><a href="#">Mick Jagger</a></li>
                  <li><a href="#">Bob Dylan</a></li>
```

end of level 3 ──────────┤
```
                </ul>
              </li>
              <li><a href="#">Web Designer</a></li>
```

end of level 2 ──────────┤
```
            </ul>
          </li>
```

end of level 1 ──────────┤
```
        </ul>
```
```
      </nav>
```

In this markup, I've included only those menu choices that are shown in **Figure 6.5**, but you can add a sub-menu to any item by clicking into the markup after the item's link, but *before* the item's closing li, and adding an unordered list with your choices. As you will see, extending the menu choices in this way requires no changes to the CSS. Let's start creating this menu by developing the horizontal top level.

THE MENU'S TOP LEVEL

Here's the CSS for the top level of this menu.

start of the visual styles ──────┤ `.multi_drop_menu {font:1em helvetica, arial, sans-serif;}`

`.multi_drop_menu a {`

makes link fill li ──────────┤ `  display:block;`

text color ────────────────┤ `  color:#555;`

background color ──────────┤ `  background-color:#eee;`

padding around link text ──────┤ `  padding:.2em 1em;`

divider width ───────┤ `border-width:3px;`

divider color–can be ───────┤ `border-color:transparent;`
color or transparent

`}`

`.multi_drop_menu a:hover {`

hover text color ───────┤ `color:#fff;`

hover background color ───────┤ `background-color:#aaa;`

`}`

background highlights when ───┤ `.multi_drop_menu a:active {`
clicked

`background:#fff;`

text color highlights when clicked ┤ `color:#ccc;`

`}`

start of the functional styles ───┤ `.multi_drop_menu * {margin:0; padding:0;}`

forces ul to enclose floated li ───┤ `.multi_drop_menu ul {float:left;}`
elements

`.multi_drop_menu li {`

makes menu horizontal ───────┤ `float:left;`

removes default bullets off lists ┤ `list-style-type:none;`

positioning context for ───────┤ `position:relative;`
sub-menus

`}`

`.multi_drop_menu li a {`

makes link fill li ───────┤ `display:block;`

adds a right border on the links ┤ `border-right-style:solid;`

background only behind ───────┤ `background-clip:padding-box;`
padding, not border

removes link underlining ───────┤ `text-decoration:none;`

`}`

`.multi_drop_menu li:last-child a {border-right-style:none;}`

temporarily hides lower levels ───┤ `.multi_drop_menu li ul {display:none;}`
of menu

FIGURE 6.6 The top level of the menu, this time with the mouse-down :active highlight.

If you separate the visual and functional styles like this in your code, be sure to add a comment explaining what you have done.

Learn more about back-ground-clip with trans-parent borders at http://css-tricks.com/transparent-bor-ders-with-background-clip.

The first thing that you'll notice about **Figure 6.6**'s CSS is that I have separated the menu's visual styles (such as the font size and the colors of the borders and the text) from its "functional mechanics" that control its layout and behaviors (as noted in the code callouts). This is good practice with a complex component like this, especially if other team members will modify your work later—they can adjust the style declarations without disturbing the functional CSS.

You can see that the only significant styling on the li elements is to float them to make the menu horizontal instead of stacked, and float the parent ul element so it encloses them. Note that this is a case where I can't use overflow:hidden to enclose floated elements, or the drop-down menus I'll add next will then not be visible; they display outside of the area of their parent list's container, the ul, and would be hidden.

For optimal user experience, all the visual styling—padding, backgrounds, borders and so on—is on the a links, not the ul or li elements, to maximize the hot area, and to provide the seamless mouseover action you learned in the previous example. To achieve this, and still visually separate the links, I apply the background-clip:box-padding declaration, which stops the links' background color extending under the border as it normally does. Now I can make the borders transparent (or solid), and thereby create gaps between the links where the underlying page shows through. By doing this, I avoid the use of margins, which would separate the links from one another. This styling gives that crisp, "no-cursor-flash" switch between the highlighted elements as the mouse moves over them—there is visual separation, but in fact, the links are edge to edge.

You may notice I've included position:relative on the li element, in anticipation of adding the sub-menus; it's not actually needed for this step. Also, on the last line of the CSS, I hide the sub-menus—it's confusing to have them display while working on the top level. I'll show how to display them when the menu is hovered in the next two steps.

The styles that I've created here for this top level will be inherited down into the lower levels of the menu, so most of the styling work on the sub-menu is already done.

STYLING THE MENU'S DROP-DOWN ELEMENT

Although it's convenient that the top-level styles are inherited into the sub-menu, some of these styles are not needed. For example, the drop-down (the second level of the list) will be a vertical menu, so I don't want the floating of the top level `li` elements that made them horizontal to be inherited. Another difference is that instead of right borders as dividers that are used on the horizontal menu, I use top borders to divide the vertical items. Also in this step, I will absolutely position the drop-down so that I can locate it precisely under its parent element, which I relatively positioned in the last step.

And while I do all this, I'll display the drop-down level menu so I can see where it is as I work, but I'll still hide the third level, which I'll attend to later.

Here's the additional CSS needed for these changes:

```css
/* visual additions */
.multi_drop_menu li ul {width:9em;}
.multi_drop_menu li li a {
  border-right-style:none;
  border-top-style:solid;
}
/* functional additions */
.multi_drop_menu li ul {
  display:block;
  position:absolute;
  left:0;
  top:100%;
}
.multi_drop_menu li li {
```

width of second level menus ⟶ `.multi_drop_menu li ul {width:9em;}`

remove inherited right borders ⊣ `border-right-style:none;`

add top borders ⊣ `border-top-style:solid;`

temporarily display level 2 ⊣ `display:block;`

position relative to parent menu ⊣ `position:absolute;`

aligns left edge of sub-menu to parent ⊣ `left:0;`

aligns top of drop-down to bottom of parent ⊣ `top:100%;`

kills inherited float—makes list stack ⊣

```
float:none;

}

.multi_drop_menu li li ul {
```

hides 3rd level ⊣

```
display:none;

}
```

FIGURE 6.7 The drop-down menu is now styled and located under its parent list item.

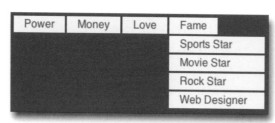

Crucial to the success of this step is the absolute/relative positioning of the drop-down. By setting its top position to 100% (with respect to the top of its relatively-positioned parent li), its top edge sits exactly at the parent's bottom edge; the visual space between the parent list element and the drop-down is actually the border of the first link in the drop-down (**Figure 6.7**).

MAKING THE DROP-DOWN MENUS WORK

Now the fun part—making the drop-down functional. I need to hide the drop-down list, and then have it appear when its parent is hovered.

```
.multi_drop_menu li ul {
```

hides level 2 ⊣

```
    display:none;
```

position relative to parent menu ⊣

```
    position:absolute;
```

aligns left of sub-menu to parent ⊣

```
    left:0;
```

aligns top of sub-menu to bottom of parent ⊣

```
    top:100%;

}

.multi_drop_menu li:hover > ul {
```

displays menu when parent hovered ⊣

```
    display:block;

}
```

FIGURE 6.8 When the mouse moves over the link, its child menu is displayed.

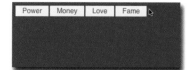

The key to making the menu work is first to hide it

hides level 2 ———————————┤ `li ul {display:none;}`

and then have it reappear when its parent element is hovered.

shows level 2 ———————————┤ `li:hover > ul {display:block;}`

This last line simply states: when a list item is hovered, display its child list. Note that I set the `:hover` trigger on the `li` element that contains the `a` link element, not the link itself. The reason I do this is that the element I want to display, the child `ul`, is not a child of the link but of the `li`, so the hover must be on that element. Additionally, I add the child selector > between the hovered list element and the child list `ul` selector, so that only the immediate child list displays (**Figure 6.8**). Without the child selector, both the second and third-level menus would display when the top level is hovered.

ADDING THE MENU'S THIRD LEVEL

Now let's make the third level of the menu function also. Actually, it already does function, sort of. If you load the code example for **Figure 6.8** in your browser and roll over the sub-menu you'll see what is shown in **Figure 6.9**.

FIGURE 6.9 The third-level list displays when its parent list element is hovered, but it is not correctly positioned.

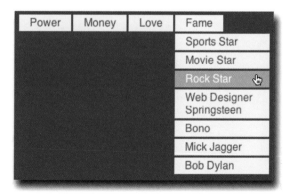

When its parent is hovered, the third-level list displays, because the preceding CSS rule with the :hover applies as much to this third-level element as it does to the second level. However, at this time the third level menu shown in **Figure 6.9** is behind its parent. Its current relationship to its second-level parent is, not surprisingly, the same as that of the second level to the top level, sitting below the hovered choice and its first item. You can see that *Bruce Springsteen* is covered by the last item of the drop-down, *Web Designer*.

What I need to do is move this third level so it sits to the right of the drop-down, with its top edge aligned with the top edge of its drop-down menu choice.

```
.multi_drop_menu li li ul {
```

position relative to parent menu ⊣   `position:absolute;`

aligns menu with right of parent ⊣   `left:100%;`

aligns with top of parent menu ⊢   `top:0;`
choice

```
}
```

FIGURE 6.10 The third level is now correctly positioned next to the second level.

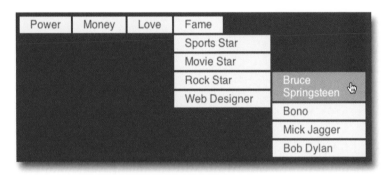

The menu is now functioning correctly (**Figure 6.10**). You can add more list elements at the top level and more sub-lists in the markup and they will all work, with no additions to the CSS. There are two more adjustments I want to make to this menu. The first, in order to make it truly a useful and reusable piece of code, is to add some alternate styles so that the top level of the menu can be organized vertically rather than horizontally, so it can be used in a navigation side bar. First I add a second class, `vertical`, to the `nav` container.

note space between class
names in HTML ────┤ `<nav class="multi_drop_menu vertical">`

Now I can write some CSS styles that will only be applied when this `vertical` class is present. Note that each of these additional `vertical` menu rules begins with

no space between class names in CSS —————— `.multi_drop_menu.vertical`

which means an element with *both* these classes on it—note there is no space between them in CSS.

top-level vertical menu width —————— `.multi_drop_menu.vertical {width:8em;}`

```
.multi_drop_menu.vertical li a {

  border-right-style:none;

  border-top-style:solid;

}
```

level 3 —————— `.multi_drop_menu.vertical li li a {border-left-style:solid;}`

```
.multi_drop_menu.vertical ul,

.multi_drop_menu.vertical li {
```

makes top level menu vertical —————— `  float:none;`

```
}

.multi_drop_menu.vertical li ul {
```

aligns level 2 menu to right of level 1 —————— `  left:100%;`

aligns sub-menu with top of menu choice —————— `  top:0;`

```
}
```

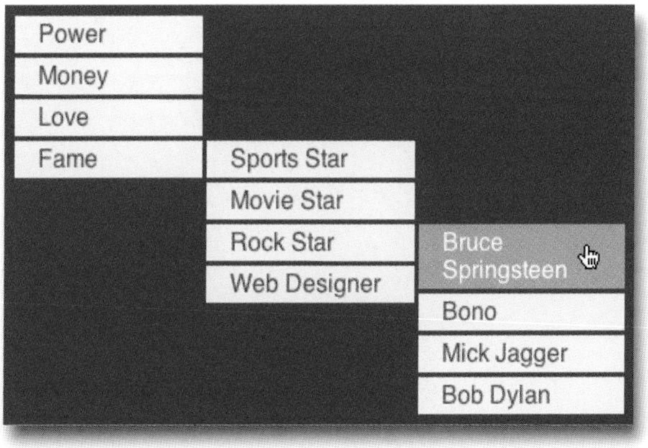

FIGURE 6.11 With the additional vertical styles, the top level of the menu now stacks vertically.

I removed the floating from the top-level li elements, so the menu returned to its default stacked state, and also from its parent ul, which was floated to make it enclose the floated li elements.

I also set a width on the nav container; without this, both nav and the top-level menu within it would expand as wide as possible. Finally, I changed the relationship of the second-level menu to the first level to be the same as the relationship I just established between the third and second levels—to the right, and with the child list's top edge aligned with the top edge of its parent list item. Note I also removed the top level's right borders and replaced them with top borders (**Figure 6.11**).

MAKING THE SELECTION PATH HIGHLIGHT

You can see that in **Figure 6.11**, only the hovered element is highlighted. To help the user know they made the right selection, I need to highlight the selection that was made at each level of the menu. This is easily achieved by replacing .multi_drop_menu a:hover with the following CSS.

```
.multi_drop_menu li:hover > a {
    color:#fff;
    background-color:#aaa
}
```

hover text color ──────────────┤ color:#fff;

hover background color ─────────┤ background-color:#aaa

FIGURE 6.12 The selection path to the choice is now highlighted at each level of the menu.

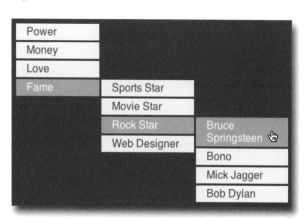

This neat little trick works because the :hover event on an element "bubbles up" the hierarchy, so by setting the hover on the li, I am setting it on all the ancestor `li` elements also. I then simply apply the `:hover` styles to each of their immediate child link elements. This greatly improves the usability of the menu, which is now complete (**Figure 6.12**).

In summary, by linking the menu CSS to your page, and adding the `multi_drop_menu` class to a container that holds an unordered list, that list will be styled into the menu layout, as you will see when I use it in the next chapter.

Forms

I highly recommend Luke Wroblewski's book on form design http://www. lukew.com/resources/web_ form_design.asp.

If you want to know more about using server-side logic to validate form data, you might want to check out my book Codin' for the Web, which covers PHP and mySQL.

Forms have a unique purpose in that they send information *from the user to the server*, while other page elements display content sent *from the server to the user*. We certainly want users to be successful in using forms; we want their feedback, opinions, contact info, and, yes folks, their credit card numbers. Large forms can become complex, and a shopping cart transaction at an e-store is an example where, without good design to support the process, users may give up in frustration. Here the quality of the design can be measured in hard cash.

The actual processing of form data is beyond the scope of this book, but I will show how forms can be styled for clarity and ease-of-use. Let's start with a look at a completed form.

The HTML Elements of a Form

Here's a finished form that I'll create in this section of the chapter (**Figure 6.13**).

HTML5 and Forms

HTML5 adds 13 new variations to the `input` tags. There are also a host of improvements, including the wonderful `placeholder` attribute that displays direction text (such as, "Enter your Customer ID!") right in a text field and magically disappears as soon as the user starts to type.

You can learn more about HTML5 forms tags and attributes, and their browser support at http://wufoo.com/html5 and http://www.html5rocks. com/en/tutorials/forms/html5forms.

FIGURE 6.13 A styled form illustrating common form elements.

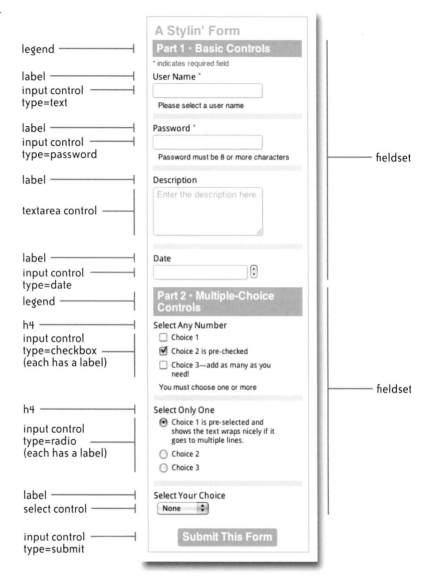

legend ─────────────┤

label ─────────────┤
input control ──────┤
type=text

label ─────────────┤
input control ──────┤
type=password

label ─────────────┤

textarea control ───┤

label ─────────────┤
input control ──────┤
type=date
legend ─────────────┤

h4 ────────────────┤
input control
type=checkbox ──────┤
(each has a label)

h4 ────────────────┤

input control
type=radio ─────────┤
(each has a label)

label ─────────────┤
select control ─────┤

input control ──────┤
type=submit

fieldset

fieldset

I'll first show the entire markup for this form, then discuss the individual HTML elements in detail.

the required form tag ──────┤
```
<form class="stylin_form1" action="process_form.php"
method="post">

<h3>A Stylin' Form</h3>
```

the container for a group of controls ————┤ `<fieldset>`

the title for a fieldset ———————┤ `<legend><span>Part 1 &#8226; Basic Controls</span></legend>`

begin single line text field ————┤ `<section>`

`<p class="note">* indicates required field</p>`

the for attribute ties the label to its control—same as control's ID ——┤ `<label for="user_name">User Name<span> *</span></label>`

the text attribute makes this input display as a text field ——┤ `<input type="text" id="user_name" name="user_name" />`

`<p>Please select a user name</p>`

`</section>`

begin password field ————————┤ `<section>`

`<label for="password">Password<span> *</span></label>`

password input text displays as bullets ——┤ `<input type="password" id="password" name="password"`
`maxlength="20" />`

`<p>Password must be 8 or more characters</p>`

`</section>`

begin multi-line text field ————┤ `<section>`

`<label for="description">Description</label>`

`<textarea id="description" name="description"`
`placeholder="Enter the description here."></textarea>`

`</section>`

begin HTML date field ————————┤ `<section>`

`<label for="special_date">Date</label>`

You can learn more about input *elements at http://htmlhelp.com/reference/ html40/forms/input.html and http://www.javascript-coder. com/html-form/html-form-tuto- rial-p1.phtml.*

`<input type="date" id="special_date" name="event_date"`
`min="2012-09-05" />`

`</section>`

`</fieldset>`

`<fieldset>`

`<legend><span>Part 2 &#8226; Multiple-Choice Controls`
`</span></legend>`

begin checkboxes ————————┤ `<section>`

```
<h4>Select Any Number</h4>

<section>

  <input type="checkbox" id="check1" name="checkset"
  value="1" />

  <label for="check1">Choice 1</label>

</section>

<section>

  <input type="checkbox" checked="checked" id="check2"
  name="checkset" value="2" />

  <label for="check2">Choice 2 is pre-checked</label>

</section>

<section>

  <input type="checkbox" id="check3" name="checkset"
  value="3" />

  <label for="check3"> Choice 3&mdash;add as many as you
  need!</label>

</section>

</section>

<section>

  <h4>Select Only One</h4>

  <section>

    <input checked="checked" id="radio1" name="radioset"
    type="radio" value="Choice_1" />

    <label for="radio1">Choice 1 is pre-selected and shows
    the text wraps nicely if it goes to multiple lines.
    </label>

  </section>

  <section>

    <input id="radio2" name="radioset" type="radio"
    value="Choice_2" />
```

begin radio buttons ────────────┤

```
    <label for="radio2">Choice 2</label>

  </section>

  <section>

    <input id="radio3" name="radioset" type="radio"
    value="Choice_3" />

    <label for="radio3">Choice 3</label>

  </section>

</section>
```

begin select (drop-down menu) ⊣

```
<section>

  <label for="select_choice">Select Your Choice</label>

  <select id="select_choice" name="select_choice">

    <option value="0">None</option>

    <option value="1">Choice 1</option>

    <option value="2">Choice 2</option>

    <option value="3">Choice 3</option>

    <option value="4">Choice 4</option>

  </select>

</section>

</fieldset>
```

begin submit button —————————⊣

```
<section>

  <input type="submit" value="Submit This Form" />

</section>

</form>
```

I'll now explain how this form markup is structured, starting at the top with the form element.

THE FORM ELEMENT

The form's markup is wrapped in an HTML form element.

```
<form class="stylin_form1" action="process_form.php"
method="post">
```

```
<!-- markup for form elements -->
</form>
```

A `form` element has two required attributes: the `action` attribute contains the URL of the file on the server that will process the form data when it is submitted, and the `method` (either `post` or `get`) determines how the data is passed to the server.

SUBMITTING THE FORM

When a form is submitted by the user, the data that the user entered or selected in each of the form's controls is sent to the server. A control is the generic name given to the form widgets that are used to collect data: text fields, checkboxes, radio buttons, and so on. The data is sent to the server in the form of a name=value pair, such as `username=chrisconsumer` with one pair for each control. *Name* is the text that you enter into the `name` attribute of the control. *Value* contains either the information that the user entered in a text field control, or the boolean state of a selectable control such as a checkbox (`1` for checked and `0` for not checked).

FIELDSETS

A set of related form controls can be grouped within a `fieldset` element. In an e-commerce site, the controls to collect the user's name and address might be wrapped in a `fieldset` with the legend "Mailing Address." A second `fieldset` might contain the controls for the credit card information, and so on.

The markup of my form example is divided into two parts using `fieldset` elements. The first `fieldset` element contains several basic label/control pairs. The second `fieldset` element contains more complex arrangements of controls: groups of checkboxes and radio button `input` elements, and a multiple-choice `select` element. The first child element of a `fieldset` must be the `legend` text element, which contains the `fieldset`'s title.

```
<fieldset>
  <legend>Mailing Address</legend>
  <!--- label/control pairs -->
</fieldset>
```

Learn how forms are processed at http://www.javascript-coder.com/html-form/html-form-tutorial-p1.phtml. There are additional form-related links at the bottom of this Web page.

Rather than assign control `name` attributes arbitrarily, you should determine these names in collaboration with your site's programmers and database manager as it makes good sense to use the given name for that data item everywhere it is referenced or stored.

As you can see, I style the `legend` elements of the two `fieldset`s into gray bars with their text reversed out of them, to separate the two sections of the form.

CONTROLS AND LABELS

A form contains one or more controls. As I mentioned, a control is the term for the form widget the user checks, selects from, or types into. Any control that can be typed into is colloquially known as a field. Each form control element, with the exception of the Submit button, has a required `label` text element that describes the data that the control represents. The following code and **Figure 6.14** illustrate this structure.

```
<label for="user_name">User Name</label>
```
creates a text field ──────────┤ `<input type="text" id="user_name" name="user_name" />`

```
<p>Please select a user name</p>
```

FIGURE 6.14 A form control and its label. Here the control is a text field. Additionally, a user direction may, and usually should, be added.

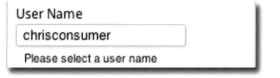

This attribute associa-tion also allows the user to select a radio button or check-box by clicking on its label.

The `label` element can wrap the control, or precede, or follow it. If the label is not wrapped around the control, as shown in the preceding code, then the label's `for` attribute *must* match the control's `id` attribute to associate them with one another. However, the relationship between them is implied, and the label's `for` attribute is not required, if the label is wrapped around the control, like this

```
<label>User Name<input type="text" name="user_name" />
</label>
```

Associating the label and the control in one of these ways is important if your page is to be successfully interpreted by assistive technology such as screen readers. I personally prefer to put the label before the control (although I put it after in the case of radio buttons and checkboxes), as this gives me more styling options.

Although I don't show this, you can add a sec-ond paragraph element with its `.error` *class if you want an error message that is different from the direction.*

In addition to the label and the control, you often want to add a user direction, especially if the supplied data must be in a specific format such as a date. There is no defined HTML element for form directions, so I use a `p` paragraph element. I also try to write directions in such a way that the text can be highlighted, usually in red, as an error message if the data entered is invalid, then I don't have to manage separate error text. I'll show how I add this highlight later in this example.

CONTROLS TYPES

You can see a full list of input attributes at https://developer.mozilla.org/en-US/docs/HTML/Element/Input.

The most common HTML form element is `input`. The `input` element is unusual in that it can display onscreen with a variety of different appearances and behaviors, from a text field to a checkbox, dependant on the `type` attribute of the `input` element. These `type` attributes include

- `text`—a basic text field
- `password`—text displays as bullets
- `checkbox`–multiple-choice button
- `radio`—exclusive choice button
- `submit`—button that submits the form
- `time`, `date`, `search`—HTML5 text field variations

Note the different `type` attribute assigned to each of these inputs in the preceding markup—this is what determines their appearance and behavior.

There is one text control that is not based on an `input` element, which is the multi-line `textarea`. Note that placeholder direction text, which displays in the field until the user types in it, is added with a `placeholder` attribute.

CHECKBOXES, RADIO BUTTONS, AND SELECTS

See a full list of HTML form elements at http://reference.sitepoint.com/html/elements-form.

These three form elements are more complex than a regular control/label combination.

- Checkboxes allow the user to make one or more choices from a number of options. Such a choice is said to be non-exclusive—making one choice from the group does not preclude making another.

- Radio buttons allow the user to make only one choice from a number of options. Such a choice is said to be exclusive—making one choice from the group deselects any previous choice that was made.

  Note that checkboxes and radio buttons are formed into a group by giving them the same `name` attribute; for the radio buttons in this example, that name is `radioset`. Each button in that set is uniquely identified by its `value` attribute; in this case, `Choice_1`, `Choice_2`, and so on. Therefore, if the user selects the first radio button, then the name=value pair passed to the server would be `radioset=Choice_1`.

- The `select` control creates a drop-down menu that appears when the user clicks on it. Within the `select` element, each menu choice is marked up with an `option` text element.

Form Markup Strategies

Because there is no defined HTML element to wrap a control and its associated label, I use a block-level `section` element for this purpose, which allows me to better organize and style the inline form controls and their `label` elements.

MARKING UP BASIC LABEL/CONTROL PAIRS

As you can also see in the preceding markup, I wrap each label/control pair in a `section` element, with the label preceding the control, like this

```
<section>

  <label>…</label>

  <input />

  <p>…</p> <!-- user direction -->

</section>
```

By wrapping each pair in the block-level section, they stack nicely down the page, and I have an enclosing parent element within which to position them.

MARKING UP CHECKBOXES AND RADIO BUTTONS

Because radio button and checkbox groups are made up of a number of label/control pairs, I mark them up with a `section` around the whole group (that gets the same CSS styles of the basic label/control pairs), and within it, a section around each checkbox or radio button label/control pair, like this

```
<section>

  <h4>Set Heading</h4>

  <section>

    <input />

    <label>…</label>

  </section>

  <section>

    <input />

    <label>…</label>

  </section>

  <p>…</p>

</section>
```

first radio/checkbox in set ⟶ `<section>`

second radio/checkbox, and so on ⟶ `<section>`

user direction ⟶ `<p>…</p>`

This time I put the label *after* the input, as this sets me up to position the label to the right of the control. While each individual control (checkbox or radio button) in the set has a `label`, I can't use a `label` element as a heading for the group, because a `label` element can only be used to label a control. I therefore use an h4 for this purpose. As mentioned earlier, I also use a paragraph tag for the user direction. Maybe a future version of HTML will provide specific elements for these purposes, but until then you will see authors make different choices for these additional elements that are needed to style forms. Now let's look at the CSS to style the preceding form markup.

Styling the Form

I'll first organize the overall layout of the form by styling the `form` element and the two `fieldset` elements.

```
                                    form.stylin_form1 {
overall width of the form ———————|    width:14em;

centers form in container ———————|    margin:20px auto;

                                      border:1px solid #bbb7ae;

                                      padding:.5em .5em .15em;

                                      }

form main heading ———————————|  .stylin_form1 h3 {

                                      margin:0;

                                      padding:0 0 .2em .2em;

                                      font-weight:600;

                                      color:#bbb7ae;

                                      }

encloses sets of controls/labels —|  .stylin_form1 fieldset {

                                      margin:0;

                                      padding:0 0 .2em 0;

                                      width:100%;

                                      border:0;

                                      }

legend has weird position ———————|  .stylin_form1 legend {
behavior, so I wrap the text in a
block-leveled span and style          width:100%;
that instead
                                      padding:.3em 0;

gray bar ————————————————————|    background:#bbb7ae;

                                      }

styles legend headings text ———————|  .stylin_form1 legend span {

                                      display:block;

                                      font-size:1em;

                                      line-height:1.1em;

                                      padding:0 0 0 .4em;
```

```
                        font-weight:700;
white text on gray bar ————|  color:#fff;

                        }
```

Now the layout looks like this

FIGURE 6.15 The `form` element and `fieldset` elements are styled.

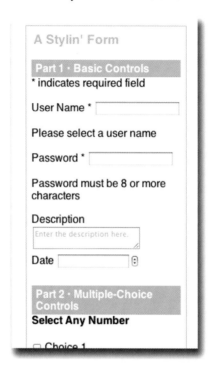

As **Figure 6.15** shows, the `form` element is now styled with padding all around it to move the content away from the sides. You can see that I have styled the `legend` element as a solid bar with its text reversed out of the bar. Because `legend`'s default position is determined by an undocumented mechanism within the browser, and not by the browser style sheet, it's impossible to control it accurately with CSS. The workaround, as I did here, is to wrap the `legend` element's text in a `span`, set the `span` to `display:block` and position that instead. Next, I'll style the controls and labels in the first `fieldset`.

```
.stylin_form1 section {
forces section to enclose the ————|  overflow:hidden;
form control and label
```

```
                                       padding:.2em 0 .4em 0;
```

visual separation between each ⊣ `border-bottom:8px solid #e7e5df;`
section

```
                                   }
```

no border on last section of ⟶⊣ `.stylin_form1 section:last-child {`
each group

```
                                       border-bottom:0px;
```

```
                                   }
```

form labels ⟶⊣ `.stylin_form1 section label,`

h4 is used to title groups of ⟶⊣ `.stylin_form1 section h4 {`
checkboxes and radio buttons

```
                                       display:block;
```

```
                                       clear:both;
```

right margin ensures label text ⟶⊣ `margin:.3em .3em 0 0;`
wraps before touching input

```
                                       padding-bottom:.1em;
```

```
                                       font-size:.8em;
```

```
                                       font-family:"Droid Sans";
```

```
                                       font-weight:400;
```

```
                                       line-height:1.1;
```

```
                                   }
```

asterisk indicating required fields ⊣ `.stylin_form1 section label span,`

```
                                   .stylin_form1 section h4 span {
```

```
                                       font-size:.75em;
```

```
                                       vertical-align:text-top;
```

```
                                       color:#f00;
```

```
                                   }
```

required fields text ⟶⊣ `.stylin_form1 section p.note {`

```
                                       font-size:.7em;
```

```
                                       color:#f00;
```

```
                                       margin:0;
```

```
                                       padding:0 0 .3em 0;
```

```
                                   }
                                   .stylin_form1 section input,
                                   .stylin_form1 section textarea,
                                   .stylin_form1 section select {
                                     margin:.2em .5em .2em 0;
creates space around the text in ⊣   padding:.2em .4em;
the input
                                     color:#000;
                                     box-shadow:1px 1px 3px #ccc;
                                     font-size:.8em;
for Firefox—uses Courier on    ⊣     font-family:inherit;
textarea without this
removes default blue focus    ⊣      outline:none;
outline                            }
style the text fields (text, pass- ⊣ .stylin_form1 section input,
word, date, textarea, etc.)
                                   .stylin_form1 section textarea {
sets the width of the fields ⊣       width:12em;
                                     border:1px solid #bbb7ae;
adds rounded corners     ⊣           border-radius:3px;
                                   }
                                   .stylin_form1 section textarea {
vertical height of textarea box ⊣    height:5em;
creates space below label    ⊣       margin-top:.3em;
                                     line-height:1.1;
                                   }
direction text              ⊣      .stylin_form1 section p {
                                     margin:.3em .75em 0;
                                     clear:both;
                                     font-size:.7em;
                                     line-height:1.1;
```

```
                    color:#000;

                    }

              .stylin_form1 section p.error {
```

colors direction text red when ———┤   `color:#f00;`
error class added

```
                    }
```

FIGURE 6.16 The controls in the
first `fieldset` are now fully styled.

As **Figure 6.16** shows, I set all the controls that are visual boxes
(inputs of the type `text`, `date`, `textarea`, and `select`) to be the same
width, styled the directions text, and added a thick bottom border
to visually separate each `section` element.

The small red asterisks at the end of some of the label elements'
text indicate the field is required; the user cannot leave it blank.
Asterisks (created by pressing Shift-8) are wrapped in `span` elements so that they can be positioned in relation to the text and
colored differently. Note also the `p.error` class for the direction
paragraphs. This class will be added onto the associated direc-

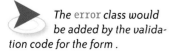

*The `error` class would
be added by the valida-
tion code for the form .*

tion paragraph if a control's data is invalid. The direction text then displays red, showing the user where a change to the data must be made before resubmitting the form.

I'll now go to work on the checkboxes, radio buttons, and the select, all of which are in the second fieldset. You can see in **Figure 6.16** that their labels are under the controls, and I want them to sit side by side. Before looking at this next piece of CSS, you may want to look at the earlier *Form Markup Strategies* section to refresh your memory on how the checkbox and radio button sections of the form are marked up.

```
.stylin_form1 section section {
    overflow:hidden;
    margin:.2em 0 .3em .4em;
    padding:0 0 .1em 0;
    border-bottom:none;
}
.stylin_form1 section section input {
    float:left;
    clear:both;
    width:auto;
    margin:.1em 0 0 .3em;
}
.stylin_form1 section section label {
    float:left;
    clear:none;
    width:15em;
    margin:.15em 0 0 .6em;
    font-size:.7em;
    font-weight:normal;
    line-height:1.2;
}
```

an inner wrapper for the label/control pairs

forces element to enclose the floated labels

radio button or checkbox

resets inherited width

top aligns with label, left stops container clipping the input

reset the inherited value

creates spacing between adjacent checkboxes, and between each checkbox and its label

reset the inherited value

```
.stylin_form1 section select {

    margin-left:.4em;

    font-size:.85em;

}
```

the submit button ⎯⎯⎯⎯⎯⎯⎯⎯⎯
```
.stylin_form1 section input[type="submit"] {
```

resets width setting from other ⎯⎯⎯
inputs
```
    width:auto;

    margin:.4em .3em 0 0;

    font-size:1em;

    font-weight:800;

    color:#fff;

    background-color:#bbb7ae;
```

changes to hand cursor when ⎯⎯⎯
over submit button
```
    cursor:pointer;

}
```

centers the submit button ⎯⎯⎯⎯⎯
```
.stylin_form1 > section:last-child {

    text-align:center;

}
```

Note that radio buttons or checkboxes behave as a group when given a common HTML name attribute. The value attribute name is passed as the value of the name=value pair.

The heading for each set of radio buttons and checkboxes looks like the labels in the first fieldset of the form, but is in fact an h4—I can only use a label element where there is an associated control, so I style the h4 by adding an h4 selector to the styling for the label elements in the first part of the form. Then I write a modified label style for the smaller labels that belong to each checkbox or radio button. I also add some styles for the select element to align it better, and make it slightly smaller by reducing its text size. The Submit button width setting no longer inherits the width of the earlier input rule, and is centered across the bottom of the form, clearly indicating it is the final step for the user (**Figure 6.17**).

FIGURE 6.17 The checkboxes and radio buttons are now styled in rows, and the submit button is styled.

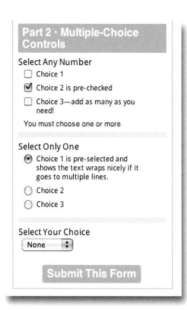

This "labels above" version of the form is now complete. I'll next show you some additional styles so that the `form` labels can appear to the left of the fields. To use this alternate style, just add the class `labels_left` to the `form` element.

```
form.stylin_form1.labels_left {
    width:22em;
    }
```
widen form to make space for left labels

```
form.stylin_form1.labels_left label,

form.stylin_form1.labels_left h4 {
    float:left;
    width:8em;
    }
```
float labels to sit left of controls

```
form.stylin_form1.labels_left p {
    margin:0 0 0 9.35em;
    padding:.3em 0 0 0;
    clear:both;
    }
```
indent directions so they sit under controls

ensures directions can't move next to floated labels/controls

space below required fields ——| `form.stylin_form1.labels_left p.note {`
message

    `margin:0 0 .2em 0;`

    `}`

wrapper for each radio button or —| `form.stylin_form1.labels_left section section {`
checkbox and its label

    `width:10em;`

    `margin-left:6.5em;`

    `padding-top:0;`

    `}`

    `form.stylin_form1.labels_left section section input {`

radio button or checkbox width —| `    width:1.25em;`

    `margin-left:0;`

    `}`

    `.stylin_form1.labels_left section input,`

    `.stylin_form1.labels_left section textarea,`

    `.stylin_form1.labels_left section select {`

creates right column of controls —| `    float:left;`

    `width:12em;`

    `}`

indents select ————————| `.stylin_form1.labels_left section select {`

    `margin-left:.2em;`

    `}`

prevents float being inherited ——| `.stylin_form1.labels_left > section input[type=submit] {`
from other inputs

    `float:none;`

    `}`

Figure 6.18a and **b** show both versions in their finished states. The "labels left" version has the `error` class applied to each of the "directions" elements.

FIGURE 6.18A AND B The labels-above and labels-left versions of the forms. The error messages are displayed in Figure 6.18b.

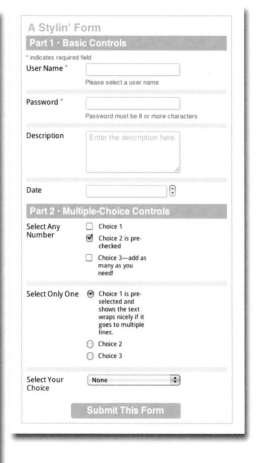

As you can tell from the large amount of HTML and CSS that was required for this example, styling a form is a complex and time-consuming job, so I have designed and commented the markup and style sheet for this prototypical form example so that it is easy for you to use this code as a basis for your own forms. Copy the HTML code blocks, or imitate their structure, to create each type of control that you need, and then link the form CSS to the page. Next, add the stylin_form1 class to the form element, and your form will be instantly styled into this layout, which you can then customize for your own needs. I do this myself, and it saves me hours every time. Now let's move on to designing a search field.

A Search Form

Almost every site offers a way to search, and you may not think of a search field as a form, but it is—a one-field form. Here is a simple search component that will sit nicely, say, in the right corner of the header bar, its typical home. The search field on Apple's site is a small, discreet component that expands when the user clicks into it, to give extra room for the search text. There isn't even a button to click—it's assumed that users know to click in, type, and press Return or Enter. The only markup needed for such a component is a `form` element containing a `label` and an `input` control. I'll wrap the form in a `header` tag for this example so that I have a `header` in which to put the search component.

```
<header>

  <form class="stylin_form_search1" action="#" method="post">

    <label for="search">search</label>

    <input type="search" id="search" name="search"
    placeholder="search" />

  </form>

</header>
```

This example also gives me the opportunity to introduce CSS3 transitions, which allow you to animate certain CSS properties—in this case, I will animate the width of the text field. Here's the CSS.

```
* {margin:0; padding:0;}

header {

    font-family:helvetica, arial, sans-serif;

    display:block;

    overflow:hidden;

    width:500px;

    margin:30px;

    border-radius:6px;

    background-color:#ddd;

    }
```

represents the page header in this example ————| `header {`

CSS3 Transitions

CSS3 transitions allow CSS properties to be animated. A change that normally happens abruptly when triggered, such as a link changing color when hovered, can occur gradually over a defined time period. A first CSS rule defines the initial state of the property and the transition. A second CSS rule defines the new state to which that property will change when the triggering event occurs.

For example, these two rules cause the border of a form input to change from black to green over 2 seconds when the user clicks in the field.

```
input {border-color:black; transition:border-color 2s;}
input:focus {border-color:green;}
```

Note that transitions require VSPs for all browsers.

Typically, transitions are triggered with a `:hover` pseudo-class rule when the user mouses over an object, or with a `:focus` pseudo-class rule when a form element receives focus. Additionally, transitions can be triggered by defining the new state in a rule with a class name selector, and then adding that class name to an element with JavaScript (or a JavaScript framework such as jQuery or MooTools) when a mouse click or other event occurs.

There are five transition properties:

`transition-property`—the name of the CSS property to be transitioned, e.g., color, width

`transition-duration`—the duration of the transition stated in seconds or milliseconds, e.g., 2s, 500ms

`transition-timing-function`—determines if the transition is smoother, or slower or faster at the beginning or end, e.g., ease-in, ease-out, ease-in-out, or linear (default)

`transition-delay`—delay before transition starts after triggering event in seconds or milliseconds, e.g., 1s, 200ms

`transition`—the shorthand version, e.g., `transition:color 2s ease-in 1ms;`

Many, but not all, CSS properties can be animated using the `transition` property. You can see a full list of these "animatables" at http://www.w3.org/TR/css3-transitions/#animatable-properties. This page gives a complete W3C-style description of the CSS3 Transitions Module. You can also find a good overview of CSS3 transitions at http://www.css3.info/preview/css3-transitions.

```
form.stylin_form_search1 {
```

a container for the label and ——| `float:right;`
input

```
    width:200px;

    margin:5px; padding:5px;

    }

form.stylin_form_search1 input {
```

```
float:right;

width:70px;

padding:2px 0 3px 5px;
```

removes default border highlight ⊢ `outline:none;`

add VSPs for other browsers ——⊣ `font-size:.8em; border-color:#eee #ccc #ccc #eee; border-radius:10px; -webkit-transition:2s width;`

```
}
```

```
form.stylin_form_search1 input:focus {width:200px;}
```

the label is required but is ——⊣ `form.stylin_form_search1 label {display:none;}`
hidden onscreen

FIGURE 6.19A AND B The small
search field slides wider when
the user clicks into it, and the
placeholder text is replaced with
the entered text.

The `form` element is "widthed" and floated right, and the `input` is floated right within it (**Figure 6.19a**). The `label` element is not displayed, although it must be present in the markup. The text within the field is created by the placeholder attribute text, which is automatically hidden as soon as the user starts typing (**Figure 6.19b**).

ADDING A CSS3 TRANSITION

In the preceding CSS, the `input` rule states that the field is 70 pixels wide, and the `input:focus` rule states that the field is 200 pixels wide. When the field receives `focus` (meaning keyboard focus; that is, the user has clicked in it, so that's where the typed characters are displayed), the field changes width. However, because of the `transition:2s width;` rule, instead of just snapping to the new size, the field smoothly expands to the new size over 2 seconds. Note that CSS3 transitions are placed on the rule with the initial state, not the final state. Transitions require VSPs—I just illustrate the webkit (Safari/Chrome) version in the CSS for this example. I'll show this component in the context of a fully-styled page in the next chapter. There is also a more advanced version of this example in the download files. For more information on using CSS3 transitions, see the sidebar, *CSS3 Transitions*.

A Popup Overlay

A popup overlay (aka a tooltip) is the name for a component that is displayed when an element is hovered. This is an effective way to provide extra information when space is limited, as users naturally move the cursor over onscreen elements that interest them. Creating a popup may sound like a simple exercise, but you will soon see why I saved it for the last example in this chapter, as I am going to use it to show you two very powerful and poorly-understood aspects of CSS: the z-index property and dynamically-generated HTML elements. I'll use three images, each with a text caption, for this exercise. Here's the HTML, which I'll mark up appropriately using the new HTML5 figure and figcaption elements.

```
<figure>

  <img src="images/pink_heels.jpg" alt="pink heels" />

  <figcaption>

    <h3>Pink Platforms</h3>

    <a href="#">More info</a>

  </figcaption>

</figure>

<figure>

  <img src="images/leopard_heels.jpg" alt="leopard heels" />

  <figcaption>

    <h3>Leopard Platforms</h3>

    <a href="#">More info</a>

  </figcaption>

</figure>

<figure>

  <img src="images/red_heels.jpg" alt="red heels" />

  <figcaption>

    <h3>Red Platforms</h3>
```

```
    <a href="#">More info</a>
  </figcaption>
</figure>
```

Note that figcaption, if used, must always be a single instance within figure, and must also be the first or last child. I first style and position the figure element into a box around the image.

```
figure {
```

sizing of image box ——————┤ `width:144px;`

sizing of image box ——————┤ `height:153px;`

space between boxes ——————┤ `margin:20px 20px;`

image border ——————————┤ `border:1px solid #666;`

positioning context for popups —┤ `position:relative;`

makes images sit side by side ——┤ `float:left;`

```
}
```

removes baseline spacing from —┤ `img {display:block;}`
under image

FIGURE 6.20 The images now have borders and are positioned side by side.

Pink Platforms
More info

Leopard Platforms
More info

Red Platforms
More info

As you can see in **Figure 6.20**, the figure elements' borders are sized to contain the images, and they are floated so they sit next to one another. The figcaption elements just display in their default position for now—the figcaption will become our popup in the next step. Note that I have set the image to display:block. I do this because images are by default inline, and are positioned to sit aligned with the baseline of text, not with the bottom of their container. This results in a small space under an image when it is placed inside a block-level element like this; changing the image to a block-level element fixes this problem. I have also relatively positioned the figure elements so that I can position the figcaption element with respect to it, which I will now do.

figcaption {

hides popups ———————┤   display:none;

relative to images ———————┤   position:absolute;

positions popup on right side ——┤   left:74%; top:14px;
of image

width of popup ———————┤   width:130px;

space around popup content ——┤   padding:10px;

    background:#f2eaea;

    border:3px solid red;

    border-radius:6px;

}

displays popup when image is ——┤ figure:hover figcaption {display:block;}
hovered

popup content ———————┤ figcaption h3 {

    font-size:14px;

    color:#666;

    margin-bottom:6px;

}

popup content ———————┤ figcaption a {

    display:block;

    text-decoration:none;

    font-size:12px;

    color:#000;

}

You can see in the CSS that I am using the same display property technique, to hide the popup caption and then show it on the rollover, that I used on the drop-down menus. In order to position the left edge of the popup inside the right edge of the figure box, I set its left property to 74%. You might expect me to use the right

FIGURE 6.21A, B, AND C The popup caption appears when I hover the related image. However, in 6.36 a and b the popups for the first and second images are under the image to their right.

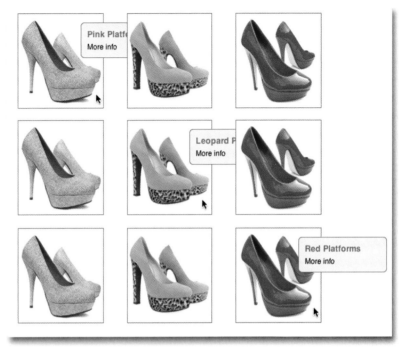

property, but that would set the relationship between the right edges of the image and the popup, not the left edges.

Stacking Context and z-index

You can see in **Figure 6.21a** and **b** that there is a problem with the first and second images' popups displaying behind the images to their right. This is caused by the figure elements' stacking order. When you put sibling elements in a container element, as here with the three figure elements inside the body element, they each create what is called a *stacking context* and their child elements stack on top of each of them. If you were to move the first and second figure elements so that they overlapped, you would see that the first figure element, *and all the child elements in its stacking context*, would appear under the second. The popup belongs to the first figures's stack, so it will by default appear behind everything in the second figure's stack.

There is a CSS property called z-index that controls the stacking order of elements, so that you can change the default stacking order. Elements with a higher z-index appear on top of elements with a lower z-index. z-index settings can range from 0 up to any number—negative values also work but are unreliable in some browsers. By default, all stacks have a z-index of auto, which is the same as 0.

However, z-index only works with elements that have a position value other than static; in other words, both elements must be set to absolute, relative, or fixed. In this situation, the popup is already absolutely positioned with respect to its relatively-positioned figure elements, so I just need to apply a z-index greater than 0 to the popup—I'll use 2.

puts the popup of the hovered image frontmost

⊣ figure:hover figcaption {display:block; z-index:2;}

FIGURE 6.22 With the z-index applied to the hovered figure element, its child popup displays over the other images.

What I have learned in situations like this is to apply the z-index on the hover state, rather than try to work out individual z-index settings for each of the elements so that overlaps can't occur. By using this "z-index on hover" technique, you can just lay out images and know that when a popup is triggered, it will become the frontmost element on the page (**Figure 6.22**).

Creating a CSS Triangle

Next, I want to more strongly link the popup to the image, and I will do this by positioning a small triangular arrowhead that points at the picture on the left edge of the popup. Here's how to make use of the angled edges of a box's border to create a triangle. I'll demo this technique using a div.

FIGURE 6.23 A triangle can be created using thick box borders.

Here's the code for the last step of **Figure 6.23**.

```
div {
  border:12px solid;
  border-color:transparent red transparent transparent;
  height:0px;
  width:0px;
}
```

As **Figure 6.23** illustrates, you can create a triangle entirely with CSS by creating a box with thick borders, and then setting its height and width to 0 and three of its borders to transparent. I'll now combine this technique with the ::before pseudo-element. Usually the ::before or ::after pseudo-element is used to add a small piece of content, such as text or an icon, but you can fully style the element box it creates just like any other element in your markup. Here, I will style the pseudo-element's box into the triangle, and position it on the popup's left edge.

red triangle box ─────────┤ `figcaption::after {`

some content required, here an ─┤ `content:"";`
empty text string

relative to popup ─────────┤ `position:absolute;`

`border:12px solid;`

`border-color:transparent red transparent transparent;`

positions triangle on box border ─┤ `right:100%; top:17px;`

collapses box to create triangle ─┤ `height:0px; width:0px;`

`}`

FIGURE 6.24 The triangle visually connects the popup to the related image.

Now the code-generated triangle is absolutely positioned relative to the popup (**Figure 6.24**), which is absolutely positioned relative to the image! With these 20 or so lines of CSS, you can display a limitless number of items with their popups. Who said programming isn't creative? Note that the `::before` pseudo-element requires some content for its `content` property or the generated element doesn't display. As I don't actually need any content, I simply use an empty text string that I create by opening and closing the quote marks. Enjoy this exercise? Way more interesting than forms, right?

Summary

This chapter has taught you how to style some of the most popular Web interface components, such as menus, forms, and popups. All the examples from this chapter are available in the download files, written in a way that makes them adaptable for your own projects. That said, there is no better way to practice your CSS skills than to build these components from scratch, as they will reinforce essential concepts and techniques relating to display, positioning, backgrounds, and other widely-used aspects of CSS. Now, let's combine the layout techniques of the previous chapter and the interface components from this chapter as I next show you how to create a complete Web page.

CHAPTER 7

A CSS3-Enhanced Web Page

IN THIS CHAPTER, I'LL COMBINE the page layout techniques from Chapter 5 and the component styling techniques from Chapter 6 to create a complete Web page. You will see many CSS3 stylings, including radiused corners, text shadows, box shadows, transitions, and transforms, that add a modern and professional look to the overall design.

The page I will create in this chapter is one that I am working on as I write this book, which is the book's new Web site. As always, I'll use this example to show new techniques that will help you on your own projects, and point out pitfalls that you might encounter.

I'll first show you how to plan your page framework, and then take you step-by-step through the process of adding the CSS for each area of the page. By the time you complete this chapter, you will understand what it takes to put together a complete Web page, and be ready to start creating pages of your own.

Structuring the Page

When you create a page of any complexity, you will write and edit hundreds of lines of HTML and CSS, so it pays to be organized. It is important to structure your code logically, and think hierarchically, so that your CSS follows the order of the HTML markup. The code for the following example is organized like this, and I highly recommend this approach. It requires a certain level of discipline, but pays off massively, as it's then easy to locate the CSS that relates to any part of the markup, and you avoid the confusing and time-wasting situation where several rules scattered through the markup apply styles to the same element. Most, of all, this approach allows my work to be easily understood and edited by me and others in the future.

Let's first look at the completed Web page as shown in **Figure 7.1**.

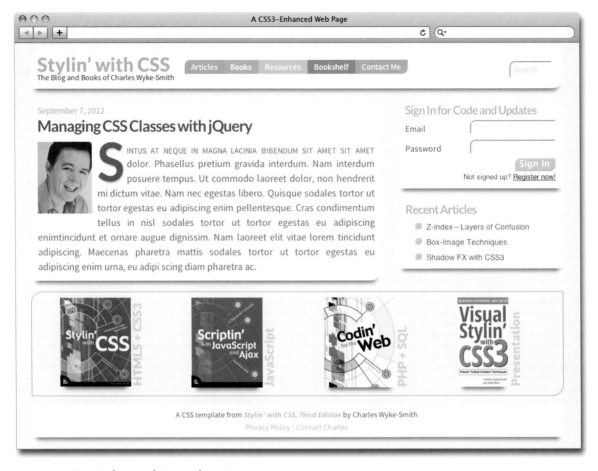

FIGURE 7.1 Here is the complete page layout.

Planning the HTML

When you first start writing HTML markup, it can be challenging to translate your visual design into the required HTML elements, so here is a good approach. Usually, you will have worked through the design issues by creating a Photoshop or Fireworks layout, or at least a pencil sketch, before starting to code the page. This is the point at which you can discuss the design with your client and then fine-tune, to ensure that the look-and-feel of the design, and the organization of the content, meets the project's needs. Then it's time to start coding the pages. The first step is to draw overlays on your layout that represent the main structural HTML.

Because HTML creates rectangular elements, you should start by looking for ways to divide your layout first into its largest possible areas to determine the top levels of your markup, and then break it down into smaller sections for the child structural elements, using rectangular boxes. Here's how that works with my page design.

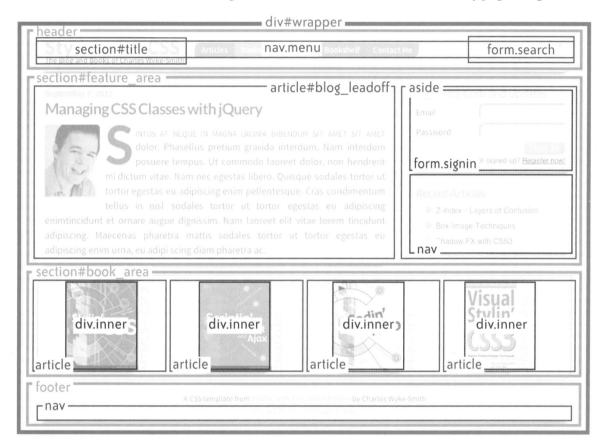

FIGURE 7.2 By looking at the box structure of the page, I can determine three structural levels.

As you can see from **Figure 7.2**, the page divides nicely into four full-width rectangles (colored orange), which will be my top-level HTML elements. Notice that I also plan to enclose the entire layout in a wrapper (colored green), so that I can easily set the overall width of the layout and center it in the browser window. This is also a good time to choose class and ID names for the main elements I will use in the markup. The header and footer HTML elements don't need a class or ID, as there will only be one of each of them,

In case you are wondering how the navigation can overlap the title and search areas, it's because I have already decided that the title and search areas will be absolutely positioned. This will cause the nav element to ignore them and it will fill the header. I will then be able to center the menu within it on the page, as you will see later in the chapter.

but the two center rectangles, both of which will be `section` elements, will each need an ID to differentiate them: `feature_area` and `book_area`.

Next, I plan the second-level structure, which I indicate with blue rectangles. I look inside each top-level element to determine the largest elements into which its content can be organized.

In the `header`, there are three groups of content: the title area to the left, the navigation menu in the middle, and the search form on the right. In the `feature_area`, I have a blog article to the left, and an `aside` area with a sign-up form and blog links list to the right. Note that I simply put an element around *both* of these components; I further sub-divide this area in the next step.

The `book_area` needs four containers for the four books. The `footer` contains text and a structural `nav` element.

Next, I need to further divide the `feature_area aside` so that I can style it into two distinct components: the form and the links. In the `book_area article`, I also wrap an element around each book image to use as a positioning context for each book's popup. These additional elements form the third level of the structural hierarchy and are indicated by purple rectangles.

That's enough planning to get started, although I may need an extra element here and there as I develop the page. I now create some initial markup to reflect this structural framework.

```
<div id="wrapper">
```

level 1 ——————————
```
  <header>
```

level 2 ——————————
```
    <section id="title">

      <!-- h1 and h2 here -->

    </section>
```

level 2 ——————————
```
    <nav class="menu">

      <!-- menu here -->

    </nav>
```

level 2 ——————————
```
    <form class="search">

      <!-- search field here -->
```

```
                                          </form>

                                        </header>

level 1 ─────────────────┤  <section id="feature_area">

level 2 ─────────────────┤    <article id="blog_leadoff">

                                            <!-- blog content here -->

                                          </article>

level 2 ─────────────────┤    <aside>

level 3 ─────────────────┤      <form class="signin">

                                              <!-- signup form here -->

                                            </form>

level 3 ─────────────────┤      <nav>

                                              <!-- blog links here -->

                                            </nav>

                                          </aside>

                                        </section>

level 1 ─────────────────┤  <section id="book_area">

level 2 ─────────────────┤    <article>

level 3 ─────────────────┤      <div class="inner">

                                              <!-- book images and rotated text here -->

                                            </div>

                                          </article>

                                          <!-- article repeats 4 times -->

                                        </section>

level 1 ─────────────────┤  <footer>

                                            <!-- footer text and nav here -->

                                          </footer>

end wrapper ─────────────┤ </div>
```

As you can see, each level of the nested boxes in the layout are represented by nested elements in the markup. Pick the most appropriate HTML element as you go; for example, the list for the menu should definitely be in a nav element.

With the structural markup complete, I'll just set the overall font and the color for the page background on the body element, and style the wrapper to provide the overall width for the layout and center it in the page.

```
body {
  font-family:helvetica, arial, sans-serif;
  background:#efefef;
  margin:0;
  }
wrapper {width:980px; margin:0 auto 20px;}
```

Now I can work my way down the page, adding content to the structural elements, and applying CSS styles.

Styling the Header

Let's start with the content markup for the header.

```
<header>
  <section id="title">
    <h1>Stylin&rsquo; with CSS</h1>
    <h2>The Blog and Books of Charles Wyke-Smith</h2>
  </section>
  <nav class="menu">
    <ul>
      <li class="choice1"><a href="#">Articles</a></li>
      <li class="choice2"><a href="#">Books</a></li>
      <li class="choice3"><a href="#">Resources</a></li>
      <li class="choice4"><a href="#">Bookshelf</a></li>
```

```
            <li class="choice5"><a href="#">Contact Me</a></li>

          </ul>

        </nav>

        <form class="search" action="#" method="post">
```

the for attribute ties the label to ⊣
its control–same as control's ID

```
          <label for="search">search</label>

          <input type="text" id="search" name="search"
          placeholder="search" />

        </form>

      </header>
```

The header markup divides into three parts: the title, the search area, and the centered menu. I'll start with title.

The Title

I absolutely position the h1 and h2 elements in the top left of the header. Here is the CSS.

```
header {
```

positioning context for title and ⊣
search areas

```
  position:relative;
```

fixed height to enclose ─────────┤
absolutely-positioned elements

```
  height:70px;

  margin:10px 0;

  background:#fff;
```

order: tl, tr, br, bl ──────────────┤

```
  border-radius:20px 0px 20px 0px;
```

negative spread brings shadow ⊣
inside box width

```
  box-shadow:0 12px 8px -9px #555;
```

prevents margin collapse on ───────┤
children

```
  padding:1px;

  }

header section#title {

  position:absolute;
```

wide enough to not force ──────────┤
text wrap

```
  width:300px;
```

tall enough for both lines of text ⊣

```
  height:65px;
```

top-left corner positioning ─────────┤

```
  left:0px;
```

```
    top:0;

  }

header h1 {

  padding:9px 12px 0;

  font-family:'Lato', helvetica, sans-serif;

  font-weight:900;

  font-size:2.2em;

  line-height:1;

  letter-spacing:-.025em;

  color:#4eb8ea;

  }

header h2 {

  padding:0px 12px;

  font-family:"Source Sans Pro", helvetica, sans-serif;

  font-weight:400;

  font-size:.9em; line-height:1;

  letter-spacing:-.025em;

  color:#333;

  }
```

font weight needed for down- ⟶ (at the `font-weight:400;` line)
loaded fonts

FIGURE 7.3 h1 and h2 are now styled. Temporary borders show the position of the elements.

The first thing to note about this markup is that I have fixed the height of the header element. As I have shown in many preceding examples, it's usually good practice to let the content set the height of structural elements so the page can expand vertically as content is added. Here, because the header contains absolutely-positioned elements that won't push against their parent containers, I have to fix the height. The content of header will rarely if ever change, so it's unlikely that content will overflow header's fixed height in the future.

Note the interesting "two-corners-rounded, two-corners-square" styling that is applied to the header element and to many other elements of the page. This unobtrusive but distinctive effect gives the layout a unique look. See the *Radiused Corners* sidebar for more details on rounding the corners of HTML element boxes.

I absolutely positioned the title (in red in **Figure 7.3**), and after determining the size and padding on its text elements, fixed its height and width to comfortably enclose them.

Note that for these headings, I am using a Google Web Font called Lato. The weight of many Google Web Fonts is set using the font-weight property, unlike browser-installed fonts, where regular and bold are the only two weights that font-weight can produce. You can learn more about Google Web Fonts in Chapter 4.

The box shadows are another distinctive part in this design. They are styled to display only along the bottom edge of the box and to be less wide than the box itself. This gives a sense of the box floating off the page. See the highlighted code in the preceding example, and get more detail on box shadows in the *Box Shadows* sidebar.

With the title in place, let's next position the search field on the right side of the header in a similar way.

The Search Form

Let's start with the markup:

```
<form class="search" action="#" method="post">

  <label for="search">search</label>

  <input type="text" id="search" name="search"
  placeholder="search" />

</form>
```

And here is the search form CSS from the example in the previous chapter. The only significant difference is the way the form is positioned within the header.

Radiused Corners

Radiused corners, the calling card of the Web 2.0 design movement of a few years ago, used to require complex JavaScript or carefully positioned graphics and nested `div`s to produce. Now it takes just one line of CSS.

The most basic syntax is

```
border-radius:10px;
```

In this case, all four borders of a box are styled with ten-pixel radius corners.

The usual box shorthands apply, except that instead of `top`, `right`, `bottom`, `left` (the usual order of the box sides), the order is `top-left`, `top-right`, `bottom-right`, `bottom-left`, because it refers to corners, not sides.

Note that you can set both horizontal and vertical radii on a corner, like this

```
border-radius:10px / 20px;
```

FIGURE 7.4 This diagram illustrates the effect of the two preceding code examples.

Figure 7.4 also illustrates why they are called radiused corners; the specified size represents the radius of a circle or ellipse that would fit inside the corner.

If you want to set both horizontal and vertical radii differently on every corner, you can write

```
border-radius:10px 6px 4px 12px / 20px 12px 8px 24px;   /* four horizontal, four vertical */
```

Note that you don't need the border to be visible to use radiused corners—as the menus in this chapter's example illustrate, the element's background color will display the rounding without the border itself being displayed.

```
form.search {
    position:absolute; width:150px;      ← wide enough for field when expanded
    top:23px; right:20px;                ← relative to top-right of header
}
.search input {
    float:right; width:70px;             ← leaves space for field to expand to left
    padding:2px 0 3px 5px;
    border-radius:10px 0px 10px 0px;
    font-family:"Source Sans Pro", helvetica, sans-serif;
```

Box Shadows

Shadows on HTML element boxes are another example of an effect that, in the days before CSS3, used to take all kinds of graphics, `div` elements, and patience to produce, but now can be created with a single line of CSS.

The basic syntax is

```
box-shadow:4px 4px 5px 8px #aaa inset;
```

The order of the styles is: horizontal offset, vertical offset, blur, spread, color, shadow inside border (the default is outside).

Minimally, you must provide horizontal offset, vertical offset, and color, which produces a hard-edged shadow of the specified width and color. If you use negative values for right and bottom, then the shadow appears at the left and top, respectively. The `inset` keyword places the shadow inside the box on the opposite side. Multiple shadow declarations can be applied, separated by commas. **Figure 7.5** shows some variations to illustrate what can be done.

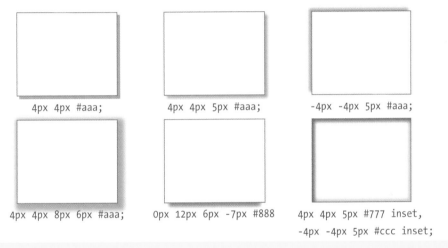

FIGURE 7.5 These six box shadows use positive and negative values to create a variety of effects.

```
                              font-weight:400;

                              font-size:1em;

                              color:#888;

removes default border highlight ⊣    outline:none;

animates field (other VSPs ─────┤    -webkit-transition:2s width;
needed
                              }

expands to this width on focus ─┤    .search input:focus {width:140px;}
```

```
.search label {display:none;}

form.search input {background-color:#fff;}

form.search input::-webkit-input-placeholder {color:#ccc;}
```

Stylin' with CSS
The Blog and Books of Charles Wyke-Smith

absolute position

FIGURE 7.6 The transition has expanded the field's width. The form's border is temporarily displayed.

Here, as the highlighted code indicates, I fix the width of the form element and then position its right edge relative to the right edge of the header element. As the temporary border in **Figure 7.6** illustrates, I make the form container large enough to contain the field at its expanded width. I won't say a lot about the search area itself, as I covered it in the last chapter, except to say that you can style the placeholder text differently from the text that the user types in the field—at least for Webkit browsers—as I show on the last line of the preceding code.

The Menu

In the interest of space, I have not shown the nested levels of the list that creates the drop-downs. You can see how to do this in the Drop-Down Menus section of Chapter 6.

I now have elements absolutely positioned on each side of the header, which removes them from the document flow, and sets me up to center the menu between them. This menu uses the CSS from the previous menu in Chapter 6 with a few minor changes.

```
<nav class="menu">

  <ul>

    <li class="choice1"><a href="#">Articles</a></li>

    <li class="choice2"><a href="#">Books</a></li>

    <!-- more menu choices -->

  </ul>

</nav>
```

The markup is the usual list of links in a nav element, but the links now have different classes to allow me to color them differently.

Here's the CSS

```
nav.menu {
  margin:19px auto;
  padding:0;
  text-align:center;
  font-size:.8em;
}
nav.menu > ul {display:inline-block;}
nav.menu li {
  float:left;
  list-style-type:none;
  position:relative;
}
nav.menu li a {
nav.menu li a {
  display:block;
  padding:.25em .8em;
  font-family:"Source Sans Pro", helvetica, sans-serif;
  font-weight:600;
  font-size:1.2em;
  text-align:left;
  color:#fff;
  text-decoration:none;
  -webkit-font-smoothing:antialiased;
}
nav.menu li.choice1 a {background:#f58c21;}
nav.menu li.choice2 a {background:#4eb8ea;}
```

aligns menu in container ⎯⎯⎯⎯ `text-align:center;`

shrink-wraps list items ⎯⎯⎯⎯ `nav.menu > ul {display:inline-block;}`

makes menu horizontal ⎯⎯⎯⎯ `float:left;`

removes default bullets off lists ⎯ `list-style-type:none;`

position context for child list ⎯⎯ `position:relative;`

makes link fill li ⎯⎯⎯⎯⎯⎯ `display:block;`

removes link underlining ⎯⎯⎯ `text-decoration:none;`

prevents pop of anti-alias change ⎯ `-webkit-font-smoothing:antialiased;`
at end of opacity transition in
Webkit browsers

```
nav.menu li.choice3 a {background:#d6e636;}

nav.menu li.choice4 a {background:#ee4c98;}

nav.menu li.choice5 a {background:#f58c21;}

nav.menu li:hover > a {

  color:#555;

  border-color:#fff;

border:0;

  }

nav.menu li:last-child a {border-bottom-right-radius:10px;}

nav.menu li:first-child a {border-top-left-radius:10px;}
```

FIGURE 7.7 The menu is now centered on the page. The absolutely-positioned title and search elements are out of the document flow, so the nav element can be full width (as shown by its temporary border).

Because the title and search areas are absolutely positioned, they are out of the document flow. The block-level nav element therefore behaves as if they are not present, and expands horizontally to fill its parent, header (**Figure 7.7**). This allows me to center the menu on the page. Let's use this example to learn more about centering with CSS.

CENTERING UNWIDTHED ELEMENTS

Centering one element within another can be difficult. With regular, static positioned elements your positioning choices are to float an element left or right, or you can use text-align on the parent element to align the element to left, right, or center. You can also center an element using auto margins. The problem with these techniques is that they require the element you want to center to be of fixed width. If the HTML list for a menu like this is generated dynamically from database information, or even if its items will be edited manually in the future, it is impossible to predict and set the centered element's width. I frequently receive email asking how to center menus within a container, so here is how to center an element that does not have a fixed width.

`inline-block` is a weird hybrid `display` property value that, as its name suggests, combines both block and inline element behaviors. Its block behavior is that it can accept both margins and padding, and can readily and validly enclose other block-level elements, while its inline behavior is that it shrink-wraps its content instead of expanding to fill its parent. This means its width is always the width of its content. Another useful `inline-block` quality is that it wraps floated elements. The problem is that the only margin value it *won't* accept is `auto`, which is the simplest way to center an element inside a larger container.

The solution is to apply `text-align:center` to the element's parent, `nav`, and then set the element you want to center to `display:inline-block`—here, the `ul` element that contains the list items for the menu. This combination produces the desired result; an element whose width is not fixed that is centered inside its parent. As the first two highlighted lines of code in the preceding example show, this is what I have done here. The menu is now perfectly centered, as its parent `nav` element ignores the absolutely-positioned elements on each side of it, and expands to fill the width of the `header`.

Just to show how nicely this works, I'll remove one of the menu's list items.

FIGURE 7.8 The menu remains centered even if the number of menu items changes.

In **Figure 7.8**, I removed the last menu item and the menu still centers perfectly on the page—ideal for a site with dynamic content where not every visitor (members and non-members, perhaps) will get the same menu choices. Note also that I do not simply style item 1 and item 5 of the menu with the rounded corner effect; this does not allow for future changes to the number of items in the menu. To make my CSS more robust, as highlighted in the preceding code, I instead style the radiused corners on the :first- and :last-child elements. Now, when the fifth menu choice is removed, the fourth choice moves into last position and correctly gets the :last-child radiused corner.

ADDING THE DROP-DOWN TO THE MENU

I'm going to use the step of adding the drop-down menu to show another example of CSS transitions.

```
nav.menu li ul {
    opacity:0; visibility:hidden;        ⟵ hides menus
    position:absolute;                   ⟵ position relative to parent menu
    width:12em;                          ⟵ width of drop-down
    left:0;                              ⟵ aligns left of sub-menu to parent
    top:100%;                            ⟵ aligns to bottom of parent
    -webkit-transition:1s all;           ⟵ sets up transition
    -moz-transition:1s all;
    transition:1s all;
}
nav.menu li:hover > ul {
    opacity:1; visibility:visible;       ⟵ both properties are transitioned
}
nav.menu li li {
    float:none;                          ⟵ kills inherited float–makes links stack
}
nav.menu li li:first-child a {border-radius:0;}
nav.menu li li:last-child a {border-bottom-left-radius:10px;}
/* for non-css-transitions browsers */
```

```
                          .no-csstransitions nav.menu li ul {
```
overrides transitions version ———| `visibility:visible;`

overrides transitions version ———| `opacity:1;`

hides menu if no css transition ———| `display:none;`
capability
```
                                        }
```
displays menu when parent ———| `.no-csstransitions nav.menu li:hover > ul {display:block;}`
hovered

Stylin' with CSS
The Blog and Books of Charles Wyke-Smith

Articles   Books   Resources   Bookshelf   Contact Me   search

Stylin' with CSS

Scriptin' with Ajax

Codin' for the Web

Visual Stylin' with CSS3

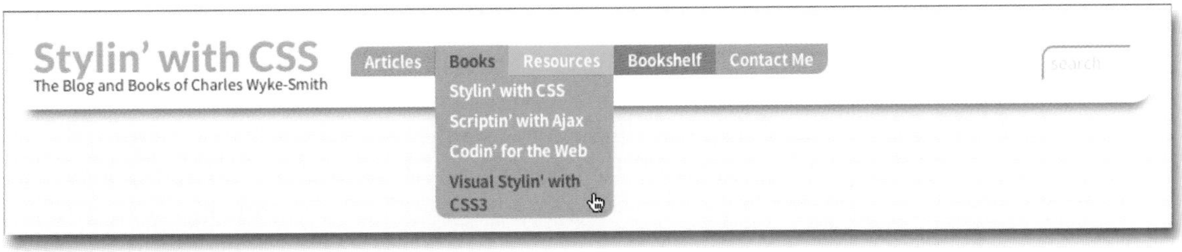

FIGURE 7.9 The drop-downs are now added to the menu.

I am using the same code for the drop-downs as the example in Chapter 6, so rather than explain it all again, I refer you back to Chapter 6 and also to the code callouts on the preceding CSS. However, there are three aspects of this version I will mention.

First, the rounded corners treatment is inherited by the drop-downs from the menu. Instead of radiused opposite corners like the menu, I want just the bottom corners rounded on the drop-down. So I remove the top-left, inherited, radiused border, and add a radiused bottom-left border—the radiused bottom-right corner is inherited (**Figure 7.9**).

Second, as the callouts indicate, I am transitioning the opacity of the menu to make it fade in. When I first tried to do this, I used only the `opacity` property. I started with the opacity at 0 (transparent), and then set it to transition to 1 (opaque/fully visible) on the hover. This did indeed fade the drop-downs in and out, but they were always there, if invisible; if I moved the cursor into the area below the menu, the drop-downs faded in, even though I had not moused over the menu itself. Next I tried adding `display:none`/`display:block`, to entirely remove the drop-downs when not hovered, which solved that problem, but then the drop-downs just turned on and off without the transition. I decided to remove display, and instead switch off the visibility property on the hover, while transitioning the opacity. The result was that the drop-down faded in but snapped off. Finally, by transitioning both the opacity and the visibility, the menu was entirely removed when transparent, and faded in and out correctly. I guess my point is that sometimes it takes a little experimentation to get the result you want. Hopefully, I've saved you a couple of hours one day. You're welcome.

Third, I have also taken the chance to show Modernizr in action here, and provide a CSS fallback for the menu functionality if the user's browser does not support CSS3 transitions. In such a case, Modernizr will write the class no-csstransitions onto the top-level HTML tag as the page loads. I use this class name in selectors for rules that only a browser that does not understand CSS transitions will then use. In those rules, I kill the visibility/opacity settings that control the menu in browsers that do support transitions, and provide less-capable browsers with the basic display:none/display:block rules to show and hide the menu, as I did in the menu in Chapter 6.

The header is now complete. Let's move on to styling the feature area that contains the blog item, sign-in form, and blog links.

Vertical Centering

Vertical centering is difficult with CSS. If you are centering a single line of text within an element of fixed height, say 300 pixels, then set the line-height of the text equal to the height of the containing element, like this

```
text-align:center; /* horizontal centering */
```

```
line-height:300px; /* vertical centering = container height */
```

To vertically center other elements, such as images, set the container's display property to table-row and then set the vertical-align property, which only works on table cells, to middle.

```
display:table-cell; /* invokes table behavior */
```

```
vertical-align:middle; /* vertical centering */
```

```
text-align:center; /* horizontal centering */
```

Neither of these solutions are particularly elegant, but CSS does not have specific properties to vertically position elements..

The Feature Area

The feature area of the page will hold the leadoff text of the most recent blog article, and in a smaller area to the right will hold a sign-in form and a list of links to recent blog articles. Here's the HTML for the feature_area.

```
<section id="feature_area">

    <article id="blog_leadoff">

      <div class="inner">

          <h4>September 7, 2012</h4>

          <a href="#"><h3>Managing CSS Classes with jQuery
          </h3></a>

            <img src="images/charles_wyke-smith.jpg"
            alt="Charles Wyke-Smith photo" />

          <p class="css_cols3">Sintus at neque in magna…</p>

      </div>

    </article>

    <aside>

      <form autocomplete="off" class="signin"
      action="process_form.php" method="post">

        <fieldset>

          <legend><span>Sign In for Code and Updates</span>
          </legend>

          <section>

            <label for="email">Email</label>

            <input type="text" id="email" name="email" />

          </section>

        <section>

          <label for="password">Password</label>
```

the required form tag

the container for a group of controls

the text label for a fieldset

control, label, and direction wrapper for styling

the for attribute ties the label to its control—same as control's ID

the text attribute makes this input display as a text field

password input text displays as ⊣
bullets

```
          <input type="password" id="password" name="password"
          maxlength="20" />

        </section>
```

submit button ─────────────────┤

```
        <section>

          <input type="submit" value="Sign In" />

          <p class="signup">Not signed up? <a href="#">
          Register now!</a></p>

        </section>

      </fieldset>

    </form>

    <nav>

      <!-- blog links here -->

    </nav>

  </aside>

</section>
```

The section element will be a full-width container, and I will float
the article and aside elements next to each other, inside it.

```
section#feature_area {
```

encloses the floated child ─────┤
elements

```
  overflow:hidden;
```

space between header and ───────┤
feature area

```
  margin:16px 0 0;

  padding:0 0 10px;

  }
```

```
section#feature_area article {float:left; width:66%;}
```

```
section#feature_area aside {float:right; width:34%;}
```

This gives me the two columns inside the container. Note I have set
these in percentages, as I am setting up this page to be viewed on
different devices, such as tablets and smartphones, and I will show
this in the next chapter. These columns will simply be the stated
percentage width of the wrapper.

I realize at this point I need to add an inner div (highlighted in the preceding HTML) inside the article element so that I can style a border around the content. Let's look at the article area styling now.

container with radiused corners and shadow
```
section#feature_area article .inner {
    padding:12px;
    background:#fff;
    border-radius:20px 0;
    box-shadow:0 12px 8px -9px #555;
}
```

link around main headline
```
section#feature_area article a {text-decoration:none;}
```

photo
```
section#feature_area article img {
    float:left;
    padding:0 10px 10px 0;
}
```

date
```
section#feature_area article h4 {
    font-family:"Source Sans Pro", helvetica, sans-serif;
    font-weight:400;
    font-size:1em;
    color:#f58c21;
    letter-spacing:-.025em;
}
```

blog headline
```
section#feature_area article h3 {
    font-family:'Lato', helvetica, sans-serif;
    font-weight:700;
    font-size:1.75em;
    color:#555;
    margin:0 0 12px 0;
```

```
                                letter-spacing:-.05em;

                                }
body text ─────────────┤ section#feature_area article#blog_leadoff p {

                                font-family:"Source Sans Pro", helvetica, sans-serif;

                                font-weight:400;

                                font-size:1.1em;

                                line-height:1.5em;

                                color:#616161;

                                text-align:justify;

                                }
drop cap ─────────────┤ section#feature_area article#blog_leadoff p::first-letter {

                                font-family:'Lato', helvetica, sans-serif;

                                font-weight:700;

                                font-size:4.5em;

                                float:left;

                                margin:.05em .05em 0 0;

                                line-height:0.6;
displays on IE10 and up ───┤   text-shadow:1px 3px 3px #ccc;

                                }
small caps for first line ───┤ section#feature_area article#blog_leadoff p::first-line {

                                font-variant:small-caps;

                                font-size:1.2em;

                                }
the right column ─────────┤ section#feature_area aside {

                                width:34%;

                                float:right;

                                }
```

FIGURE 7.10 The styled article element of the feature_area.

September 7, 2012

Managing CSS Classes with jQuery

SINTUS AT NEQUE IN MAGNA LACINIA BIBENDUM SIT AMET SIT AMET dolor. Phasellus pretium gravida interdum. Nam interdum posuere tempus. Ut commodo laoreet dolor, non hendrerit mi dictum vitae. Nam nec egestas libero. Quisque sodales tortor ut tortor egestas eu adipiscing enim pellentesque. Cras condimentum tellus in nisl sodales tortor ut tortor egestas eu adipiscing enimtincidunt et ornare augue dignissim. Nam laoreet elit vitae lorem tincidunt adipiscing. Maecenas pharetra mattis sodales tortor ut tortor egestas eu adipiscing enim urna, eu adipi scing diam pharetra ac.

These stylings bring together several elements from earlier in the book. Of note is the a link around the h3. Putting an inline element around a block-level element used to be a big no-no, but with HTML5 it is now valid to wrap a link around any element, which of course makes it much easier to make things clickable.

As you can see in **Figure 7.10**, the photo is floated left so the text wraps around it, and then I use the drop-cap/small-caps combo that you saw in Chapter 4 to add some visual interest and provide a smooth lead-in to the text. I also added a text shadow to the drop-cap to lift it off the page. Next, I'll style the form.

Styling the Sign-In Form

I ask readers to sign up to download the code examples for the books, so that I can provide updates and keep in contact with them. On this home page, I provide a sign-in form, with a link to a sign-up form for first-time visitors. The home page form is marked up in the same way as the form in Chapter 6. Here's the HTML

```
<form autocomplete="off" class="signin" action="process_
form.php" method="post">
    <fieldset>
        <legend><span>Sign In for Code and Updates</span>
        </legend>
        <section>
            <label for="email">Email</label>
```

the text label for a fieldset ⟶

the email field ⟶

the for attribute ties the label to its control—same as control's ID ⟶

Text Shadows

Text shadows are very similar to the box shadows that you saw in the *Box Shadows* sidebar earlier in the chapter. Here is the syntax

```
text-shadow:4px 4px 5px #aaa;
```

These styles in order are: horizontal offset, vertical offset, blur, and color. Note that unlike box shadows, text shadows do not have a spread setting. Minimally, you must provide horizontal offset, vertical offset, and color, which produces a hard-edged shadow of the specified width and color. If you use negative values for right and bottom, then the shadow appears at the left and top, respectively. Multiple shadow declarations can be applied, separated by commas. **Figure 7.11** shows some variations to illustrate what can be done. For a more advanced use of text shadows, check out my eBook, *Visual Stylin' with CSS3*.

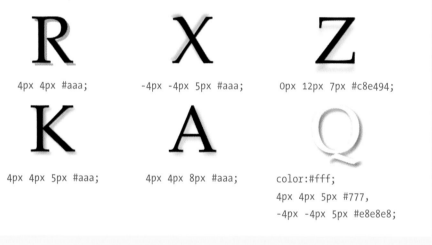

FIGURE 7.11 These six type shadows use positive and negative values to create a variety of effects.

the text attribute makes this input display as a text field
```
<input type="text" id="email" name="email" />
</section>
```

the password field
```
<section>
    <label for="password">Password</label>
    <input type="password" id="password" name="password" maxlength="20" />
```

hidden unless error class added
```
    <p class="direction">Wrong user name or password</p>
</section>
```

the submit button
```
<section>
```

```
        <input type="submit" value="Sign In" />

        <p class="signup">Not signed up? <a href="#">Register
now!</a></p>

      </section>

    </fieldset>

  </form>
```

Here I take only the CSS I need from the form example in Chapter 6 and modify it for this particular form.

```
form.signin {
```

overall width of form ————————┤   `width:19em;`

```
  float:right;

  background:#fff;

  border-radius:10px 0 10px 0;

  box-shadow:0 12px 8px -9px #555;

  }
```

removes default fieldset border ┤ `.signin fieldset {border:0; margin:10px 14px;}`

```
.signin legend span {

  font-family:'Lato', helvetica, sans-serif;

  font-weight:700;

  font-size:1.3em; line-height:1.1em;

  color:#4eb8ea;

  letter-spacing:-.05em;

  }

.signin section {
```

encloses the form control and ——┤ `overflow:hidden;`
label

spacing between form elements ┤ `padding:.25em 0;`

```
  }

.signin section label {

  font-family:"Source Sans Pro", helvetica, sans-serif;
```

```
                                    font-weight:400;

                                    float:left;
```
width of label column ——————⊣ `width:5em;`

right margin pads text from input ⊣ `margin:.5em .3em 0 0;`
```
                                    font-size:1em; line-height:1.1;

                                    color:#555;

                                    }

                                  .signin section input {

                                    float:right;
```
width of input column ——————⊣ `width:10.5em;`
```
                                    margin:.2em 0 0 .5em;
```
creates space around input text ⊣ `padding:3px 10px 2px;`
```
                                    color:#555;

                                    font-size:.8em;
```
removes default blue focus ————⊣ `outline:none;`
outline
```
                                    border-radius:10px 0 10px 0;

                                    }
```
removes yellow background in ⊣ `input:-webkit-autofill {color:#fff !important;}`
webkit
```
                                  .signin section input[type=submit] {
```
aligns button with right edge of
inputs   ⊣ `float:right;`

resets width setting from fields ⊣ `width:auto;`
```
                                    margin:0 2px 3px 0;

                                    padding:0px 8px 3px;

                                    font-size:1em;

                                    font-weight:800;

                                    color:#fff;

                                    border:none;

                                    background-color:#d6e636;
```

```
                          box-shadow:1px 1px 2px #888;

                          }
```

not signed up? text ─────────┤ `.signin section p {`

```
                          float:right;

                          clear:both;

                          margin:.2em 0 0;

                          text-align:right;

                          font-size:.8em;

                          line-height:1;

                          color:#555;

                          }
```

link in sign-up text ─────────┤ `.signin section p a {color:#333;}`

```
                          .signin section p a:hover {

                          color:#777;

                          text-decoration:none;

                          }
```

error message ─────────┤ `.signin section p.direction.error {`

```
                          display:block;
```

colors direction text red when ──┤ `color:#f00;`
error class added

```
                          }
```

hides error message ─────────┤ `.signin section p.direction {display:none;}`

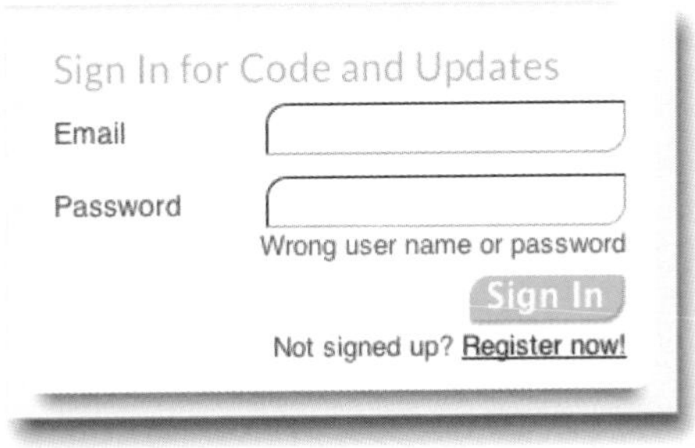

FIGURE 7.12 The styled sign-in
form displaying an error
message.

No matter how simple, a form always seems to require a lot of code! Most of this example's code is fairly straightforward though, and the callouts explain the key points. One thing I want to mention is the error message, which is hidden until it's needed (**Figure 7.12**): just add the `error` class onto the `p` element (which already has the `direction` class on it) to make it appear. However, the intention is for this class to be added programmatically if needed by the form's validation code. As the person responsible for coding the UI, it's your job to add this usually-hidden error message HTML element and the CSS to display it, and let the programming team work out how and when to add the class that invokes that CSS to make the error message appear.

The Blog Links

Below the form are the blog links. As usual, I have marked up the links as an unordered list.

```
<nav>

  <h3>Recent Articles</h3>

  <ul>

    <li><a href="#">Z-index&mdash;Layers of Confusion</a>
    </li>

    <li><a href="#">Box-Image Techniques</a></li>

    <li><a href="#">Shadow FX with CSS3</a></li>

  </ul>

</nav>
```

Here's the CSS!

```
section#feature_area nav {
```

overall container width ———┤ `  width:19em;`

aligns to right edge of section ——┤ `  float:right;`

space above and below ———┤ `  margin:15px 0 0;`

padding above and below content ——┤ `  padding:.6em 0em .75em;`

`  background:#fff;`

`  border-radius:10px 0 10px 0;`

```
                           box-shadow:0 12px 8px -9px #555;

                           }

                       #feature_area nav h3 {

horizontal space for title ─────┤   padding:0 14px;

                           font-family:'Lato', helvetica, sans-serif;

                           font-weight:700;

                           font-size:1.3em;

                           text-align:left;

                           color:#aaa;

                           letter-spacing:-.05em;

                           }

                       #feature_area nav ul {margin:0 0 0 20px;}

                       #feature_area nav li {

                           padding:.7em 0 0 2em;

positioning context for bullets ──┤   position:relative;

                           list-style-type:none;

                           }

custom list bullets ─────────┤ #feature_area nav li::before {

empty string for unneeded ────┤   content:"";
content

relative to list items ────────┤   position:absolute;

size bullet ──────────────┤   height:10px; width:10px;

position bullet ───────────┤   left:12px; top:12px;

the bullet shape ──────────┤   border-radius:5px 0 5px 0;

bullet color ─────────────┤   background-color:#d6e636;

                           box-shadow:1px 1px 2px #888;

                           }

                       #feature_area nav li a {

link becomes full width ───────┤   display:block;
```

remove default underline ——————|

```
text-decoration:none;

font-size:.9em;

color:#616161;

}
```

`#feature_area nav li a:hover {color:#000;}`

The styled links area sits directly under the form area. Both are within the aside element that is floated next to the article element (**Figure 7.13**).

FIGURE 7.13 The aside is now complete with the addition of the blog links.

By floating the nav element in the same way as the form element above, I am able to position it directly under the form. While the rest of this element is a standard list styling, the bullets are interesting, as I wanted them to reflect the "two-radiused, two-square corners" of the design. So, rather than create a graphic for the list marker, I used a ::before pseudo-element to create a 10 pixel-square element and round two of its corners. A tiny one-pixel shadow helps to pop it off the page.

The Book Area

The four book covers are presented in a row across the bottom portion of the page. With the popups and the rotated text, there are some interesting features to this part of the page. Here's the HTML.

```
<section id="book_area">

<!-- this section repeats four times -->

<article class="left">

  <div class="inner">
```
rotated type ─────────────
```
    <h3>HTML5 + CSS3</h3>

    <img src="images/stylin_cover.png" alt="Stylin' with CSS
    cover" />
```
popup ─────────────
```
    <aside>

      <ol>

        <li><a href="#">Download the Code</a></li>

        <li><a href="#">Table of Contents</a></li>

        <li><a href="#">Buy this Book</a></li>

      </ol>

    </aside>

  </div>

</article>

<!--- end of book code repeats -->

</section>
```

The HTML code is very simple, and as the callout indicates, it repeats four times, once for each book. Let's now look at the associated CSS. First, I show the layout of the books and the rotated text, and then the popups.

full-width element ─────────────
```
section#book_area {

  clear:both;

  border-radius:20px 0px 20px 0px;

  border:1px solid #f58c21;
```
space top and bottom ─────────────
```
  margin:8px 0 16px;

  overflow:hidden;

}
```

four columns for the books ────┤ `#book_area article {`

      `float:left;`

      `width:25%;`

      `padding:10px 0;`

      `background:none;`

      `}`

wrapper around books ────┤ `#book_area article .inner {`

positioning context for popups ─┤   `position:relative;`

wraps each book ────────┤   `width:140px;`

centers each book within its ───┤   `margin:0 auto;`
article element

      `}`

rotated text ─────────────┤ `#book_area .inner h3 {`

      `position:absolute;`

      `width:160px;`

positions text on right side of ──┤   `left:112%; bottom:5px;`
book

turns the text—needs VSPs ───┤   `transform:rotate(-90deg);`

sets rotation point at start of ──┤   `transform-origin:left bottom;`
text—needs VSPs

      `color:#ccc;`

      `font-family:'Lato', helvetica, sans-serif;`

      `font-weight:900;`

      `font-size:1.4em;`

      `text-align:left;`

      `}`

different offset for narrower ──┤ `#book_area article.right:last-child h3 {left:85%;}`
book cover

shadow under each book ────┤ `#book_area article img {box-shadow:0 12px 8px -9px #555;}`

Within the full-width section element (#book_area), I floated four article elements, each with 25% width. Within each of these I centered a widthed inner div that contains the book image. This gives me a nicely spaced row of book covers (**Figure 7.14**). The aside element that will be styled into the popup is currently hidden.

FIGURE 7.14 Each book in the book area has its descriptive title rotated and positioned along its right edge.

The rotated text is positioned using two functions (capabilities) of the CSS3 `transform` property. The first, `transform-origin`, sets the origin of the transition to the bottom-left corner of the `h3` element's box. The origin is the point about which the transformation occurs—as if I've stuck a pin through the element at that location. Then I rotate the `h3` element ninety degrees using the `transform` property's `rotate` function, and finally move it up 5 pixels to fine-tune the location. I provide a brief overview of the `transform` property in the *CSS3 Transforms* sidebar, and you can learn more about CSS3 transforms in my eBook, *Visual Stylin' with CSS*.

Now it's time to add the popups to each book. I'll take the popup from Chapter 6 to a slightly more advanced level in two ways. First, the popups on the right side of the page will now appear to the left of the book covers so that the popups aren't cut off by the browser window. Second, I style the arrow on the side of the popup to give the illusion that the box's border also runs around the arrow, and is part of the box. As is often the case with these seemingly small but significant design touches, there is quite a bit of code behind them.

If you look back to the preceding markup, you will see that I added left or right classes to each of the `article` elements that contain the books, so that I can apply specific CSS to left- or right-position the popups and their arrows. Heeere's the CSS!

shared styles for all popup boxes start here ┤ `#book_area article aside {`

hides popups ─────────┤ `    display:none;`

relative to inner div around images ──────┤ `    position:absolute;`

`    z-index:2;`

width of popup ───────────┤ `    width:200px;`

CSS3 Transforms

If you have worked in a graphics program like Adobe Illustrator or Adobe Fireworks, you will probably have rotated, scaled, or skewed text or other elements. Now you can create these same effects in the browser using CSS3 transforms (as shown in **Figure 7.15**).

There are two CSS3 transform properties, `transform` and `transform-origin`. Let's start with `transform`.

The `transform` property has functions, not simply values, associated with it. The functions allow you to specify both the type of the transform and the values that will be used in the transform calculation.

The format of a transform is `transform:functionName(numerical value or x,y)`

The transform functions are

- `scale`—make an element larger or smaller (values larger than 1 scale the element larger, values smaller than 1 scale the element smaller), for example `transform:scale(1.5)`

- `rotate`—rotates an element by a specified number of degrees (positive values rotate clockwise, negative values rotate counter-clockwise), for example `transform:rotate(-30deg)`

- `skew`—slants an object along its x or y axis (if only one value is stated, then y axis is not affected), for example `transform:skew(5deg, 50deg)`

- `translate`—moves an object by a specified distance along its x and y axis (this is similar to relative positioning as the initially occupied space remains), for example `transform:translate(-50px, 20px)`

The `transform-origin` property sets the point about which an element is transformed. By default, this point is at its vertical and horizontal center, so if you rotated an element, it would behave as if you had stuck a pin right in the middle of it, and would rotate about that point. You can set the `transform-origin` to a different point of the element with other position keywords (`top`, `right`, etc). You can also set the `transform-origin` point, even outside of the element's bounding box, with positive and negative numerical units.

no transform applied

`transform:skew(10deg);`

`transform:skew(-10deg,30deg);`

`transform:rotate(20deg);`

`transform:rotate(20deg);`
`transform-origin:bottom right;`

`transform:translate`
`(30px,-30px);`

FIGURE 7.15 Here are some examples of transforms.

```
                          background:#fff;
```
space around popup content ———┤
```
                          padding:10px 2px 5px;

                          border:2px solid #f58c21;

                          border-radius:10px 0px 10px 0px;

                          box-shadow:4px 4px 16px #555;

                          color:#555;

                          font-family:"Source Sans Pro", helvetica, sans-serif;

                          font-size:.8em;

                          line-height:1.5em;

                          }
```
shows popup when book is ———┤ `#book_area article:hover aside {display:block;}`
hovered
```
                          #book_area article aside li {
```
vertical spacing and left pad on ——┤
list items
```
                          padding:.25em 0 .75em 1em;
```
removes default bullets off list ———┤
items
```
                          list-style-type:none;

                          line-height:1.2em;

                          }
```
text links ——————————┤ `#book_area article aside li a {`
```
                          text-decoration:none;

                          font-size:1.2em;

                          color:#616161;

                          }
```
highlights links on rollover ———┤ `#book_area article aside li a:hover {`
```
                          color:#333;
```
end of shared popup styles ———┤   `}`

two left popups ——————————┤ `#book_area article.left aside {`

positions popup on right side of ——┤ `left:84%;`
left images
```
                          top:14px;

                          }
```

two right popups ————————| `#book_area article.right aside {`

positions popup on left side of ——| `right:84%;`
right images

   `top:14px;`

   `}`

orange triangle box ————————| `#book_area article aside::after {`

some content required—using ——| `content:"";`
empty text string

relative to popup ————————| `position:absolute;`

   `top:33px;`

   `border:12px solid;`

collapses box to create triangle ——| `height:0px; width:0px;`

   `}`

orange triangle position and ————| `#book_area article.left aside::after {`
color for left popups

   `right:100%;`

   `border-color:transparent #f58c21 transparent transparent;`

   `}`

orange triangle position and ————| `#book_area article.right aside::after {`
color for right popups

   `left:100%;`

   `border-color:transparent transparent transparent #f58c21;`

   `}`

white triangle box ————————| `#book_area article aside::before {`

some content required—using ——| `content:"";`
empty text string

relative to popup ————————| `position:absolute;`

   `top:37px;`

   `border:8px solid;`

collapses box to create triangle ——| `height:0px; width:0px;`

ensures white triangle is topmost ─| `z-index:100;`

   `}`

white triangle style, position, and ⊣
color for left popups

```
#book_area article.left aside::before {

    right:100%;

    border-color:transparent white transparent transparent;

}
```

white triangle style position, and ⊣
color for right popups

```
#book_area article.right aside::before {

    left:100%;

    border-color:transparent transparent transparent white;

}
```

The popup is an absolutely-positioned element, positioned relative to the inner div around each book. In the popup example in Chapter 6, I simply positioned a red pointer triangle on the side of the box (**Figure 6.24**). In this example, I have greatly improved this effect; the side of the popup appears to push out to form the pointer and the border runs around it (**Figure 7.16**). This effect is achieved by laying a second triangle that is slightly smaller and white—the same color as the background of the popup—over the orange underlying triangle, with their vertical edges aligned. Now the orange triangle creates the effect of the border.

I added the white triangle with the ::before pseudo-element and the orange with the ::after pseudo-element, and used absolute positioning and z-index to position them precisely one on top of the other on the edge of the box. The result is very pleasing and it's easy to believe that the popup and its pointer is a single element.

The confusing aspect of this code is keeping track of what is left and what is right. For example, the popups for the two books on the left are positioned to the right of those books, and their pointer triangles are on the left side of the popup. The opposite of this is true for the two books on the right.

Here's where you see the top-down approach I mentioned earlier. As the callouts in the preceding code explain, first comes the CSS

FIGURE 7.16 **A space-saving popup on each book provides links to additional information.**

that is common to all four popups—their size, padding, border colors, and content. Then comes the positioning code to place two of the popups to the right of the first and second books, and two of the popups to the left of the third and fourth books. This is followed by the pointer triangle styles common to the popups of all four books. Next comes the styles for the triangles for the popups of the two left books, and then the triangles for the popups of the two right books.

The coding maxim that this approach is based on is called DRY—don't repeat yourself—and the objective is that you end up with a "single and authoritative source" for any given piece of data.

While it's a lot to explain, this code is logically sequenced and avoids the kind of repetition where all the styles are restated in their entirety for each popup. It's worth spending a little time either studying or recreating this example so you can understand this organization for yourself, as it will help you break down the task of coding multiple elements with similar but not identical stylings and behaviors. Most of all, this approach results in code that you and others can easily understand and maintain.

Let's finish off this page by adding the footer.

The Footer

The footer of the page is a good place to put a statement about who has created the site and some links to business-related parts of the site such as disclaimers, terms of service, contact info, privacy policies, and copyright notices. Here's the HTML.

```
<footer>

  <p>A CSS template from <a href="http://www.stylinwithcss.
  com"><em>Stylin' with CSS, Third Edition</em></a> by
  Charles Wyke-Smith</p>
```

```
    <nav>
      <ul>
        <li><a href="#">Privacy Policy</a></li>
        <li><a href="#">Contact Charles</a></li>
      </ul>
    </nav>
  </footer>
```

This is the CSS.

```
footer {
  padding:.5em 0 .35em 0;
  text-align:center;
  border-radius:10px 0px 10px 0px;
  background:#fff;
  box-shadow:0 12px 8px -9px #555;
}
footer p {
  font-family:"Source Sans Pro", helvetica, sans-serif;
  font-weight:400;
  font-size:.85em;
  letter-spacing:-.05em;
  color:#555;
}
footer p a {
  font-family:"Source Sans Pro", helvetica, sans-serif;
  font-style:italic;
  font-weight:700;
  font-size:1em;
  color:#4eb8ea;
```

space above and below content ⊣ padding:.5em 0 .35em 0;

centers content ⊣ text-align:center;

text line styling ⊣ footer p {

link in text line ⊣ footer p a {

```
      text-decoration:none;

      }

    footer p a:hover {

      color:#777;

      }
```

list of links ——————————| `footer ul {`

shrink-wraps list ——————————| `  display:inline-block;`

```
      margin:4px 0 0;

      }

    footer li {
```

removes default bullets ——————| `    list-style-type:none;`

makes list horizontal ——————| `    float:left;`

```
      font-family:"Source Sans Pro", helvetica, sans-serif;

      font-weight:400;

      font-size:.85em;

      }

    footer li + li a {
```

dividers between links ——————| `    border-left:1px solid #ccc;`

```
      }

    footer li a {
```

removes default underlining off ——| `    text-decoration:none;`
links

```
      color:#aaa;
```

space between links ——————| `    padding:0 5px;`

```
      }

    footer a:hover {

      color:#777;

      }
```

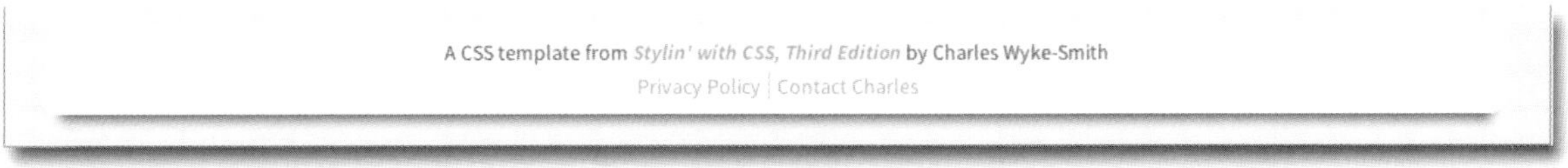

A CSS template from *Stylin' with CSS, Third Edition* by Charles Wyke-Smith
Privacy Policy | Contact Charles

FIGURE 7.17 The styled footer contains a text element and a list element.

There is nothing here that you haven't seen before. The content is centered using `text-align:center` (**Figure 7.17**). The paragraph inherits this setting and its text is then centered within it. Note that `text-align:center` would not normally center a list of links like this as it is made up of block-level elements that would normally be full width. However, because I applied `display:block-inline` to the `ul` it shrink-wraps the `li` elements. This effectively gives it width so it is then centered by the `text-align:center` setting. As you may remember from the menu styling, using this `display:block-inline` technique means the width is still fluid, so new elements can be added or removed and the list will still center. Note that applying `auto` margins instead of `text-align:center` would center the list equally well.

Summary

That completes this layout and this chapter. I hope you have seen how starting with the structural layout, using the techniques I showed in Chapter 5, and then adding in the components you learned to create in Chapter 6, allows you to rapidly develop complete pages.

I am going to continue working with this example in the next chapter, because today, Web sites are not just viewed in a wide layout for a large monitor like the one I created in this chapter. Your Web pages need to be responsive to the size of the device on which they find themselves. What you don't want to do is maintain several different sized layouts and try to deliver the right one to each size of device. Instead you want to be able to create pages that can sense their environment and load the appropriate CSS to style the markup to make the layout fit the device. I'll use the final chapter of this book to show how responsive sites are created.

CHAPTER 8

Responsive Design

TODAY'S WEB PAGE LAYOUTS NEED TO BE RESPONSIVE to the many different environments in which they are displayed. There is a big difference between good user experience on a large monitor and on a mobile phone. A multi-column layout may make sense for a large monitor, but on a phone each column is so narrow as to be unreadable; a single, "serialized" column layout becomes the only feasible solution. It is then very easy and natural for the viewer to scroll the screen with a swipe gesture as she reads.

Today, using a CSS feature called media queries, it is now easy to detect the screen dimensions of the user's device, and then provide alternative or additional CSS to deliver a more optimized experience for that screen. Creating sites that are device-aware in this way is known as responsive design.

In this chapter, I'll start with the page that I constructed in Chapter 7 that was designed to display on a desktop browser, and show you the steps to optimize it for display on progressively smaller devices.

> *Here I am modifying the browser version for smaller screens, but there's a lot to be said for designing for "mobile first." Check out Luke Wroblewski's article at http:// www.lukew.com/ff/entry.asp?933 and his book,* Mobile First, *published by A Book Apart.*

Large Layouts on Small Devices

I use the iPad and iPhone as the alternative devices in these examples, but the concepts I illustrate here apply equally to other tablet and smartphone devices. Let's start by looking at the Chapter 7 page (with its fixed 980-pixel wide layout) on smaller devices such as tablets and smart phones.

> *iPad and iPhone screen and interface component dimensions can be found at http://upstageapp.com/ resources.*

The iPad' screen is 1024 by 768 pixels, and because the layout of this page is set to 980 pixels, it scales to fit very nicely on the 1024-pixel wide iPad in its landscape (horizontal) orientation (**Figure 8.1**). When I turn the iPad to the portrait (vertical) orientation, the page layout does not fill the display.

FIGURE 8.1 The Chapter 7 Web page is very readable and fits well on an iPad in landscape orientation, but in portrait orientation the page is rather small and does not fit the vertical format.

Now let's look at the page on the iPhone, as shown in **Figure 8.2**.

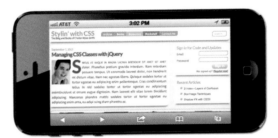

FIGURE 8.2 When displayed on the iPhone in landscape format, the page fits horizontally, but is nearly unreadable. When displayed vertically, the page is even smaller.

As you can see, both the iPad and the iPhone automatically size the page to fit, but the layout simply doesn't work on the small iPhone screen. In particular, the text is too small. The user would have to

The Elements of Responsive Design

There are three key aspects to responsive design

- **Media queries**—these are CSS constructs that allow CSS rules to be delivered to a browser based on specific browser charactistics, usually the screen or browser width.

- **Fluid layouts**—by setting the overall width of a page in relative units such as ems or percentages, the layout can scale to a device's screen size.

- **Flexible images**—by sizing images in relative units you can prevent them from being larger than their containing elements.

These concepts were first introduced by Ethan Marcotte in his seminal May 2010 article on A List Apart http://www.alistapart.com/articles/responsive-web-design.

use a stretch gesture to enlarge the page to make the text readable, and would then only be able to see a small area of the page at any given time. In portrait format, which is the most natural way to hold a smartphone, the page is smaller still.

The obvious conclusion here is that one size does not fit all, and what is needed is a way for the page to detect the size of the device on which it finds itself and modify its layout accordingly—in short, it needs to be responsive. Let's look at what it takes to achieve this outcome. The first step is to learn about media queries.

Media Queries

Android devices have a variety of screen sizes. This site lists media queries for targeting iOS, Android, and Windows-based devices http://pugetworks.com/blog/2011/04/css-media-queries-for-targeting-different-mobile-devices.

Media queries are CSS code containers, and the CSS within them is only applied if certain conditions are met, such as if the page is currently printing, or if it's displaying on a particular type or size of device. A media query can be in one of two formats, the `@media` rule and the `link` tag `media` attribute.

The @media Rule

The first format, the `@media` rule, allows a media query to be included within the CSS of a style sheet or within a `style` tag, like this:

```
@media print {

  nav {

    display:none;

  }

}
```

This rule states that if the page is being printed, then the element is not displayed.

Observe that in this example I am nesting the CSS rule inside the `@media` rule, which seems a little strange at first. However, while CSS rules can be added within media queries, the media queries themselves cannot be nested inside one another. Here's another hypothetical example (more relevant to the problem with the examples in **Figures 8.1** and **8.2**) that includes a maximum screen width.

only applied if the browser ——┤ window is no larger than 568px

```
@media screen and (max-width:568px) {

  .column {float:none; width:96%; margin:0 auto;}

}
```

In this example, if the page is displayed on a screen and that screen is no wider than 568 pixels, then the CSS unfloats elements with the class `column` to form a single vertical stack that is 96% of the width of the screen and centered within it.

Read an interesting article about making your graphics display at appropriate resolution on Apple Retina and other high-resolution screens at http://coding.smashingmagazine. com/2012/08/20/towards-retina-web.

An iPhone 4's screen is 320 by 480 pixels, but an iPhone 5 screen is 320 by 568 pixels (at least in terms of the browser and media queries, because pixel doubling is used—the physical pixels are double these amounts in both directions). By setting the `max-width` to the largest dimension of the larger iPhone 5 screens, I can ensure that the columns are unfloated and stack on all iPhones.

In short, this rule states that the device must identify itself as a screen (such as a browser or smartphone) with a maximum screen width of 568 pixels. This rule therefore would not be applied to an iPad, whose screen is 1024 by 768 pixels.

Now let's see the second way to format media queries as the `media` attribute of a `link` tag.

About Media Queries

MEDIA TYPES

The most commonly-used media types are:

- `all`—Suitable for all devices

- `handheld`—Intended for handheld devices (typically small screen, monochrome, limited bandwidth)

- `print`—Intended for paged material and screen in print preview mode

- `screen`—Intended primarily for color computer screens

- Other media types include `braille`, `embossed`, `projection`, `speech`, `tty`, and `tv`

Learn more about these media types at http://www.w3.org/TR/CSS2/media.html.

Note only one media type can be used by a browser window at any given time. Also, media types are supported all the way back to IE6, but media features are only supported by IE9 and above. Usually, this is not a problem, as you want to use media features to detect modern devices such as tablets and smartphones.

MEDIA FEATURES

These are descriptions of the device feature to be tested and many begin with min- or max-. The most commonly used are:

`min-device-width` and `max-device-width`—these relate to the size of the screen on the device.

`min-width` and `max-width`—these relate to the viewport width, i.e., the width of the browser window.

`orientation` (`portrait` or `landscape`)—allows different CSS to be applied if the device is positioned in an orientation where the height is greater than the width, or if the width is greater than the height, respectively.

If you want to use media queries to create a layout that reformats as the user sizes the browser window, use `min-width` and `max-width`. You can see a full list of media features at http://www.w3.org/TR/css3-mediaqueries/#media1.

You can use the logical operators `and`, `all`, and `not` to combine media types and media features.

The `only` keyword hides style sheets from older browsers that don't support media queries. Learn more about operators at https://developer.mozilla.org/en-US/docs/CSS/Media_queries#Operator_precedence.

A good primer on media queries can be found at http://www.javascriptkit.com/dhtmltutors/cssmediaqueries.shtml. You can make media queries work on IE8 and below with the Respond.js polyfill—see Polyfills in the Appendix..

The Link Tag Media Attribute

If you have a large number of CSS rules that you are applying with a media query, you may prefer to use the `media` attribute of the HTML `link` tag to conditionally load a separate style sheet. As you have seen, the `link` tag is used to link style sheets to your HTML pages, but by stating specific conditions in the `link`'s `media` attribute, the style sheet then only loads if those conditions are met. Here are the same examples I showed with the `@media` rule, but this time, in a linked `media` attribute.

```
<link type="text/css" media="print" href="css/print_styles.
css" />
```

```
<link type="text/css" media="screen and (max-width:568px)"
href="css/iphone_styles.css" />
```

Check out Andy Clarke's list of `@media` rules for targeting different devices at http://www.stuffandnonsense. co.uk/blog/about/hardboiled_ css3_media_queries.

The outcome is the same—the CSS rules are applied if the conditions in the `media` attribute are met. The second of these two examples would not load if the page was viewed on a large desktop monitor or iPad, but would be applied if the page was viewed on a smartphone. The most straightforward way to apply media queries is to have them take effect at various break points.

About Breakpoints

The term breakpoint refers to the screen width at which a media query takes effect and is written like this

```
@media screen and (max-width:640px) { /*css rules here*/ }
```

In this example, that breakpoint is set at a screen width of 640 pixels. If a device's screen width is equal to, or less than, the screen width defined at the breakpoint, it will have the related CSS applied to it.

You sometimes want to set breakpoints to match particular device screen widths, but I have found that what is most important is simply that the layout remains usable as it gets smaller. In other words, instead of thinking about matching breakpoints to device widths, simply start slowly sizing down the browser window, and choose breakpoints for new styles when the current layout no longer makes sense. Then you are not targeting a particular device, but simply providing alternative layouts at various ranges of screen widths that can work for any device that has a screen width within that range.

By reducing the browser window width, you can immediately get an idea of how the layout will appear on smaller devices, but obviously, you want to test on those smaller devices, too. Tablets are of similar dimensions to small monitors, so a media query with a breakpoint at 1000 pixels (i.e., that will deliver styles to screen widths of 1000 pixels or less) is going to format tablet-sized screens. Before I do this, let's see how to override the "scale-to-fit" behavior of the iPhone and iPad.

The Viewport Meta Tag

As you saw in **Figures 8.1** and **8.2**, the iPad and iPhone scale a monitor-size Web page down to fit on their smaller screens. It's a great party trick, but, especially on the iPhone, it almost always means that you then have to stretch the page larger and slide it around to actually read anything because the text size is so small. Because my layout will be designed to fit these smaller screens, I am going to override this auto-scaling feature. The way this is done is by adding an HTML `meta` tag into the head of the page.

```
<meta name="viewport" content="width=device-width; maximum-scale=1.0" />
```

This `meta` tag tells the browser to fit the content to the width of the screen and not to scale it. While this ensures that the layout fits as you designed it, it can introduce a known bug in iOS devices, i.e., iPad and iPhone. I discuss this bug and how to fix it later in the chapter.

> When I get to a layout width where I want to set a breakpoint, I use the dimensions display on the marquee on my screen capture software, Ambrosia Software's SnapzProX, to tell me the pixel width of the layout.

> There is a lot more to the meta viewport tag than I have room to discuss here. Learn more at http://developer.android.com/guide/webapps/targeting.html.

Optimizing the Layout for Tablets

The Chapter 7 Web page (aka the layout) currently has a fixed width of 980 pixels and centers within the browser window when the window is wider than the layout. When the browser window is narrower than this, as it is on a tablet or smartphone, the right side of the layout starts to be cut off by the browser window, so I will set my first breakpoint at just above this width, at 1000 pixels. If the browser becomes narrower than this breakpoint, I want the layout to become fluid, so that it scales to fit within the browser window. This is easily achieved, as all the structural elements are at `auto` or percentage widths, so simply by setting the fixed-width wrapper to a percentage width, the entire layout becomes fluid.

> The percentage width illustrates the second of the three aspects of responsive design—a fluid layout.

98% ensures small horizontal ——| `#wrapper {width:98%;}`
margins

However, once the layout becomes fluid, there are a number of issues to address.

FIGURE 8.3 On the 768-pixel wide screen of the iPad in portrait format, the elements run into one another.

Figure 8.3 shows that, as the layout width narrows—here at 768 pixels wide on the portrait-oriented iPad—the navigation menu soon overlaps the title to its left, and the form and links area below overlap the blog text. It's clear that the current menu positioning and the two-column layout below the header don't work at smaller screen widths.

So, I'll make some changes to the layout at this 1000-pixel break point. Let's first look at the CSS and then I will explain the changes I have made.

```
breakpoint 1000px ─────────┤ @media only screen and (max-width:1000px) {

                             body {

add right margin to prevent scroll ┤   margin:0 8px 20px;
bar clipping
                             }

layout becomes fluid ─────────┤ #wrapper {width:98%;}

                             header {
```

increases header height for ——————|
repositioned menu
prevents collapse of nav top ——————|
margin

```
    height:100px;

    padding:1px 0 0 0;

  }

header nav.menu {
```

moves menu down below title ——————|
and search

```
    margin-top:65px;

  }
```

no longer needed ——————————————|

```
section#feature_area {padding-bottom:0;}
```

makes blog leadoff full-width ——————|

```
section#feature_area article {
```

no longer needs to be floated——————|
full width
fills layout width ——————————————|

```
    float:none;

    width:auto;

  }
```

makes aside full-width ——————————|

```
section#feature_area aside {

    float:none;

    width:96%;

    width:auto;

  }

section#feature_area aside form {
```

moves form to left of aside ——————|

```
    float:left;
```

matches nav top margin ——————————|

```
    margin:15px 0 0 0;

  }

section#feature_area aside nav {
```

decreases width on blog link ——————|
area

```
    width:17em;

  }
```

end 1000px max-width media ——————| }
query

Figure 8.4 shows how this new layout improves the iPad display in portrait view. While the iPad's landscape orientation width is greater than the 1000-pixel breakpoint (and so is unaffected, as shown in **Figure 8.1**), the iPad portrait view's vertical format now displays more appropriately in the new, less-than-1000-pixel, fluid layout.

FIGURE 8.4 When the layout gets narrower than 1000 pixels, the CSS in the media query is applied. The menu moves down and the right column's elements reposition under the large left column.

As you can see in **Figure 8.4**, the new rules applied by the media query increase both the height of the header and the top margin of the menu. These changes move the menu into this newly created space at the bottom of the header and it now sits below `title` and `search`.

The `feature_area` also changes. The two child elements of `feature_area`, `article` containing the blog leadoff and `aside` containing the form and blog links, are unfloated and reset to their default `auto` widths. They then sit under one another, instead of side by side, and fill the width of the layout. Within `aside`, the `form` element is floated left, so `form` and `nav` now sit left and right, respectively, under the blog article (`nav` is already floated right). I also slightly reduced the width of the `nav` element on the right so that it doesn't hit the form on the right before the layout reaches my next desired breakpoint at 640 pixels—more on that in a moment.

I didn't need to do anything to `book_area` at this time; because I originally set the container for each book to 25% rather than a fixed width, the books and their associated type simply move closer together at the narrower width.

On the iPad, or in a non-mobile browser window whose width is reduced, this less-than-1000-pixel layout provides a much improved user experience. Now let's see what happens when the layout gets even smaller.

Optimizing the Layout for Smartphones

However, this improved state of affairs only lasts so long. Below about 640 pixels width (as we approach smartphone dimensions), the form and the link elements in the second row collide and the books below them start to overlap.

I'll now create a new breakpoint at this width.

```
@media only screen and (max-width:640px) {

  header {height:100px;}

  header nav.menu {width:94%;}              ← relatively more horizontal margin

  section#book_area article {                ← the blog post

    width:auto;

    float:none;

    margin:0; padding:0;                     ← now each book container is full width

  }

  section#feature_area aside form,

  section#feature_area aside nav {           ← the blog links

    margin:10px auto;                        ← adds top and bottom margins

    float:none;

  }

  section#book_area article .inner {         ← full-width pic wrapper

    width:98%;

    margin:0 0 0 5px;

  }
```

unrotate the rotated text ─────┤

```
#book_area .inner h3 {
    -webkit-transform:none;
    -moz-transform:none;
    -moz-transform-origin:none;
    transform:none;
    position:static;
}
```

makes the image size relative to ─┤
the device width

```
#book_area article img {width:40%;}
section#book_area {
    background:#fff;
    padding: 0 10px 10px;
    margin:0 0 10px;
}
```

display the popup content next ─┤
to the image

```
#book_area article aside {
    display:block;
    position:static;
    float:right;
    margin:0; padding:0 0 20px 0;
    font-size:.8em;
    border:none;
    width:55%;
    box-shadow:none;
}
```

hides the triangles on the ─────┤
popups

```
section#book_area article aside::before,
section#book_area article aside::after {
    display:none;
    }
}
```

FIGURE 8.5 The single column landscape-oriented layout displays nicely on the iPhone (and iPad).

FIGURE 8.6 In portrait orientation, the layout fits well but the header area elements are still too big.

This CSS applied by this 640-pixel breakpoint makes even-more significant changes than the 1000-pixel breakpoint. First, the containers for the form and blog links that were side-by-side are now unfloated and full width so these two elements now stack. Second, the book covers' containing elements, that were in a row next to each other, are now also stacked. It no longer makes sense to have the rotated text headings next to the book covers and, because these headings precede the books in the markup, as soon as I remove the text rotation and reset their position property to the default `static`, they obligingly position themselves above each book. The popups also no longer make sense, so I unhide and unstyle them and position their links next to each book. These changes create the single-column, serialized layout that works well on smartphones; now all the major elements of the page are full width and stack one under the other.

Note that I also set the image widths to 40% as shown in **Figures 8.5** and **8.6**, so that they can't be larger than the layout. The images I am using here are quite small, but if you have images that might be larger than the width of their container on a smaller device, then include this CSS in your style sheet

```
img {max-width:100%;}
```

and it will ensure they never become larger than their container, without affecting their capability to resize if smaller. This illustrates the third aspect of responsive design—flexible images.

Because all the stacked elements are set to a percentage of the browser window, the layout readily reformats when the device is rotated between landscape and portrait orientation.

Fine-Tuning for Portrait Format

There are two issues with the header in the iPhone portrait format that still need to be resolved, as illustrated in **Figure 8.6**. First, the menu wraps, and second, the search area overlaps the headings. Both these problems can be easily fixed, so let's add a media query that kicks in when the iPhone is in portrait format. I could use the `portrait` keyword in the media query, but I don't want this scaling to occur in portrait orientation on the larger-screen iPad. Instead, I'll use a `max-width` setting of 320 pixels, which is the width of the iPhone in portrait orientation.

portrait iPhone ─────────────┤

reduces height of header ──────┤

makes text smaller ───────────┤

makes text smaller ───────────┤

moves search up ──────────────┤

scales down and moves menu up ┤

increase link sizes to give ──────┤
better target

```
@media only screen and (max-width:320px) {

  header {height:80px;}

  header #title h1 {font-size:1.25em;}

  header #title h2 {font-size:.75em;}

  header .search {top:12px; right:4px;}

  header nav.menu {font-size:.55em; margin-top:50px;}

  nav.menu ul li a {

    padding:5px 4px;

    margin:0;

  }

}
```

FIGURE 8.7 The layout now fits nicely on the 320-pixel width of the iPhone.

This CSS, as displayed in **Figure 8.7**, reduces the size of the title headings, and moves the search up into the top-right corner. By setting a smaller relative font-size the menu gets smaller, as its size is entirely determined by the text size of the links and the padding around them. Because of the smaller text and menu elements, I can reclaim precious vertical height by slightly reducing the height of the header.

With the layout now formatted to provide optimal user experience on devices from wide-screen monitors, down to the narrow width of a smartphone in portrait orientation, it's time to take care of the small details that complete this responsive layout.

Finishing Touches

There are two issues that still need to be addressed. These relate to ensuring that the well-documented redraw and scaling bug of iOS (the Apple mobile operating system) is fixed, and that the drop-down menus also work on touch devices.

The Scaling Bug in Safari Mobile

Safari Mobile (the iPhone browser) has a bug that can cause scaling and redraw problems when the screen is rotated between portrait and landscape orientations (**Figure 8.8**).

FIGURE 8.8 When rotated from portrait to landscape orientation, a bug in Webkit can cause screen redraw problems.

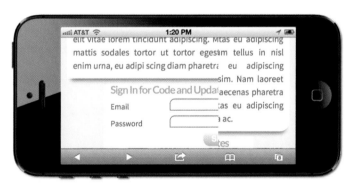

There is a JavaScript fix for this Webkit redraw problem, which I have included in the head of the HTML file for the completed example. You can also learn more about this issue at http://webdesignerwall.com/tutorials/iphone-safari-viewport-scaling-bug and obtain the code to fix it at https://gist.github.com/901295.

Making the Drop-Down Menus Work on Touch Screens

There is one final problem that needs to be addressed: the drop-down menus don't work on touch devices. You will remember that in the last chapter, I used a combination of the opacity and the visibility properties to make the drop-down menus fade in and out, using this CSS

hides the drop-down ─────

```
nav.menu li ul {

    opacity:0; visibility:hidden;
```

transitions both opacity and ─────
visibility

```
    -webkit-transition:1s all;

    -moz-transition:1s all;

    transition:1s all;

}
```

shows the drop-down when ─────
hovered

```
nav.menu li:hover ul {opacity:1; visibility:visible;}
```

It turns out that touch devices skip the :hover rule when you try to transition the visibility property, which is not entirely surprising, as it is moving between simple boolean on/off states—either hidden or visible—and so is not an ideal candidate for a transition. The menus won't work on touch screens unless I remove the visibility property, but when I do this, non-mobile browsers show the menu if you move the mouse below the menu, where the menus are entirely transparent but still "visible" to the mouse. The workaround is to use Modernizr to detect whether the device is touch enabled, and if so, remove the visibility transition. The way this works is that if a device is touch enabled, Modernizr adds the class touch to the root html element, so I can then write:

Here is an excellent article on using Modernizr: http://webdesignernotebook. com/css/how-to-use-modernizr.

modernizr touch screen detect─ ─────
transitioning visibility breaks
touch menus

```
.touch nav.menu li ul {

    -webkit-transition:1s opacity;

    -moz-transition:1s opacity;

    transition:1s opacity;

}
```

This rule is therefore not applied on non-mobile devices (devices with no touch capability), but on touch-enabled devices, this rule causes the menus to appear when the associated menu choice is touched. However, the drop-down now closes instantly rather than fading when you tap anywhere else on the screen. Because the only real advantage of the fade-out is that you can move the mouse back onto the menu if you accidently move off it, the "snap-off" effect is just fine on the no-mouse touchscreen.

Note that this menu only closes when you touch elsewhere on the screen because touching anywhere triggers the scaling bug code (which I described in the preceding section of the chapter), which forces JavaScript to run—and that alone is enough to cause the menu to realize it's no longer being hovered and close. Another way to achieve this "touch-anywhere-to-close" effect is to simply trigger any JavaScript function—here's a simple example of a jQuery function that actually does nothing—"noop" means "no operation", but just calling it by touching the screen anywhere closes the menu.

```
(function(){  $(window).on('touchstart',$.noop);  })();
```

If you don't want to use jQuery, just add `ontouchstart="  "` *to the* body *tag of the markup. This also causes JavaScript to run, and closes the menu.*

Of course, this a total hack, but as JavaScript expert Isaac Shapira who showed me this said "It's an elegant hack." If you find you don't need the scaling bug fix, then just adding this line of code should close the menu.

There is a lot of talk in the blogosphere about how to make drop-down menus work on touch devices. Here is an example of the experimentation that is going on: http://css-tricks.com/convert-menu-to-dropdown.

I finally figured out how to make this drop-down menu work on both mouse-based and touch-based devices as I was writing this book. That said it is definitely a work in progress on touch devices, and I will continue to refine it, so check out my blog for progress on making it more robust and any other issues that I discover. It seems to work well on the iPad and iPhone, and limited number of Android devices on which I have tested it.

So there it is—a Web page that displays appropriately on almost any device on which someone chooses to view it. As mobile devices become yet more relevant (and are already the only means of Web access for an increasing number of the world's population), developing responsive sites will only become more important.

Conclusion

That completes, this exercise, this chapter, and this book. In this chapter, you have seen how responsive design uses media queries, fluid layouts, and flexible images to enable the same Web page to be appropriately displayed on a range of device sizes. I don't have perfect solutions to the issues of responsive design, and no one does. It is the cutting edge of Web design today and the techniques, browsers, and hardware are all evolving rapidly.

CSS, and especially CSS3, is itself a thousand evolving possibilities that are all at different stages, so it's not something that you can wait on to be finished. You just have to jump in and learn what works and what doesn't today, and adapt to what changes tomorrow. What is clear is that the Web is moving to a new level of capabilities as HTML5 and CSS3 become increasingly robust and can support more application-like experiences. I hope this book has opened your eyes to these possibilities and inspires you to take your great idea and make it a reality.

Technical Notes

Writing CSS

CSS is the mechanism for styling HTML. Almost every example in the book begins with a block of HTML code that I then style with CSS. HTML is shown like this:

```
<p>A HTML paragraph element</p>
```

HTML ignores all white space, returns, and tabs, except within text, where single spaces are respected, but more than one space is ignored. This gives you options for formatting. For example, these are all equivalents and display: An HTML paragraph element.

```
<p>An HTML paragraph element</p>

<p>A HTML        paragraph      element</p>

<p>

  An HTML paragraph element

</p>
```

CSS is shown like this:

```
p {color:red;}
```

CSS also ignores white space, tabs, and returns, so these are equivalents:

```
p {color:red;font-size:20px;line-height:1.2;}

p {color: red; font-size: 20px; line-height: 1.2; }

p {

  color: red;

  font-size: 20px;

  line-height: 1.2;

  }
```

The first two examples show a rule with multiple declarations on one line (the second example simply has more white space). The third example shows a rule with one declaration on each line. All three examples produce the same result. When writing CSS, I mix both of these styles (many declarations on one line, or one declaration on each line). Also, although declarations with a rule can be placed in any order, I organize them in the following sequence:

Display related

Position related

Margins, padding, and borders related

Font/text related

Decoration related

For example:

```
.demo {
  display:block; position:absolute;
  height:100px; width:300px; left:10px; top:10px;
  margin:0 5px; padding:10px;
  font-size:10px; line-height:1.2;
  background-color:#eee; border:1px solid; border-radius:6px;
}
```

This sequence places what I consider the most important information about the element first—how and where it is positioned on the page—and ends with the least important—how it is visually decorated. Sometimes, I'll change this order and, say, put a margin first if that is the most important aspect of that particular rule. I find this approach of grouping related declarations on the same line to be a good balance: simply putting all of a rule's declarations on one long line makes the CSS hard to read, but putting each declaration on its own line results in very long style sheets, and a lot of scrolling. It's a matter of personal preference, of course; there is no right or wrong way. I mix these formats in this book, sometimes to accommodate space issues or so that I can add a callout comment against each declaration.

However, one organization tip that I highly recommend is to list your CSS rules in the style sheet in the same order as the markup they style, rather than just tacking each new rule on the end as you write it. Take a look at one of the longer style sheets in the download files, such as the form in Chapter 6, and you will see that the CSS rules are in exactly the same sequence as the HTML they style. Style sheets can get very long and it's hard to keep track of which rules apply to an element if they are not sequenced in this way.

Testing Your Code

You will spend part of your time writing CSS and other code, and part of your time debugging; that is, determining why it doesn't work the way in which you expected. I like the aphorism, "Debugging is the systematic erosion of your assumptions." In other words, it is about determining the difference between what you believe the code is doing and what it is actually doing.

It is very helpful in this regard to be able to clearly see which CSS rules are being applied to a particular HTML element. Because of the CSS Cascade, many different CSS rules can potentially set a CSS property but only one can have the last say and set that property to its final value. For example, a font style on the HTML body tag will be inherited by all the text elements on the page, but if a different font style is specified for a particular text element, that style will be used, overriding the inherited value from body. Often, identifying the winning style is not so obvious, so here is how you can see all the matching styles for a given element, and determine which ones are actually being applied. I'll use an extract from my *Visual Stylin' with CSS3* eBook as a demonstration of how to do this.

As **Figure Appendix.a** shows, by right-clicking a page element in the browser (here, Safari), and choosing *Inspect Element* from the popup menu, the Web Inspector opens. The Web Inspector displays both the HTML element (bottom-left pane) and a listing of CSS rules that match the element (bottom-right pane) as shown in **Figure Appendix.b**.

FIGURE APPENDIX.A (On right) Right-click an element and choose *Inspect Element* to open the Web Inspector (or *Inspect Element with Firebug* if installed in Firefox).

FIGURE APPENDIX.B (Below) The Web Inspector window for this element.

The CSS listing shows that while the p rule specifies Open Sans as the font to be applied, this style is being overridden (indicated by the strike-through) by the more specific .basic_borders_large .demo8 p rule above it, and the element is being displayed in the Niconne font. You can point at an HTML element in the HTML pane and its styles will then show in the CSS pane.

It is, of course, incredibly helpful to see which styles are actually being applied to a given HTML element as you develop your CSS. If you change a style, but the element is not affected, it's time to pop open the Web Inspector to see if the rule you are changing, or a different one, is actually being applied to element. Note the close (x) button in the top-left corner of the Web Inspector to close the window when you are done.

I highly recommend Firebug, a more advanced code inspector, that can show the DOM structure and also help debug JavaScript, is available as an Add-on for Firefox. To install, choose Add-ons from the Tools menu of Firefox, search for Firebug in the Add-ons Manager, and follow the simple install steps.

Supporting Older Browsers

HTML5 and CSS3 offers so many powerful and easy-to-implement features that it's natural to want to use them and not worry about older browsers that don't support all this new coolness. However, that is not reality and certain new CSS3 features will simply not work, or in some cases, cause display issues in browsers that don't support them. Good examples are the `display:table` and `box-sizing` properties, which are very handy when creating columns, as I explain in Chapter 5, but can result in broken layouts in IE6 and IE7. So it's definitely worth testing your pages in older browsers, and providing alternative code for those browsers where needed.

Until recently, the way to support browsers with different capabilities was browser sniffing. This meant using JavaScript to check the browser's user agent string that contains the browser name, and serve up code to address the shortcomings of that browser. However, ultimately what matters is not what browser is being used, but what features that browser supports. That why today's approach is not to worry about the browser itself, but to detect the features it does or doesn't support, and then provide fall-backs or polyfills to work around any missing capabilities.

Fallbacks

A fallback is code that is provided to older browsers as an alternative to the CSS3 that they don't support.

The most simple fallback is to do nothing, and in many cases, you can get away with this. For example, if you are using CSS3 radiused corners, they will not display in IE6 and IE7; users of these browsers will see square corners. And that is probably just fine—those users won't know what they are missing, and rounded corners are unlikely to be critical to successfully viewing the content. In other cases, you need to provide alternative CSS for non-supporting browsers.

As a simple example, pre-IE9 browsers don't support multiple backgrounds, so the fallback is to simply add a single background image declaration before the background images declaration.

```
.someElement {background-image:url(images/basic_image.jpg);}
```

```
.someElement {background-image:
  url(images/cool_image1.jpg),
  url(images/cool_image2.jpg),
  url(images/cool_image3.jpg);
  }
```

All browsers would read the first background rule, but only browsers that can display multiple backgrounds would be then be updated with the second rule. If a browser doesn't understand a CSS declaration, because it contains CSS it doesn't support, or the declaration contains an error, then that declaration is skipped, and the browser starts reading again at the next declaration. So IE8 and earlier would ignore this second rule and would display `basic_image.jpg`.

CONDITIONAL COMMENTS

Note that if you truly are only targeting IE, then you can add fall-backs with conditional comments like this:

```
<!--[if lte IE 8]>       <!-- an IE conditional comment -->
    <link src="ie_only.css" rel="stylesheet" />
<![endif]-->
```

This special style of HTML comment is ignored by non-IE browsers so the code within it is only executed by IE browsers. Here I load a style sheet with extra styles if the browser is IE8 or lower. You can use `lte` (less than or equal to), `lt` (less than), `gte` (greater than or equal to), `gt` (greater than), or just a browser number such as `IE 6`, to specifically target different versions of IE.

Sometimes, if a required feature is entirely missing from a browser, and supplying alternative CSS is not enough, then you need to use a polyfill.

Polyfills

Paul Irish has compiled a comprehensive list of polyfills at https://github.com/ Modernizr/Modernizr/wiki/ HTML5-Cross-Browser-Polyfills.

A polyfill is the term given to a piece of JavaScript code that gives a browser functionality that it would not otherwise have. There are numerous polyfills for just about every CSS3 and HTML5 feature, from video playback to drop-shadows, to allow you to teach old dogs (or at least old browsers) new tricks.

To add a polyfill, download it and put it in a folder with your site. I create a folder called helpers for this purpose. Then add a `script` tag into the head of the page.

```
<script type="text/javascript" src="helpers/selectivizr.js">
</script>
```

A useful way to determine if a polyfill is needed is with Modernizr. Modernizr (http://modernizr.com) is a JavaScript file that enables you to determine the HTML5 and CSS3 features that a user's browser supports by adding a list of classes to the top-level `html` tag of the page, indicating which features are supported, and by setting the properties of the `modernizr` JavaScript object so that you can then test for them with JavaScript. The added classes are most useful when working with CSS.

Here are some useful polyfills:

- **html5shiv.js** (http://code.google.com/p/html5shiv) enables IE8 and below to recognize the new HTML5 elements such as `section`, `article`, `nav`, and so on.

- **selectivizr** (http://www.selectivizr.com) enables advanced CSS selectors such as `::first-child` to work in versions of IE (6, 7, and 8) that do not natively support them.

- **IE9.js** (http://code.google.com/p/ie7-js) fixes many IE bugs and missing features across IE6 through IE9.

- **CSS3Pie** (http://css3pie.com) gives IE6 through IE9 the capability to support visual CSS3 features such as radiused corners, background gradients, border images, box shadows, and RGBa colors.

- **Respond.js** (https://github.com/scottjehl/respond) makes media queries work in older browsers.

- **-prefix-free** (http://lea.verou.me/projects) adds Vendor Specific Prefixes (VSPs) to CSS3 declarations that need them (see the *Vendor Specific Prefixes* sidebar in Chapter 4 for details).

- **borderBoxModel.js** (https://github.com/albertogasparin/borderBoxModel) enables the CSS3 box-sizing property in IE6 and IE7.

These polyfills are the ones that I use most and are incredibly useful when providing support for older browsers, especially Internet Explorer. Additional technical information can be found at www.stylinwithcss.com.

Index